Gypsy and Traveller Ethnicity

This book explores the notion of Gypsy and Traveller ethnicity, providing a much-needed critique of the conceptual basis of racial and ethnic categorisation of these groups. Using an analysis of the post-war housing situation to illustrate a connection between social and economic conditions, Brian Belton also examines legislation affecting Gypsies and Travellers.

Gypsy and Traveller Ethnicity argues that the position of Gypsies and Travellers largely arises out of social conditions and interaction rather than political, biological or ideological determinants. In a bold and entirely original manner Belton demonstrates how the 'ethnic Traveller' is socially generated as a cultural, ethnic and racial categorization, this offers a rational explanation of the development of an itinerant population that is more informative than interpretations based on 'blood', ethnicity or race.

Brian A. Belton is Senior Lecturer at the YMCA George Williams College, London. His research focuses on the nature of culture, race and ethnicity, and oral history, particularly in relation to sport and community.

Gypsy and Traveller Ethnicity

The social generation of an ethnic phenomenon

Brian A. Belton

Routledge
Taylor & Francis Group

LONDON AND NEW YORK

First published 2005 by Routledge
2 Park Square, Milton Park, Abingdon, Oxfordshire OX14 4RN

Simultaneously published in the USA and Canada
by Routledge
711 Third Avenue, New York, NY 10017

First issued in paperback 2014

Routledge is an imprint of the Taylor and Francis Group, an informa business

Typeset in 10/12pt Baskerville by Graphicraft Limited, Hong Kong

British Library Cataloguing in Publication Data
A catalogue record for this book is available from the British Library

Library of Congress Cataloging in Publication Data
A catalog record for this book has been requested

ISBN 13: 978-1-138-87449-7 (pbk)
ISBN 13: 978-0-415-34899-7 (hbk)

In memory of Jimmy Stone, the Bonny Downs Gypsy
Boys and their sacrifice

Contents

Illustrations

Figures

Tables

Acknowledgements

This book has been written over a period of research that really has no beginning within the span of my life. I was born surrounded by the echoes of Gypsy culture and was brought up in constant contact with the complexities, joys and woes, the inescapable consequences of that association.

This being the case, these pages cannot house the necessary acknowledgements of a lifetime of interaction, bewilderment, learning, arguing, fighting, resisting, embracing, fostering, rejecting and understanding. As such this is a symbolic tribute but I hope I can mark the most fruitful associations that have helped me extract the pictures that follow from the realm of 'almostness'. The most pragmatic collaborator in that process was Rosy, the mother of my son. She has been a tireless editor, bold consultant, honest critic and kind encourager. Other, more tangential contributors can be found in the pages of this book. From the people closest to me, to others I knew for only a few minutes. They populate and punctuate the analysis and, I hope, bring it to life. Family, friends and enemies. The living and the dead. Bastards and saints, lovers lost and found . . . and, playing between the chapters, my (and Rosy's) son, who has lived with this work the whole short time he has danced on this earth. I dedicate this book to him; a life busily making and remaking his identity. For him I hope the bonds of ethnicity will never define him, the corral of race never hold him or the exactitudes of culture, defined outside him, impede his progress in looking for himself, a search which at its best has no end. These, my wishes for Christian and all human kind, were the seed of the crop of words I now offer to you.

A priest once offered me peace – amriya on that priest. I seek not peace but barearav, chachimos, darane svatura, chere and desrobireja. This is why I wander still.

Introduction

This book is an exploration of the social generation of the notion of Gypsy and Traveller ethnicity. Using quantitative and qualitative data, it seeks to problematize the conceptual basis of racial and ethnic categorization of this group and heighten the general awareness of the diversity and difference that exist within the Traveller population in the face of the conventional view of this group that, in short, effects an homogenization of Travellers into a distinct ethnic/cultural/racial grouping.

The work examines legislation that has had, and is likely to have, an impact on Gypsies and Travellers. This is linked to an analysis of the post-war housing situation[1] in order to illustrate a connection between social and economic conditions, legislation affecting Gypsies and Travellers and the visibility and general consciousness of the Gypsy and Traveller population. The book argues that the position and categorization of Gypsies and Travellers largely arises out of social conditions and interaction that are attributable to the disciplinary social form, rather than discrete political or ideological determinants.

In the pages that follow I will demonstrate that Gypsy and Traveller identity is founded on a life-style that contradicts the discipline of the housing market. I will argue that itinerant ways of life are repressed by disciplinary society as they represent a symbolic threat to the order. I go on to critique individual emotional or moral explanations for the repression of travelling forms of existence and suggest that these are largely symptomatic of a more profound aetiology of repression, set in the social structure. The book puts forward the notion that itinerancy is the object of control as it is antithetical to the structure of contemporary society. A travelling life-style is considered as only a symbolic threat because as a phenomenon it provides an example of defiance of disciplinary society. Ambulant ways of life are not able to provide a mass alternative to the housing market. On this basis the book presents a critique of theories that portray discrimination against Travellers as arising out of psychological dispositions premised on race or ethnicity. The book puts forward a theoretical structure focusing on the social generation of Travellers as a cultural, ethnic and racial categorization over a broader tableau than has been previously attempted, whilst the analysis is focused on the situation pertaining to post-war Europe and some data generated in the United States and Australia, I believe that the position I establish in this work is applicable to a much wider constituency than the United Kingdom. Given its theoretical underpinnings it is likely that the analysis that follows provides a model for a broader understanding of the travelling population across western Europe, North America and the post-industrial world.

In what follows I explore ethnicity and the politics of culture relating to Gypsies and Travellers (centred as they are on the homogenization and categorization of the travelling population), including contemporary issues connected with discrimination and how this relates to forms of social exclusion, primarily in the form of housing provision. This amounts to an examination of space, place and location in the light of current issues facing Travellers as embodied, for example, in the Traveller Law Reform Bill 2002.[2] In the process I will offer a rational explanation of the development of an itinerant population that is less ambiguous and more informative in terms of the social nature of the Gypsy and Traveller position than interpretations based on 'blood', 'breed', 'stock' ethnicity or race that dominate the literature.

Biographic/ethnographic connections

I write this book from the point of view of someone who was brought up with a clear knowledge of his own background in what might be called the English Gypsy tradition. The work is based on years of formal and informal activity related to Traveller issues. From my earliest days, my family travelled from our East London home to the hop-fields of Kent, where I played and worked with a colourful mixture of Gypsy, Gorgio (non-Traveller) and Traveller children. As a sixteen-year-old I stood on a pub table at Horsmonden horse-fair, a regular family event, and sang to the applause of what I considered 'my people' 'I'm a True Didikois'. As a teenager I attended and was repelled by cock and dog fights. I have witnessed bare-knuckle boxing, both organized and impromptu, at closest range at 3 a.m. on 17 June 1972 in a gravel pit in Essex. I fought in front of a crowd of Irish Travellers and English Gypsies, losing a purse of £50 an hour later. I have practised as a professional youth and community worker with Traveller families on and off sites. I have served on a national organization concerned with Traveller education and have written, lectured, spoken and argued about Traveller issues from Canning Town to the South Atlantic, from Shanghai to Lusaka.

The travelling population

The travelling population of England is, in the main, described in the literature concerned with this group as un-problematically made up of people of a definite 'type'. This approach is often portrayed as being generated through hereditary considerations; Travellers are seen as the product of biological inheritance. This essentially ethnic and racially oriented analysis is not always overt. However, texts do make definite references to Gypsies as an ethnic group or race.[3] In this book I argue that the Traveller population of England has emerged out of the complexity of modern society, the flux of economic and social history, out of a melding of people from a diverse range of backgrounds. What follows suggests that this group is, to a significant extent, socially generated and through a systematic and critical assessment of the current view of Travellers in England I propose that this population does not constitute an ethnic or racial whole. I question the unproblematic description of this group as a homogeneous collective, whether defined as Traveller, Romany, Gypsy or other.

The book seeks to address the lack of a contextual and social perspective in theory relating to Travellers. It explores Gypsy identity, considering the part social influences play in the generation of this population and attempts to develop a more structured understanding of this identity in particular and the concept of ethnicity in general. Whilst the work does not look to undermine the notion of Traveller and Gypsy identity, it proposes that the individuals and groups that make up this category have a wide social base. I argue that this identity is created and maintained not only by tradition and hereditary but also by social and ideological factors.

As such, the book examines the interconnectedness of Traveller identity, relating to and setting it within social and economic processes of the contemporary era, what might be understood as an exploration of the dynamics of antecedent events. This approach mirrors the method favoured by Montesquieu; the analysis of the material and cultural environment and human interaction with the surroundings.[4] It also connects with a sociological heritage as exemplified in the Chicago School tradition of social and cultural research.

The first chapter analyses the nature of Traveller identity. I argue that, in the main, the literature relating to Traveller identity:

1   Neglects serious sociological analysis of the Traveller population.
2   Assumes that Travellers have an unproblematic shared ethnic, racial and cultural origin.
3   Overtly and covertly proposes a Gypsy ethnicity but does not provide a rigorous analysis of ethnicity or race.

I suggest that the above are the consequence of the reliance on a fragmented and partial historical and anthropological analysis. I undertake a theoretical evaluation of Traveller ethnicity and critique the literature focusing on Traveller issues. I begin this task by taking a Weberian, social constructivist position that ethnicity is a product of social action. From this perspective I critically assess a number of themes and theoretical standpoints drawn from the literature, including the range of phenomena that are seen by theorists as embodying and expressing ethnic differences, including political affiliation, ritual and rite, language, travelling, and self-determination. This part of the work provides the reader with an overview of the current paradigm of Traveller identity.

Building on the findings of Chapter One, Chapter Two starts by looking at the nature of ethnicity, how it has been defined within anthropological and sociological theoretical discourse. This exercise demonstrates that the notion of ethnicity has encompassed the meaning and social use that was once the province of the concept of race. I argue that adoption of and/or the conscription to an ethnic identity arises out of the emotional, sentimental and psychological considerations that express shared social positions, and the need for common identity. I suggest that ethnicity is also the product of broad economic and social phenomena. The second part of the chapter presents an innovative stance considering ethnicity as a product of social, economic and colonial relations.

Taken as a whole the chapter presents the argument that, contrary to the literature focusing on Traveller identity, ethnicity is not reliant on family, hereditary, biological or 'blood' transmission. The first part of the chapter can be understood to be concerned with *what* ethnicity is whilst the second part examines *how* it is generated and maintained. The combined analysis initiates an exploration of the social *meaning* of ethnicity, in particular with regard to the Traveller population.

Having argued in the previous chapter that ethnicity is a category arising out of social interaction, continuing with the search for the social *meaning* of Traveller ethnicity, Chapter Three looks at definite social situations and economic phenomena that can be understood to contribute to the designation, adoption or continuance of Traveller identity. This analysis reiterates that travelling life-styles may not always be an 'ethnic inheritance', but are also likely to be endorsed, embraced, chosen or obliged by social and economic considerations.

The chapter points out how the growth in the Traveller population since the Second World War coincides with housing shortages. This suggests that the Traveller population is likely to have been swollen by the recruitment of formerly homeless people, with little or no previous connections with Travellers or an itinerant life-style. I argue that this situation needs to be considered when analysing the character and development of the English Traveller population if a realistic understanding of this group is to be achieved and to offer valid social meaning. This position is reinforced by an analysis that encompasses interview material, examples drawn from the popular media, specific Traveller and family biographies and analysis of data relating to the registration for homelessness alongside the Department of the Environment caravan counts (over a 20-year period). This latter exercise offers an additional empirical framework to complement the current understanding of the Traveller population. It represents a quantitative and qualitative sociological contribution to the literature, putting forward data that will demonstrate a pattern of development within the Traveller and homeless populations, illustrating that at least part of the Traveller population and those seeking to register as homeless may have a related/similar social genus. This material further confirms that the travelling population may be understood as a social rather than an ethnic phenomenon.

Chapter Four looks at examples of contemporary legislation that have affected the Traveller population. It critically examines the possible impact that this activity has had on the development of the Traveller population. Guy's point that prior to the legislative activity of 1960s 'most authorities had far more

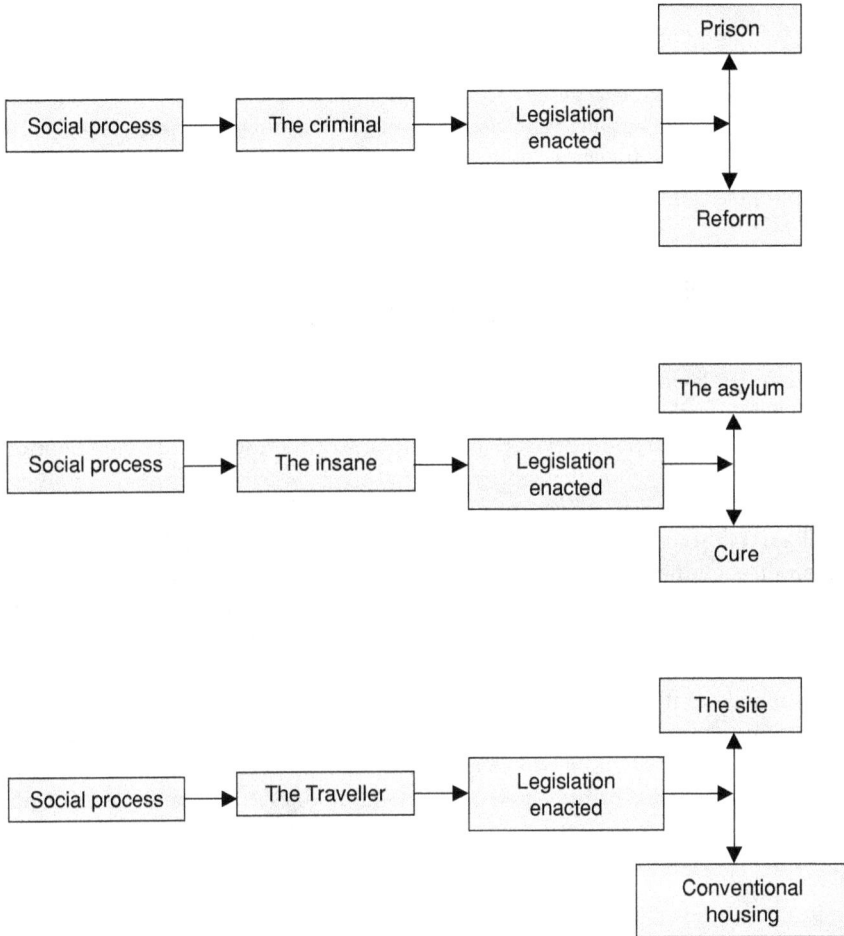

Figure 1 The disciplinary social process and categorization.

pressing problems to deal with than complaints against a few Rom' and that 'when they did act against Roms perhaps they were playing a deeper game'[5] is heeded. The chapter suggests that the legislative activity impacting on Gypsies can be connected to a wider housing discipline. It is argued that the lineage of legislation affecting Travellers following the Second World War has an underlying relationship that works to establish a norm of housing provision. I suggest that this discernible line of development within the legislation has over time made travelling culture more untenable.

I further argue that the caravan-site can be interpreted as a form of punishment for those who choose or are obliged to resort to itinerant/transient homes. I suggest that itinerant Travellers have, in effect, been treated as 'housing deviants';

being people with no fixed address, employment or ready social taxonomy, they cannot easily be controlled; their movements and activity may not be conveniently observed and recorded. I demonstrate how recent legislative activity (The Traveller Law Reform Bill 2002) can be seen to address this situation and integrate caravan-dwelling into the realm of the legitimate housing market.

Chapter Five is concerned with a Foucauldian analysis. This proposes that the ethnic category arising out of social processes becomes a focus of discipline. This can be understood to give rise to a similar response stimulated by other categories (see Figure 1).

Overall Chapter Five suggests that the development of the Traveller population is connected to forms of social discipline. This analysis continues the concern for an exploration of the social meaning of Traveller ethnicity.

The overall analysis contained in this book promotes an understanding of Travellers, emphasizing the constant growth and the dynamism of this group. The work is an effort to develop an awareness of the intricate development of social, racial and ethnic categorization and provide a broader understanding of the make-up and social constitution of the Traveller population. As such, the book establishes a social meaning of ethnicity with regard to the Traveller population through the critical examination of social, political and cultural forces that create Traveller identity. This being the case it seeks to add to rather than undermine the understanding of the Traveller population in the British context.

However, the work is also something of a confirmation of Hetherington[6] who has pointed out that we now choose social/familial type affiliations and identities and are not limited to 'primary groups', such as fixed biological associations. In the contemporary situation people are apt to become part of what Hetherington has described as 'neo-tribes' and 'elective communities'.[7] This is consistent with the ideas of Harvey *et al.*[8] who demonstrate how old cultures are reinvented to serve the new/current needs of a particular group of people.

1   Who are the Travellers?

Introduction

The literature relating to Gypsies and Travellers is complex in its diversity and quality. It ranges from stories/biographies or collections of anecdotes[1] to disciplined and rigorous academic study[2] and the beginnings of a socio-historical approach.[3] All of this material has at least some interpretative value, in terms of understanding the position and perception of Gypsies and Travellers. However, the direction of this book is, to some extent, dictated by the research concerning itself with English Gypsies and notions of Gypsy/Traveller identity and ethnicity. As in the rest of the book, this chapter will not attempt to make a distinction between Travellers and Gypsies as there seems to be no agreement about the boundary between these labels[4] and some doubt concerning the integrity/authenticity of either.[5] As such the terms have been used interchangeably.

The field of literature called on throughout the book represents the most influential thinking referring to the historical, sociological, cultural and anthropological analysis of Gypsies and Travellers in the British context since the end of the Second World War.[6] It relates to the topics of concern to the book: identity and population generation.[7]

The literature demonstrates that during the post-Second World War period Gypsy identity has been energetically subjected to a focus that has had a kind of anthropological character. For example, Lucassen *et al.*[8] have assessed the work of Fraser[9] as representing the tradition of Gypsy research and although they concede that Fraser displays a vast knowledge of the existing literature they argue that his analysis is, 'Mainly leaning on linguistic research'[10] and upholding the idea that Gypsies are the direct descendants of a people of Indian ethnic/racial origin who have managed to maintain their ethnic integrity since being obliged to flee from their primordial homeland. For Lucassen *et al.*,

> . . . this interpretation is not unproblematic and is in many respects based on speculation mixed with a fair proportion of teleological and wishful thinking. Fraser and others with him, refuses to integrate competing evidence in his analysis and only uses what fits with his preconceived idea of one Gypsy people.[11]

The type of analysis used by Fraser[12] has influenced most of the ideas relating to Traveller identity. The rigour of the enterprise has varied greatly. Most of the research has over-emphasized the role of genealogy and/or heritage in establishing Traveller identity. The position is, in short, one of biological determinism. This has been covertly or overtly postulated in the form of a Gypsy ethnicity and/or related concepts such as race and culture. For example: 'Roma, commonly known as Gypsies, a traditionally nomadic people found throughout the world. The Roma share a common biological, cultural, and linguistic heritage that set them apart as a genuine ethnic group.'[13]

To a large extent this ignores the sociological and everyday (macro) social context within which the very diverse groups that make up the Traveller population exist.[14] The literature tends not to give appropriate consideration to social conditions, context, activity and interaction that may contribute to the development and maintenance of this population.[15]

What follows looks to begin to redress this situation by offering a more sociological perspective, including, later in the work, statistical analysis, in order to suggest a significant social influence on the development of the Traveller population.

The impression given by much of the literature is that those groups loosely labelled as Gypsies are a homogeneous ethnic group and/or race (maybe made up of a number of ethnicities). Although other categories of Traveller are identified, such as Didikois (a contested expression, taken to mean mixed blood Gypsies or being 'of Gypsy blood'), these groups have, latterly, been referred to under the collected category of Travellers and portrayed within a continuity of history and origin. Lucassen *et al.*[16] demonstrate the flaws in this approach and relating to Fraser[17] argue that there has been little consideration of the influence of the labelling of itinerant groups as Gypsy and how this given identity might be adopted by those so labelled. They go on to make the point that Fraser has also failed to adequately deal with the fact that those identified as Gypsies have intermingled with host populations from the Middle Ages whilst ignoring that the notion of a 'people' is a relatively recent concept associated with nationalistic ideology that emerged in the nineteenth century.[18]

Okely refutes the idea of exotic origin and the idea of a 'Gypsy race'. She points out that in Britain there are those known as 'real' Gypsies and other groups who are seen to be in some way 'counterfeit'. This latter group are dismissed as drop-outs from mainstream society whilst the former are perceived as a definite 'race', a 'pure-blooded' group, with roots (evidenced by linguistic traits) in India. According to Okely these rurally based, more or less extinct people are regarded as inherently self-sufficient and as having nobility not found in the 'mixed blooded' groups. However, she dismisses all this as a fictional stereotyping that says more about society's needs to project its desires onto 'other' mythical groups.[19]

However, Okely's position is made in order to develop a notion of homogeneity in terms of the Traveller population. She argues that this group is intrinsically connected to society. She argues that Travellers do not exist in a type of social vacuum and that collectively they constitute a unique group internationally, not falling into a nomadic group in the traditional anthropological sense, being interdependent with wider society.[20]

For Okely, Gypsies maintain an essential difference that connects them, even though this can be given up or lost:

> They share a resistance to wage-labour, a multiplicity of self-employed occupations, often a need for geographical flexibility and an ideological preference for trailers or caravans. Among all groups there are extremes of wealth or relative poverty, some may move into housing, some may 'pass' into the dominant society, marry people outside the ethnic group and choose to take up wage labour.[21]

Although seemingly moving away from the notion of an exotic origin, this analysis still mystifies the nature of the Traveller population. It portrays Travellers as the same but different, connected but separate. Okely, to an extent, can be seen to be replacing 'exotic origin' with 'ideological preference' to underpin what she continues to call an ethnic group.

In this chapter I will illustrate and analyse the situation Okely describes. I will challenge what Lucassen *et al.* have identified as the dominant contortion of Gypsy origins. For them, most of those involved in the study of Travellers, whilst understanding that the term 'Gypsy' is a social construct used to identify particular travelling groups, continue to consider and refer to this population as a 'people' or a racial/ethnic type.[22]

This analysis provides the main thrust of the first part of the work, which argues for a wider aetiological basis of the Traveller population. Following a Weberian analysis, I contest that Traveller activity is part of the constant flux of human social organization:

> race creates a 'group' only when it is subjectively perceived as a common trait: this happens only when a neighbourhood or the mere proximity of racially different persons is the basis of joint (mostly political) action, or conversely, when some common experiences of members of the same race are linked to some antagonism against its members of an obviously different group.[23]

The most pertinent part of Weber's position for this work is that:

> ethnic membership does not constitute a group; it only facilitates group formation of any kind, particularly in the political sphere. On the other hand, it is primarily the political community, no matter how artificially organized, that inspires the belief in common ethnicity.[24]

This argument can be seen as both a disconnecting force (in terms of an entire population) and a pressure that connects and mixes various categories, groups and types (like Gypsies). This book sets out to demonstrate that the Gypsy and Traveller population is a rich mixture of culture and very much part of the society in which it exists but, in Weberian terms, it coagulates and arises out of political pressures. This chapter seeks to provide a consideration of social, political, cultural and economic forces as contributory factors to, and generators of, itinerant and travelling life-styles. This perspective, as will be illustrated below, is for the most part neglected in the area of study.

The literature recognizes the multifarious character of the Traveller population, but at the same time it contains an undercurrent that presents Gypsy connectivity. This position is problematical;[25] it suggests a tenuous collective of Gypsyness, grouping people together around fragmented similarities of language, ritual or tradition, often with little correlation between these considerations. For example, a group may share snippets of language, but have very different life-styles. It is an exercise that would not be dissimilar to an attempt to define contemporary Britishness or Irishness for example in terms of habit, tradition or even language.

Although it may be important for individual and group identity to emphasize various ethnic boundaries, tastes, style and so on, the effort to seek to identify habits or defining traditions/traits on behalf of a particular group, that has an effect of merely distinguishing or categorizing, seems to be highly questionable in terms of its political or social motives. The practice of aggregation of Traveller identity may also result in outcomes that amount to little more than subtle forms of discrimination. For example, an underlying theme (although not the overt contention) in the literature[26] is the implication that people, once identified as Gypsies, belong on a site. A human being categorized as a Gypsy has a logical place in these terms (as, under the South African apartheid regime, blacks belonged on a Bantu).

The practice of defining 'Gypsy' characteristics from a very broad life-style basis (living in a caravan) and what is a diverse collection of people, from a range of social, ethnic and cultural backgrounds[27], might be likened to the making of claims about 'white' racial tradition or ethnically 'black' behaviour. Such distinctions are racist in themselves in that they fail to consider, and in effect deny the existence of, the wide and varied nature of cultural traditions and ethnic identities within this very limited taxonomy of colour. It is valuable to ask what purpose there is in labelling uniquely 'Gypsy' behaviour or 'ways'.[28] How could such distinctions have anything other than extremely limited applicability in a multi-racial, multi-ethnic, cross-cultural society? Although this work cannot really address this propensity it is hoped that the book will act as a question mark over the literature.

Difference defined

Analysis of the literature identifies five main forces that are used to postulate Gypsy connectivity:

1   Ritual and rite
2   Language

3   Travelling
4   Self-identification
5   Romanticism

These are elaborated below.

The perceived nature of difference is directed by social and psychological motives, although the consideration of broader social issues is conspicuous by its absence. It is not the purpose of this book to seek a reason for this, but such a gap served to generate a critical reading which enabled my research to focus on the social processes impacting on the generation of the Traveller population.

Although Lucassen *et al.* go much further than others in demonstrating that Travellers derive from various origins[29] and critique what they call, 'The inadequacy of traditional answers'[30] found in research surrounding Gypsies and other itinerant groups, they continue a traditional, if an uneasy consensus within the literature, that sees there being a Traveller population that might be thought of as a single entity[31] being made up of a diversity of ethnic types, where inclusion into the whole seems to be based on rather open qualifications. From this perspective it might be reasonably asked if travelling sales-people might be considered to be Gypsies. This group, as occupational Travellers, could be seen as a modern equivalent to the Tinkers or Show-people, whom Acton[32] connects with Gypsy identity. Workers obliged to live alongside their moving employment on civil engineering projects, in caravans, could also be recruited to the Gypsy population. For Acton[33] there is no clear overriding indication of what is needed to be part of this collectivity. However, for Clebert, Gypsy culture is quite closed. For him Gypsies are 'an ethnic whole' who have maintained the 'singleness of their race' for more than a thousand years.[34]

Calling oneself a Gypsy, Traveller or New Age Traveller, self-ascription, seems to be, for most of the writers, a major factor in terms of establishing Traveller identity.[35] However, only Rehfisch[36] states overtly that the main marker of Gypsy identity is self-ascription. For all this, the social categorization Gypsy is, at least in part, created by groups and individuals in the wider social field, following Weber's[37] understanding. One manifestation of this wider social field might be academics of the type that write about Gypsies.[38] Given the feelings of ethnic discontinuity that appear to exist within the Traveller community,[39] those groups that make up the category Gypsy would seem less likely to see themselves as part of a tight whole than interested non-Gypsies. Of course, the most obvious Gypsy trait to the outside world is caravan-dwelling, so it would seem the most likely person to be a Gypsy would be one who ascribes this label to themselves and who lives in a caravan, but this seems a vulnerable and uncertain measure of ethnicity.

It can be suggested that the five factors of Gypsyness collectively produce a range of responses to those conscripted to or adopting Traveller/Gypsy identity. For example, fables about travelling are intimately connected to the romance of the Traveller life-style. Also, exotic language, unity in difference and political affiliation are hard to separate in the Traveller context. There is some overlap in these factors of interpretation, especially as none of them exist as isolated aspects of identity; they are interrelated and mutually supporting. On this basis the material that follows seeks to illustrate that Traveller identity has been subject to a limited and questionable analysis.

Underlying unity in difference

Samuels provides an example of how the literature sometimes presents Gypsies as a distinctive racial grouping. He cites such distinguishing factors as an extensive, common history; a conscious sense of difference; the presence of folklore; birth into a closely related community with marriage confined to the same; being a nomadic, minority group with a common dialect.[40]

At the same time, most of the literature suggests that the idea of a homogeneous Traveller population is tenuous and thus questionable, implying that the whole *race* is made up of a number of different ethnicities. There is an obvious tension here. An insistence on an underlying or primal unity is built on the basis of diversity. For example, Acton at points argues against a clear or distinctive racial or ethnic Gypsyness, seeing the Traveller population as a 'disunited and ill-defined people', who possess 'continuity, rather than a community, of culture'.[41] He refers to distinctive origins and ethnic categories, for example Romani speakers leaving India 1,000 years ago,[42] the presence of a 'caste hierarchy', but goes on to question the validity of this, arguing that one or a number of 'sociocultural continuums' exist in relation to Gypsies. Acton's position is further complicated by his definition of different categories of Travellers.[43]

It is clear that Acton replaces an ethnic or 'caste hierarchy' with a series of social boundaries. It is difficult to discern from his analysis exactly what difference this makes. Neither does he specify how 'continuity' is distinct from 'community'. In effect Acton is arguing that Travellers are a distinct group. He presents diversity as a key factor which for him is based on Gypsy and non-Gypsy stereotypes, producing 'ethnic sub-group categories'. This analysis superficially suggests that Gypsy ethnicity is socially generated,[44] but social and cultural identity are not central to Acton's theoretical analysis. What seems to be of primary concern to Acton is an effort to make a case for the existence of a whole by attention to the sum of diverse groups that are portrayed as parts. In short this argument implies a homogeneity of difference but within this it is conceivable that any group could be adopted as Gypsy.

As such, Acton[45] is not too far from Clebert[46], who also depicted a wholeness or homogeneity arising out of obvious heterogeneity and diversity. Both use the same mixture of romanticism and historical conjecture when establishing a notion of Traveller identity.[47]

For Clebert there is a general failure, 'to appreciate' Gypsies as 'a whole people', who are 'jealous of their ethnic unity, conscious of their racial originality', being a 'unique example of an ethnic whole perfectly defined'.[48] For him, Gypsies have never 'consented to any alteration as regards to the originality and singleness of their race'.[49] He then goes on to consider, 'The indispensable distinctions', 'within Gypsy ethnology', they being a 'race' who differ in custom, look and dialect. This contradiction in conviction is ameliorated by Clebert's argument that this 'ethnic whole' is held together by the maintenance of 'original roots' and 'a basic tongue'.[50] Although criticized by many of those involved in the study of Gypsies over the years,[51] I call on Clebert as he exemplifies the propensities of many of those who have denounced him. Like him, much of the literature formulates claims about race and/or ethnicity that are not backed up by any solid evidence. Clebert is echoed by other writers who categorize Travellers unproblematically as a definite racial or ethnic group. For example Kenrick and Puxon write of the arrival of Gypsies in the United Kingdom at the turn of the sixteenth century.[52] This claim is based on documentary evidence of the time that labelled any foreign group of uncertain origin as Gypsy.[53] However, Kenrick and Puxon, like most other writers, assume that the sixteenth century had a reliable taxonomy of racial types (peoples) comparable with contemporary understanding, a postulation which is highly questionable.[54]

Liegeois[55] takes a European perspective, and at times, a worldview of the history and character of Gypsies. He consistently makes the point that what he is looking at when referring to Gypsies is 'a rich mosaic of ethnic fragments';[56] a collection of different groups, with different names. He can thus be understood to be agreeing with Clebert and Acton's[57] interpretation. He argues for an overall connection between these groups, although this is fragile and tenuous in nature. Liegeois argues that the world population of Gypsies is the sum 'of small diverse groups'. For him, Gypsies are connected by a flexible and constantly changing structure, which is derived from their consistent persecution.

Liegeois contends that contemporary studies of Gypsies are inaccurate because they do not allow for the very complex and 'multi-faceted reality' of Gypsy identity. For him, portrayals of Gypsies are slanted by over-generalization and are based on stereotypical images, which are hundreds of years old. He argues that such a group cannot be adequately described in generalities, 'any synthesis'[58] necessarily being an over-simplification. At this point Liegeois seems to hold a duel understanding; Gypsies can be taken to be a very diverse, loosely connected group, but at the same time we must see this synthesis as doubtful.

According to Liegeois,[59] Gypsy culture is not unchanging or passive. The diverse grouping that he refers to as Gypsies cannot really be thought of as having a straightforward line of development. Although he does use generalization throughout, he constantly reiterates that the character of those groups that share Gypsy identity is diverse. Reinforcing this point he informs his reader that there is no single word for a Gypsy type in the various Romany dialects. This contradicts the likes of Clebert, Fraser and Hawes and Perez,[60] but it is a much more secure analysis in the light of Willems and Lucassen *et al.*,[61] the latter showing the basic historical analysis of Traveller origins to be spurious and the former clearly indicating the ethnic label 'Gypsy' to be primarily socially generated.

Much effort is expended in the literature justifying the 'exotic' version of Gypsy origins, tradition and language being cited as cementing factors. This argument, as Liegeois[62] suggests, is a fragile basis on which to found theories of identity. He provides a more flexible view of those placed in the category of 'Gypsy' than Clebert,[63] seeing them as a grouping with a diverse range of social, political, cultural and ethnic origins, but his position ties him to the 'diversity = unity' analysis that Acton[64] and Clebert promote.

Okely makes the point, like Liegeois, that Gypsy identity is amorphous. In common with Acton she sees the groups that constitute the Gypsy population as having a range and mixture of backgrounds. In her second chapter, 'Modern Misrepresentations', she suggests that Travellers have been portrayed as 'victims of cultural disintegration'.[65] She argues that they are not a separate or complete cultural group. For her, Travellers have changed with the dominant order, in that they are and have been connected to and are interdependent with the wider economy. This, according to Okely, is exemplified by the presence of rural and non-rural groups of Gypsies. Although Okely represents what might be thought of as a soft position, relative to Clebert and Acton she continues to portray Traveller identity as a collective connected by difference, a contradiction that does not help her analysis.

Hawes and Perez also argue that travelling people have 'never constituted homogeneous group' and that 'they are a most disunited and ill-defined people'.[66] Taking the lead from Acton, they see Gypsies as possessing a 'continuity rather than a community of culture'.[67] They support Liegeois, seeing Gypsies as 'a whole, whose component features are linked to one another; a structure that is not rigid but ever-changing', and state:

> The Irish Travellers in particular, whose Celtic origins and background to some extent set them at odds with the rest, are nevertheless so closely iden-tified, interbred and integrated with the Gypsies, over at least 200 years, that their experience is directly related to our purposes.[68]

Hawes and Perez draw attention to post-war problems of homelessness,[69] the extensive encampments along the Thames marshes, which they refer to as 'sprawl-ing shanty towns', and 'the post-war housing shortages' that coincided with the rise in ownership of mobile homes to a total of 150,000.[70] They state that these issues gave rise to the 1960 Caravan Sites Act and also point out that this legislation was not primarily concerned with Gypsies and Travellers, its rationale being to control the unlicensed sites. However, they do not see this situation as having any great impact on the make-up or social perception of the Gypsy population.

More recent legislation effuting Gypsies[71] can also be clearly seen to address broad social issues rather than a particular ethnic group.[72] Given the recent history of itinerancy, it is difficult not to speculate that those seen as New Age Travellers may well have counterparts throughout history and that these groups would be likely to interact both with other itinerant groups and settled populations: 'With each new piece of legislation, there was less and less attempt to differentiate between the various kinds of itinerant. The 20th century equivalent, in some respects; is the advent of New Age Travellers.'[73] This recognition that New Age

Travellers have predecessors contradicts the assertion that Hawes and Perez make that this group are a 'more recent kind of Traveller' who are, for them, a 'quite different group of nomads'.[74] However, they recognize that shortages of social housing, together with other considerations create 'loose groupings of articulate people from the settled population . . .', but for Hawes and Perez their 'origins are considerably different from those of the traditional Gypsy or Irish Traveller'.[75] How they have this intimate knowledge about origins is not explained, but their link between housing shortages and those taking up an itinerant life-style does confirm the diversity of origin of the travelling population and demonstrates the role of social forces in its development.

This comparatively recent set of considerations, alongside the historical evidence makes it hard to ignore the potential admixture of Traveller origins. Hawes and Perez recognize the numerous socio-economic pressures which might have caused people to take up an itinerant life-style in the Elizabethan period and how peddlers, hawkers, vagrants and beggars would have been likely to mix as an underclass[76] and they suggest that there have been constant additions to the travelling population from the settled community over time. As a result it becomes difficult to sustain a notion of a traditional, blood lineage of Travellers. On the contrary their position does seem to support the probability that Britain's Traveller population is essentially a social phenomenon rather than an ethnic or racial type.

Hawes and Perez do not clearly articulate or establish the relationship that Travellers have to the State because the social reality/origin of Travellers is given no definite meaning. Their argument is vague in terms of the social generation of the Traveller population being seemingly distracted by their effort to promote a notion of a collective origin of the group. The analysis follows the tendency of the romantic tradition established by other writers, for example Kenrick and Clark[77] and Clebert, who suggest that the Traveller population is the result of family, blood or even tribal lineage. A position of this type allows such writers to theoretically champion an oppressed ethnic group, and fight the cause of minority rights, but it obscures other possible forms of group generation arising out of the relationship between the Traveller population and social phenomena affecting a much wider constituency.

Sutherland demonstrates the omnipotence of this perspective. She looks at the social, political and ceremonial patterns of groups of *Rom* in the USA (in particular around the town of Barvale, California). She applies the Romani term *kumponia* to these activities and interactions. Sutherland, in her effort to uncover the economic organization of 'Rom in America',[78] refers to a number of formally travelling family groups under the collective name of *Rom*. Like other writers (some using the other generic labels, Gypsy or Traveller for example), she deploys this as an umbrella term for varying collections of current and former nomadic peoples, including *Machwaya, Mikailesti* and *Gurkwe*. She provides no explanation of her rationale for this other than seeing the connections between the life-styles she describes as evidence of this ethnic typology.

Most of the people Sutherland[79] writes about were not full-time nomads, although constant and consistent travelling interspersed by short to long sedentary living was not uncommon.[80] Sutherland goes on to look at economic relations between these groups and between the whole category of *Rom* and non-Travellers, including welfare considerations.

The main weakness of Sutherland's analysis is that what is being portrayed is a group of families that have either carried nomadic traditions from their East European origins or adopted this way of life since arriving in the United States.[81] The basic connection between these groups is their background as travelling people. Their customs, traditions and economic structures have no necessary Rom, cultural or ethnic bias. Sutherland does not seem to see the possibility that the cultural and economic ways of the community she examines could emanate from a shared life-style and migrant background as much as from a cultural tradition set in an ethnic framework of Romhood. This can be seen from Sutherland's critique of Clebert's attempt to identify Gypsy occupational categories, like musicians or metal workers. In short, she argues that Rom have a very wide range of economic relations, proposing that the basic tenet of these relations is co-operation between Rom for the exploitation of non-Gypsies.[82] She gives little consideration to the possibility that this occupational network may be life-style generated, rather than part of an ethnic mechanism; it may be materially energized and not culturally rooted.

This unproblematic connection between ethnicity and behaviour is taken up by others.[83] For example, Miller[84] examines what she calls the 'American Rom', specifically focusing on an 'Ideology of Defilement'. But again, the basic weakness in this work is that it assumes that various groups of nomadic people are a homogeneous ethnic category – Rom. The problem with this argument is highlighted by Guy[85] when he states that, 'How Roms should be characterized is a basic problem'. He goes on to point to the confusion amongst social anthropologists who have not been able to identify conclusive, objective criteria of the ethnic group. He cites the attack made by Barth[86] on this whole approach. For Barth, 'the ascriptive aspect is logically prior to any objective characteristics of the ethnic group'.[87]

This position seems to be indicating that there is a propensity amongst social anthropologists to create ethnic types on the basis of certain observed characteristics, which appear to have similar elements. Thus, it could be argued that caravan-dwelling is an ascriptive aspect, this exists prior to the anthropologist labelling it an objective characteristic. The possibility that a range of people, from varying backgrounds and ethnic groups, could live in caravans is not addressed, especially if they can be described as carrying other ascriptive aspects[88] that in turn become objective characteristics. These other ascriptive aspects may have more to do with caravan-dwelling life than any ethnic propensities. This possibility is not considered.

In contrast, Kornblum, looking at Boyash Gypsies, noted that a family, the Ivonovichs, although not Gypsies, maintained a 'nomadic style of existence', as such, their situation and relationships were defined by their itinerant way of life and the consequent upheavals involved in such a life-style. It was this that brought them to adopt Gypsy ways as they often required the support that the Gypsies were in a position to give.[89] Kornblum noted certain ascriptive aspects that corresponded to the objective characteristics of Gypsy life-style, but saw that this did not automatically lead to being part of a Gypsy category. This conclusion was based on the relative comfort expressed or observed amongst non-Gypsy migrants and Gypsies. Although an entire catalogue of ascriptive aspects might have been fulfilled by this family, the rather abstract and vague notion of comfort excluded them from being seen/portrayed as Gypsies. For Kornblum[90] the Ivanovichs' relative discomfiture with a travelling life-style showed them to be involved in a temporary response to the economic/social position they found themselves in at the time and not expressing a permanent ethnic or genealogical propensity.

Willems agues that those studying Gypsies focus on similarities whilst, to a great extent, ignoring differences between groups. For him, the insistence on the distinctiveness of Gypsies has resulted in a lack of comparative studies of groups in approximately similar circumstances.[91] His conclusion, when discussing Dutch Travellers, is not too far from Korblum's position:

> When several years ago, a colleague of mine in the company of British anthropologist Judith Okely, visited a caravan camp in Leiden, they saw parallels with British and Irish Gypsy-Travellers. They knew for certain that these were Gypsies. The Dutch women living in the caravans, however, were having none of it and stressed that they were native Dutch. That social surroundings can, as it were, compel people to behave in a certain way is something that Gypsy specialists do not acknowledge sufficiently.[92]

Willems goes on to demonstrate the prevalence of this type of analysis:

> The writers of an analysis of begging of Gypsies in seventeenth-century western Europe omit to mention that at the time the number of beggars was, in any event large. Elaborate discussions of the deceptions perpetrated by Gypsies throughout the German countryside in the eighteenth century lose much of their ethnic charge if we realize that a legion of drifters struggled to extract themselves from the swamp of poverty through ruses and tricks.[93]

The collective analysis in Rehfisch and Rehfisch suggests that there may be some consistent patterns of activity amongst groups of Travellers, but it demonstrates that there is no overriding connection between the very disparate groups that make up the category, apart from the need, wish or obligation to travel. Even this is questionable, as Guy[94] points out. This could link Gypsies to Bedouin, Bushmen, Aborigines and Inuit, any and all of the worlds' itinerant peoples. Are they all Gypsies? It can be seen that there has been a failure on the part of writers on Gypsy issues to explain the Traveller population as a distinct group based on tradition, habit or life-style.

This propensity has a history. As Willems has explained, the idea of the existence of a Gypsy type has become the predominant paradigm. The existence of other travelling folk, from pilgrims to vagabonds, the assortment of social outsiders that have roamed from the earliest of times, have all but been left out of the analysis.[95] Here Willems is pointing to a historical process that has merged various travelling groups into one all embracing category – Gypsies. Many of these itinerant groups travelled for economic reasons rather than an ethnic drive or a racial urge. These groups would have included show-people, weavers, landless labourers, knife-sharpeners, drovers, beggars and so on.[96] The ascriptive aspect (travelling), although existing prior to categorization by anthropologists, has been used by the same to define all these groups under one *ethnic* label.

Allegiance to the model Gypsy

The confused analysis that arises out of this situation, wherein a range of travel-ling/itinerant groups fall into one homogeneous, ethnic category, made up of a diversity of cultural types is exemplified by O'Nions. She argues that when Gypsies are seen as 'simply a social bonding of nomads with no distinctive culture or group identity', this is no more than 'a myth'.[97] She goes on to assert that the perception that they are no more than a 'social group of nomads', more or less undistinguishable from the rest of society, threatens 'Gypsy identity'.[98]

O'Nions sees this identity being sustained after five hundred years of co-existence with a host or dominant population. She argues for a definite and distinct Gypsy ethnic/racial group, seeing the idea of assimilation as futile[99] but[100] she advances her position on a confused and contradictory analysis:

> The fact that some have been absorbed and are indistinguishable from any ordinary member of the public, is not sufficient in itself to establish loss of . . . an historically determined social identity in [the group's] own eyes and in the eyes of those outside the group . . . despite their long presence in England, Gypsies have not merged wholly in the population as have the Saxons and the Danes . . . They, or many of them, have retained a separate-ness, a self-awareness, of still being Gypsies.[101]

O'Nions starts out by arguing that 'five-hundred years of co-existence with the dominant population' have resulted in there being no 'true-Gypsies'. She suggests that nomadic groups have merged to such an extent that any differentiation is 'meaningless'.[102] However, she goes on to postulate a lasting separateness (unlike the Danes and Saxons) within a level of assimilation. This position is flawed in that, moving beyond the likes of Acton[103] who propose difference within unity, O'Nions is arguing that Gypsies have been totally assimilated yet, as a group, remain distinct.

The usefulness of this analysis is that it reiterates a traditional propensity within the study of Travellers. O'Nions falls into a double bind that, according to Willems[104], has marked the historical analysis of Traveller populations. For him, the character of Gypsy identity has been obfuscated by the nature of research into Gypsy identity (most of the writers looked at in this chapter have been affected by this). Willems notes how the early writers interested in Gypsies collected historical and mythological fragments relating to a range of travelling/ itinerant groups. From this somewhat random collage they developed a Gypsy racial history and identity. According to Willems, writers like Fraser have followed and built on this foundation. When, as might be expected, no true Gypsy type can be identified[105] that corresponds to this, what might be thought of as primal model, it is concluded that this category has disappeared, having been integrated/assimilated to a greater or lesser extent according to the level at which they correspond to the ideal type.

Although Willems,[106] later alongside Lucassen and Cottaar,[107] strongly implies that the Traveller population is a socially generated phenomenon, being made up of a variety of ethnic types brought together (for the academic and juridical gaze only) by socio-historical forces, including the rise of nationalism,[108] he does not elaborate on the underlying social forces and economic relations that can give rise to the creation of and/or conscription to an ethnicity. Neither does he postulate, in any definite manner, possible 'external' binding factors between Travellers.

Political affiliation

One means of looking at links between travelling people is through political affiliation. This is demonstrated within the literature to some extent, although it is often seen to connect people through a shared life-style rather than a common ethnicity. The social and cultural problems faced by New Age Travellers are indicative of this. This argument has been complemented by English law restricting itinerancy. Methods of law enforcement have created degrees of unity between itinerants that could be understood as political solidarity. It may be argued that itinerancy is part of these peoples' rites, rituals, traditions and culture, but it is not this that binds them politically. What unites this group is a common feeling of oppression and injustice. This may well be the catalyst of a shared identity unrelated to ethnic or racial considerations.[109]

Most of the post-war legislation affecting Travellers has a wider constituency impacting on other sections of society. For instance, the Caravan Sites Acts of the 1960s made caravan-dwelling much more difficult, both for what were seen as traditional Travellers and those who might have chosen or been obliged to take up such a housing resort. Before the Caravan Site Acts of the 1960s, it was relatively easy to use caravan-dwelling as an alternative to what might be called the 'norms' of the housing market (rented or mortgaged 'bricks and mortar'). Although Travellers have been most likely to suffer ill treatment from the effects of enforcement, having relatively restricted recourse/less access to the apparatus of social protection, legislation of the kind exemplified by the 1994 Criminal Justice and Public Order Act or even the likes of the 1960 and 1968 Caravan Site Acts, demonstrates the socially corrective power that embodies action limiting the activity of, in the case of the 1994 Act, tens of millions of people. Such legislation is not centrally concerned with relocating the relatively small Gypsy population, or ethnic cleansing, as Hawes and Perez would have it. This would be paradoxical as a primary aim of State activity of this scale.

The one-dimensional focus on the effects of the above legislation on Travellers in the literature suggest laws affecting Gypsies have little direct consequence for a wider social constituency. It also distorts the meaning of Gypsy and Traveller identity as it promotes a perspective that legislation is aimed specifically at a type rather than more social outcomes. This approach invites eugenic interpretations of these groups[110] that concentrate on racial/ethnic distinctions and fail to adequately take sociological perspectives into consideration. The general social impact of legislation is often relegated to a secondary status in the literature focusing on Traveller issues because the primary focus is on a racial/ethnic type or category. The path of analysis is as follows:

- Concentration on interpretation of legislation (such as the 1994 Criminal Justice Act) as an attack on ethnic/racial interest.

Which leads to:

- The obscuration of the meaning/purpose of legislation[111] as a vehicle for far reaching social discipline.
- The portrayal of a far reaching tool of social normalization as being primarily an incursion on minority life-styles.

In the final part of his analysis, Liegeois[112] makes it clear that the main motivation for Traveller organization that reaches as far as a notion of Gypsy nationalism can be linked with the persistently harsh treatment of those living an itinerant life-style. But this harassment, for Liegeois, seems not to be premised on notions of race or ethnicity, but on non-Gypsies feeling threatened by travelling people[113], seeing nomadism as hazardous to civil society.[114]

Historically, modern methods of control can be seen to be no more than recent variations on a traditional theme. For Liegeois expulsion has been historically unsuccessful. The alternatives have been prison, factory confinement and constant police surveillance on the peripheries of society.[115] The site, being on the fringes of society, fits well into this control system. What might be called housing dissidents, those unable or unwilling to take up conventional, sedentary forms or modes of housing, can be assigned or obliged to move to the site. The view of the site as a locale or means of control is confirmed by Liegeois.[116] According to him Gypsies can see sites as 'traps', facilitating police surveillance. He argues that sites across Europe fit this description. It is not unusual to find guardhouses at the entrance and social amenities placed at a focus point where, panoptican like, the whole site might be observed,[117] making sites areas of confinement and control. It could be argued that this exemplifies the sin of itinerancy. These ideas are looked at more closely in Chapter Four.

Liegeois[118] argues that Gypsies have been a constant target for persecution and although he fails to consider the fact that any legislation affecting itinerant groups or those living outside housing norms has an impact on Gypsies and non-Gypsies alike, what becomes clear from his analysis is that many groups of people have been categorized as Gypsies. It seems that unconventional and/or transient ways of life are the basis of persecution rather than Gypsyness. However, this is not an overt part of the analysis Liegeois puts forward; his focus is more on forms of categorization and identity rather than on questions of origin and cultural meaning.

Okely[119] is aware of the political advantages of creating a homogeneous Gypsy identity; that a racial/ethnic grouping can prove useful to groups that have no other means of combating oppression. As Stuart Hall has pointed out: 'Paradoxically, marginality has become a powerful space. It is a space of weak power, but it is a space of power nonetheless.'[120] For Hall the weak and oppressed are placed at the margins of society and as such have no access to the conventional routes to power. This being the case they make the source of their marginality an asset. Okely does not overtly state that this may be a primary force behind the manufacture of an analysis that suggests that Travellers have common origins, but she does state that the notion of the distinct category of Traveller is as much a social construction as the result of genetic/biological considerations.[121]

According to Okely a 'Gypsy race' does not exist. But she goes on to note that the portrayal of collective racial and persecutory elements have the capacity to supply impetus for solidarity. However this perspective may also be counterproductive. Okely appears to suggest that oppression can become a means to gain resources. Therefore it is in the interest of the self-proclaimed oppressed to continually assert (preserve) their oppressed (deficit) status. Okely recognizes that all roles ascribed to Gypsies by non-Gypsies, 'trickster, exotic or victim', carry the 'risk of self degradation and a dangerous sense of unreality'.[122] This is an insightful point. The adoption of roles described by others is something warned against in the colonial context;[123] the process can be part of the wider control nexus – 'we are not as worthy as they, that is why we have an inferior status'. This analysis highlights the possible political and social outcomes of ethnic categorization. However, Okely does not expand on this point. In fact what looks like the start of an informative analysis of the social meaning of ethnic categorization regresses by way of her claim that the ethnic boundary of Gypsyhood is based on pollution beliefs, founded on the practice of 'inner purity'.[124] This argument subscribes to the exotic origin analysis, although she refutes the notion of Indian derivation. Okely appears to be putting forward a contradictory position, but it allows her to acknowledge what might be called the social generation of the Traveller population, whilst at the same time maintaining a link with the romantic tradition of writing about Gypsy origins.

In terms of the political dimension as a cementing factor of Gypsy ethnicity, Norman Dodds[125] can be seen as something of a pioneer. He was the first post-Second World War writer on Gypsy issues to chart the progress of legislation affecting Gypsies and Travellers. Following the Second World War Dodds was also one of the most energetic of parliamentary pro-Gypsy activists.

Dodds' analysis aims to compare and contrast the treatment of Gypsies in various countries, but the main part of his work is devoted to his experience of campaigning on behalf of Travellers between the late 1940s and early 1960s. Although initially something of an integrationist, Dodds ends up making a case for sites. He recommends that 'we should have to find suitable sites where they could live . . .'.[126] As such, he can be seen as one of the precursors of a movement that continues up to the present time, that seeks, on behalf of Travellers, to pressurize for Traveller rights.[127] When analysed these rights are of a very different nature relative to non-Traveller rights. Dodds thus can be seen as one of the innovators of a social differentiation of rights in respect of Travellers and non-Travellers, this being premised on the need and requirement for sites to facilitate a Gypsy life-style. He asks:

> What do Gypsies want? A piece of ground, with a hard course so that they are not plodding in the mud all the time. They also want what each must have – water, sanitation facilities for ablutions. A camp site should be large enough to take 50 or 100 caravans. Such a community would warrant at least a wooden building, which would serve as a school at the beginning.[128]

This thinking promotes the site as the rightful/natural place of the Traveller. The site and the Gypsy become as synonymous as Inuit and igloo, or Native American and reservation, the Black and the ghetto, the Jew and the concentration camp, in other geographical and historical contexts. However, this describes the movement that came out of post-war parliamentary sentiment, more than Dodds' own perspective. He saw the contemporary legislative activity relating to Travellers as amounting to 'segregation laws' equivalent to the South African apartheid regime.[129] This suggests that his own instincts were against the notion of the site as the would-be natural resort of the Traveller.

The value of the material set down by Dodds is that it adds to the analysis of the rationale behind the Caravan Sites Acts of the 1960s. The conspicuous absence of any explanation as to why Travellers came, suddenly, to be seen as a problem during a time of great housing shortage, together with a focus on Travellers as a traditional type, with a need for new and specific rights, is revealing. Travellers are not seen as a group 'of' society, with existing rights that are simply denied or withdrawn. Dodds, whilst writing within this framework, does suggest that the so-called rights proposed for Travellers are closer to constraints, in that he invites comparison with the rights of Blacks in South Africa in terms of designated homelands. These seeming rights also echo the rights of Native Americans with respect to reservations and convict rights relative to the prison. This raises the question as to why a population that Dodds sees as approximating 100,000 should incite such strong political reactions and provokes the conclusion that other factors underlie the nature of legislation affecting Travellers.

According to Liegeois, those who qualify as Gypsy can be determined by political motives[130] rather than other considerations. This is perhaps why Liegeois considers the people with whom Gypsies live as being crucial in terms of establishing and confirming Traveller identity. He seems to imply that the category of Gypsy relies on social identification. For Liegeois, Gypsies have built strength in resistance to discrimination, and have asserted their identity through opposition to non-Gypsies.[131] He suggests that collective oppression has, at times, given rise to an almost nationalist whole, in that it has created a concrete political affiliation, including representation at United Nations level. He concludes that Gypsy identity is based on social experience as much as any other consideration.[132]

According to Liegeois,[133] Gypsy solidarity is made more difficult because conventional forms of political organization are antithetical to Gypsies. He does not elaborate on this contention, although given that, according to Liegeois, the Gypsy population is very diverse, it may be that many of those designated to be part of this group do not see their so-called representatives as working for their interests. It may be that this amorphous category does not see itself as a homogeneous whole, under the label of Gypsies. More precisely, the apparent lack of Gypsy solidarity betrays the disparate nature of the Traveller population. This, again, throws doubt on notions of shared identity or origin, the basis of organization perhaps being more a form of social categorization than some fundamental connection of ethnicity, blood, race or shared origin.

Those who are active in promoting the Traveller population as a definite collective may well be attracted by other motives. As Liegeois states:

> The Gypsies, like many other minorities, are highly marketable these days. The fashion for Gypsies has now become a feature of the environment in which they live. This threat to turn their culture into spectacle is a danger more difficult to apprehend than the effects of the various regulations or of social work and schooling. There is now a risk that lack of respect will give way to pseudo-respect. In some ways this is worse, because it is garbed in an insincerity and fraternalism that are more dangerous than the paternalism that preceded it.[134]

Here we can see a critique of the romantic tradition found in the literature and Liegeois clearly identifying the motivation of some writing on Gypsy issues. The identification of the other, seen in a positive light, marks out uniqueness and difference that can easily be reinterpreted as strange and/or alien. In an academic and intellectual environment it is difficult to sustain a doctrine of innate human differentiation based on race[135] that includes prescriptions that certain types belong in particular places. However, it is acceptable to make a position supporting ethnic diversity or distinctiveness and campaign for the rights of labelled individuals and groups to be placed in their own cultural space, for instance, the trailer, on the site. It may not be that some writers on Gypsies have a conscious hidden racist agenda; however, as Liegeois recognizes, the desire for ethnic categorization might be stimulated by unconscious forms of class anxiety, discrimination and prejudice. The potential for discriminatory motivation is especially disturbing when ethnic categories seem to be based on very insubstantial premises.

Acton argues that 'New Gypsy politics'[136] arose from clashes between Gypsies and non-Gypsy society during the 1960s. According to him, this was the result of economic and cultural changes, both in society and amongst Travellers, which caused a loss of role for Travellers and/or contradiction between Traveller and non-Traveller situations. This restricted, what might be called Gypsicentric perspective, does not consider the wider implications of local and central government policy that affected Gypsies. Acton seems convinced that legislation and enforcement activity is the product of discrimination and prejudice exclusively directed at Travellers. No alternative social analysis is put forward; Acton fails to consider the possible wider meaning of the political activity affecting Travellers in the 1960s and, as such, is unable to comprehend the relationship the resulting legislation had to a more general promotion of housing/family norms and social discipline. The essence and spirit of the Caravan Sites Acts of the period can be seen as part of a much broader concern about the family and community life that was changing dramatically at that time. For example, housing shortages were a contradiction to traditional perceptions of family life and the political values related to the family as an institution; for the family to be maintained as a viable social unit, families had to be housed. At the same time the adoption of alternative life-styles, based on communal values rather than nuclear consumer units, represented a more permanent threat to housing and other market norms. The seeming simple answer would have been a greater State commitment to forms of social housing, however this would have contradicted the move towards the privatization of housing supply, that was all but complete by the mid 1960s.[137] As such, what might be called housing discipline had to be enforced in legislation and the threat of law.

Acton[138] does make an effort to set the analysis of Gypsy politics and situation in a wider context, but he is unable to see the issues affecting Travellers as part of a general social dynamic. It might be argued that this is not his aim, but a project seeking to explain political activity and change concerning any given social phenomenon must look to its context for meaning. What Acton offers does not provide meaning, it describes events and issues and as such its use in terms of exposing the nature of Traveller existence and activity is limited by a restrictive and ultimately separatist analysis. This is emphasized by his late but detailed examination of Gypsy nationalism[139] that concludes by suggesting that this movement is both positive and valid.

Hawes and Perez[140] effect a similar position, but use a notion of oppression as the engine of categorization. Emotive expressions, including 'Ethnic cleansing', 'holocaust', 'apartheid' and 'clearances', pepper the claim that 'official violence' is being perpetrated against groups that seem to pose a threat to 'collective well-being'. Such oppression is portrayed as having a historical consistency in terms of the treatment of Travellers. For Hawes and Perez contemporary legislative activity represents a 'draconian change of direction' and a 'radical shift in policy'.[141] The consultative document of 1992[142] that was a precursor to the 1994 Criminal Justice and Public Order Act, for them, signalled an end to 'the co-operative approach to policy on Gypsy and Traveller issues that had existed since 1965'.[143]

Hawes and Perez quote Acton[144] when making a case for a move from Elizabethan 'State racism' to the 'sincere benevolence' of Victorian society. They characterize non-Traveller involvement at this point as a mixture of 'manipulative benevolence' and 'the continuation of the direct repression backed by legal measures[145] – both these characterizations might be applied to the Traveller Law Reform Bill 2002.[146] This analysis seems little different from what the writers call the 'era of consensus' when one takes a critical perspective on the activity of the 30 years prior to 1993.

Hawes and Perez see the long-term aim of current policy affecting Gypsies as being aimed at altering Traveller life-style in a manner that would extinguish this group's culture, which for Hawes and Perez is based on mobility 'as a basis for ontological security'. As such the outcome of such policy is the absorption into the house-dwelling population with the consequent relationship to 'one place'.[147] Here Hawes and Perez appear to be unable to differentiate between the essentially sedentary experience of site living and an itinerant way of life. Because the Caravan Sites Acts of the 1960s contained provision for the building of sites does not, in effect, make this legislation any better than the impact Hawes and Perez see resulting from the 1994 Criminal Justice and Public Order Act. Indeed, they point out that the effect of the 1960 Caravan Sites Act was to reduce the number of sites.[148]

This analysis offers little more than a psychological explanation for the social and political position that Travellers find themselves in. This is expanded upon when Hawes and Perez put forward the simple idea about the need to change,[149] but the analysis lacks a solid strategy on which to build for the same. At worst the general theme of their work engenders aimless guilt. The authors seemingly set themselves a rather modest mission:

> In facing the detailed formulations of public policy as they relate to the provision of services for Gypsies and Travellers, particularly the provision of legal sites, the book attempts to identify those elements which could be said to represent discriminatory or oppressive measures against this minority group.[150]

They follow this statement with the wish not to enter into the debate on ethnicity. This hesitancy is understandable given the very vulnerable nature of any theory relating to a Gypsy ethnic type, but given the phraseology that Hawes and Perez use in making their argument, and the subtitle of their book,[151] their desire to avoid a discourse on ethnicity seems to lack analytical conviction. Indeed, the analysis is similar to Acton's.[152] Like Acton they define official activity as an effort to control Travellers and ignore the effects of legislation on a much broader swath of society. This perspective is premised almost exclusively on psychological responses to ethnic/racial categorizations and amounts to a restricted interpretation of legislation, seeing it as being energized and framed with the comparatively small Traveller population as an exclusive target. In a sense the argument perceives Travellers in a ghetto focus.

The erection of a 'sameness through difference' construct places Gypsies within an apparently fixed identity. This categorical chamber situates Travellers within the parameters of an ethnicity, with most writers using a covert biological corral alongside behavioural, attitudinal and traditional considerations.[153] This essentialist position focuses on notions of blood and race. It is usually primised on the physical make-up of the body, but in the case of Travellers it is seen to emanate from where the body is situated, that is no fixed location. Whilst providing some ground for political solidarity and strength, this essentialism is also used as a political tool to deflect a range of social ills onto groups of people who are primarily categorized as Gypsies over and above their immediate origins. As such, political affiliation or identity politics founded on being a Gypsy is a double-edged sword, which seems, at least via the indications of the popular media, to cut more one way than the other.

Ritual and rite

According to Boas[154], customs, rituals and habits are of vital importance in the maintenance of societies. He drew on the romantic vision of culture as heritage and habit, the role of which is to allow the past to shape the present. Tradition and history moulds individual behaviour, and culture arises out of this. For Boas, the particularity of cultures is essential for continued social stability. Durkheim's[155] 'collective representation', the beliefs, values and symbols that are common to any particular society, served as a means of perceiving the environment, giving it meaning. According to Durkheim, individual modes of thinking and feeling are shaped by collective representations imposed by the society of which they are part.

According to Radcliffe Brown: 'Every custom and belief . . . plays some determinate part in the social life of the community.'[156] Goldschmidt argues that ritual is used 'at points of culturally defined crisis', 'which focus on the group and reinforce its unity'. According to him rituals manipulate human feelings to create a common sentiment and reaffirm social ties. For Goldschmidt, in order to cope with stress they reorient feelings connected with life crises, ameliorating fear and guilt. In total they create an emotional environment that helps those involved work together for shared desires.[157] Burns puts forward the argument that:

> Ritual, like etiquette, is a formal mode of behaviour recognized as correct, but unlike the latter it implies the belief in the operation of supernatural forces. Religion is characterized by a belief in, and an emotional attitude towards, the supernatural being or beings, and a formal mode of approach – ritual – towards them.[158]

This being the case, rite and ritual appear to be markers of general social affiliation rather than specific ethnic boundaries. It would seem that ritual and rite are first social bonding agents. Ritual relates to ethnicity as a secondary effect. Ritual and rite mark out one social or community group, but these cultural markers may not be shared by another group who occupy the same ethnic category. This seems to be the case amongst Travellers. For example, Clebert[159] chronicles the various everyday traditions, habits, beliefs and life-styles of the very diverse groups to whom he ascribes the umbrella title of Gypsies. Whilst he shows there to be certain shared elements of activity, interest and tradition within this Gypsy grouping, the level of allegiance to and from these phenomena is not consistent across the whole of the Gypsy population referred to. Neither has this claim for distinct traditions been subject to any comparative analysis with host communities who might share so called Gypsy interests and traditions as profoundly as any group within those categorized as Gypsy.

Okely states that Gypsies do have coherent ethnic boundaries,[160] based on various traditions and what she calls 'rites'. She later reinforces this argument by stating that Gypsies do not take on the beliefs of the wider society.[161] For Okely, cultural separation between Gypsies and non-Gypsies is based on 'images of opposing systems'. The two populations, according to Okely, see themselves as distinctive groups and as such evolve and follow distinctive ethnic paths. For her, this can be crystallized in 'the Gypsies' symbolic work' that 'is seen as subversive'.[162] This subversion seems to be premised on the informal nature of much of the work traditionally associated with Travellers, but given the rise of the car-boot sale and odd-job culture of post-Thatcher, Blairite Britain, this would seem to be a more wide-spread symbolism. This apart, it is possible to argue that this general notion of separateness seems to contradict Okely's ideas about the inter-dependent and connected nature of the relationship between Gypsies and the wider society.

Another question arises from symbolic work being given such a defining role in Traveller identity. Given the strong emphasis placed on belief and values in the various definitions of ritual and rite, can work, as the central locale of Traveller symbolism, sustain a social identity and by implication, ethnic identity? Gypsy rites based around hygiene, or cleanliness[163] can be cynically understood as middle class and academic interpretation of essentially working-class traditions, home-spun lore engendered through a lack of education and inadequate health care and inherited good advice.[164] The very cross-cultural interaction that Okely points out can be seen, by anyone brought up in, or influenced by, pre-war working-class traditions, habits and received medical wisdom deformed into coded behaviour that may be interpreted as superstition, as the source of many of what Okely understands to be customs and rites. Given these considerations, the rites, rituals and symbolism that Okely sees as so central to ethnic identity can be criticized as fragile markers of differentiation. She seeks to make a case for ethnicity being partly based on a distinct symbolism, ritual and rite, looking to identify a Gypsy type of behaviour and from this to extrapolate an ethnic character. The question that this analysis begs is why can we not see other behaviours, within different groups, being based on symbolism, rites or rituals, as creative of ethnicity?

It appears that a Traveller life-style incurs some central values and beliefs around separateness and the need, want and/or wish to be travelling. If a travelling population were to have distinct rituals and rites, activities that were central and confirming of a way of life, it would seem that they would need, by definition, to be connected with these aspects of their existence. Okely does begin to depart from the traditional views maintained in the literature on the nature and future of Travellers, putting forward the notion that housing Gypsies does not necessarily mean an end to Gypsy identity[165] and that the separation between Gypsies and non-Gypsies is, in part, a social construction,[166] but she does not develop these ideas.

Language

Writers on Gypsy issues, as this section will seek to demonstrate, have consistently seen language as an important marker of ethnic identity. However, in common with ideas relating to ritual and rite, the claims made for language as an effective bonding agent within the homogeneity of the Traveller population do not stand up to critical scrutiny. Okely for example argues that language alters and moves independently from groups of people. For instance, the dominant language of Ireland is English, but this does not mean that the Irish are English, only that this shared language demonstrates a relationship founded on any number of factors, such as colonialism, conquest or trade for example.[167]

Acton makes the case for persistent and widespread use of Gypsy languages[168] to confirm the separateness and distinctiveness of Gypsies. However, the language link as a marker of ethnicity is somewhat brittle. Fraser points out that the history of linguistics cannot be used to establish the ethnic and/or racial roots of ancient Romani speakers – there is no necessary connection between race and language.[169]

Even where a whole mode of verbal communication is evident, this does not necessarily indicate a separate language, ancient origins or a distinct heritage. Donall P. O'Baoill, Head of Structural Linguistics at Institiuid Teangeolaiochta Eireann, has stated that the creation of Irish Traveller Cant came about in the last 350 years. For him this means of communication doesn't constitute a distinct language as its structure is indelibly connected to English.[170]

Various activities, social and employment groups, all have specialized language particular to them. Even alongside unique ritual and rite, dress codes and social structures, this does not give rise to ethnic categories enveloping such groups. If one looked at a housing-estate in Glasgow, and another in Moscow, it is likely that one would find similar traditions and perhaps even shared fragments of language (particularly in respect of consumerist contexts; advertising, television and cinema for example). This does not demonstrate a strong connection between the origins of people, it reflects the interchange and mobility of culture. If one goes on to compare what one could call the estate rites with those of Travellers, one could again find similarities, probably more between the Glasgow estate and urban Scottish Travellers and the Moscow estate and western Serbian Gypsies respectively.

Clebert indicates that the most definite bonding agent of Gypsyness is that of language. He asserts that, 'A century of gypsiology has proved that this language is of Indian origin.'[171] He then goes on[172] to provide a detailed analysis of elements of Romani, pointing out possible derivatives from,[173] and kinship with, Sanskrit and Hindi. However, he eventually makes the point that this language, 'in its purity' is practically dead, in that it is not used by Travellers. Even the fragments that are still used are not understood between various groups of Travellers.[174]

Fraser relies on connections between elements of language of some communities and the names that a range of nomadic groups give to themselves for his presentation of Gypsy homogeneity. According to him the Gypsies' extensive use of their 'name for men of their own race' allows for the assumption of a common ethnicity based on language.[175]

Even if one were to accept the debt that Romani has to language with its roots in the sub-continent (being the cradle of the Indo-European family of languages, comparative linguistics has suggested that the East is the root-source of all European languages) this has questionable validity as a definite 'proof' of the Indian origin of the descendants of former users of Romani.[176] Languages are not restricted genetically, they are socially learnt, they move via political, social, environmental and geographical channels. It has been suggested that Gypsy groups adopt a core vocabulary to the grammar of the host countries. They have also been influenced linguistically through trading posts and cultural transmission.[177] As such, the move from language to people is not necessarily a logical or unproblematic step.[178] For example, a Chinese person living in the USA may speak perfect English, having command of not a word of Mandarin, but this is no guide to racial identity.[179] On this basis it is difficult to sustain the place language holds as a defining element of Gypsyness.

Travelling

Mobility is seen by many writers on Traveller issues to be a marker of ethnic identity but as Guy[180] argues, travelling as a form of ethnic/racial identification is tenuous. As I will argue later in the book, the resort to caravan living may not be one of choice. This was exemplified at a global level when a young Gypsy in conversation with Hillary Clinton was reported to have stated, 'I would like to live in a larger house'.[181] It is also likely that many people living in caravans or involved in an itinerant way of life are not Gypsies.[182] Guy[183] makes the point of how difficult it is to say anything very certain about Gypsy traits. He critiques Clebert's claim that, 'the Gypsy is primarily and above all else a nomad',[184] arguing that in countries with the largest numbers of Rom the majority of them are sedentary.[185] Liegeois[186] argues that not all Gypsies are nomads. According to him, since the Second World War travel has become difficult, given local authority and boarder controls. The industrialization of Western Europe has restricted the economic adaptation of Gypsies whilst the accompanying urbanization has made the setting up of camps increasingly problematic. For Liegeois the strength of Traveller groups lie not in a shared nomadism but their diverse lives and their 'absorption or borrowing from the cultural environment in which they find themselves'. This 'is achieved without weakening the essential and distinct collective identity'.[187] Hawes and Perez also suggest that nomadism is no guide to Gypsyness and that a Gypsy need not be a nomad, and concede that when discussing the situation of Gypsies it is impossible not to acknowledge, 'that large numbers of people who live in caravans do not conform to generally accepted notions of what is meant by that term'.[188]

According to Sandford a quarter of those included in the 1967 Government Survey of Travellers in England and Wales said that they had lived in houses. He also refers to a group of people he became aware of whilst in the process of research who took up a travelling life-style 'thus forming a new generation of Gypsies'.[189] Thus not all Gypsies have sub-continental ancestry. This claim of instant ethnic/identity generation is deeply problematic. One might adopt the life-style of an Inuit or an indigenous Australian, but this does not mean that one would then be part of a new generation of the group into which one has assimilated. One would not be regarded by society as an ethnic snow-dweller or Aborigine. Can an individual claim identity or even ethnicity or race because they have somehow melted into the host group? This may be possible in terms of entities like nation-states, wherein one may be enveloped within a political/geographical boundary, but the categories of race or ethnicity involve much more inflexible notions that call on concepts relating to what might be thought of as internal states of the individual; blood, stock, instinct and nature. Such facets are reliant on the semi-mystic genealogy often supported by selective scientific references to genotypes and inheritance.

Self-identification/ascription

Self-identification is cited by a number of writers as a means by which a Traveller ethnicity may be postulated.[190] When analysing the position of Irish Travellers, McCann, O'Siochain and Ruane argue that this is not a phenomenon that can be answered by resort to historical research. For them the central issue is how Irish Travellers comprehend their own experience from the perspective of the present.[191]

This is maybe the least helpful marker of Gypsy identity. Just to say, 'I am a Gypsy' , or that, 'I understand myself to be a Traveller', does not imply any consistent or agreed set of criteria. One could mean that one is a wanderer, a mystic, one who lives in a caravan, or the individual making the claim could be a deluded lunatic living in a fantasy world. Statements of this type can mean anything and everything. However, by its very elasticity, self-ascription is appealing to certain individuals who want to belong to a different, exotic, oppressed ethnic group, perhaps feeling that they might gain some kind of kudos, influence, respect or power from this identity. For all this, flexibility can have an equally negative impact; one is only who one says one is and no more.

Okely[192] sees 'self-ascription rather than objective traits' as the most appropriate means of identifying Travellers. This coincides with Barth's view as cited by Guy.[193] For Barth, an ethnic group is constituted by those who identify themselves as a category that might be distinguished from other categories of the same order. At the same time this group will be recognized by others. Thus,

Gypsy identity is established, for Okely, in terms of commitment to the same. However, she appears to back-track on this position, stating that familial and kinship relations are necessary in terms of claiming Gypsy identity.[194] From here she goes on make the same kind of assumptions as Miller[195] and Sutherland[196] by assuming that various groups of nomadic people are a homogeneous ethnic category. This contradictory stance is further complicated by her later claim that Travellers are connected to and interdependent with wider society[197] but that Gypsy status is ascribed by birth, one Traveller parent being required for a legitimate Gypsy identity.[198] She argues that non-Gypsies who marry into Gypsy groups are not to be allowed to forget their origins. Okely does not elaborate on how this is achieved, but claims a former Gorgio (non-Traveller) will be able to participate in day-to-day life and that their children will be incorporated into a given Traveller community. This interpretation is somewhat confusing when she later states that the biological model for Gypsies is misleading as many Travellers are as close to non-Travellers as they are to Travellers, although her position is perhaps made a little clearer by her argument that:

> The principle of descent provides a method both for inclusion and exclusion. Thus, Gypsies, like any ethnic group, have procedures for releasing or absorbing a number of individuals without weakening their boundaries. Ascription by the individual is subsidiary to the group's continuing self-ascription.[199]

This position seems to give a secondary importance to descent, it being over-ridden by group ascription, but it is hard to conceptualize how descent can be subsidiary to ethnic self-ascription. Okely does not show how she established the presence of such a hierarchy. The notion is also problematic given that identity is not a one-way process, needing both social and self-ascription.[200]

From Okely's analysis[201] it is not clear to what extent Traveller identity can be based on heritage/genealogy. Even the presentation of 100-year-old 'Traveller names'[202] brings little security in terms of establishing a continuity of Traveller identity via lineage, given that no evidence is provided about local non-Traveller names or the presence of other names in the Traveller population looked at. Other considerations also have to be taken into account. As Okely points out, Travellers may not give their real names to people they are relatively unfamiliar with. Many English Travellers have chosen to be known by the comparatively common and anonymous title of 'Smith'.[203] One of the most common names Gypsies call themselves is Smith.[204]

Other theorists are no clearer about self-ascription and Gypsy identity. For example, Rao proclaims: 'I shall use the word "Gypsy" as a general term to cover all persons claiming to be "Rom", irrespective of their cultural, linguistic or religious differences; and whatever the degree of their nomadism or sedentarization.'[205] This argument is followed by the assertion of 'the certitude of a common Indian origin for all the Gypsy groups'.[206] The consequence of this position is that if one claims to be a Gypsy one has an Indian origin and identity.

This theorization fails to offer substantive evidence or coherent explanation. It seems that the researcher has found no firm basis for theoretically relying on self-identification as a substantive indicator of ethnic identity. In contrast it appears to be a highly fragile marker of Traveller ethnicity. The overall impression given by the research in Rehfisch and Rehfisch[207] is that the answer to the question of 'who is a Gypsy?' is, 'a Gypsy is anyone who says they are', but this is not secure. Another answer to the same question might be someone who has, or say they have, one Gypsy parent. Of course, both of these contentions could amount to the same thing. How could anyone reliably check if ones parents were Gypsies? Even if I may be able to prove that my father was/is a Gypsy and thus justify my own claim to Gypsyhood, in order to substantiate my father's Gypsyness I would have to show that at least one of his parents was a Gypsy and so on. Given the outsider status traditionally associated with Gypsies, excluded as many of them would have been, by choice and circumstance, from the bureaucratic interventions of community and State, it would seem that the reliance on public records would to be a tenuous and very limited means by which to establish the Gypsy lineage of all but a very few beyond two generations. For the most part one would need to rely on hearsay or family legends. Interesting and meaningful as such phenomena are as narrative, they cannot be regarded as a concrete foundation on which to build an ethnic identity.

Romanticism

Many writers looking at Traveller issues romanticize Traveller culture and lifestyle.[208] O'Nions critically asserts that a romanticized image of Gypsies is often fostered. This portrays them with horse and wagon as part of an archaic, rural idyll.[209] This depiction of a 'pure' yet 'foreign', pastoral, roving type, involved in esoteric employment (fortune-telling for example, palms/crystal ball) and 'clan' pastimes (bare-knuckle boxing, cock fighting) encompasses many of the ethnic markers outlined above, including exotic notions attached to origin, nomadism, tribal affiliations and language. Concepts of blood and the natural abound. Clebert exhibits the full range of the flaws in writing relating to Gypsies,[210] notions of 'stock', 'purity',[211] 'mother tongue' and 'blood' run throughout, but these terms are never really explained. A diverse range of people, 'all kinds of real Gypsies, by whatever name they may be known', are seen to be 'united in the same love of freedom' and their 'eternal flight from the bonds of civilization, in their vital need to live in accordance with nature's rhythm'.[212] The nobility and grand separateness of the Gypsy as both victim and free person dominates the character of the text. Biblical origins are explored alongside what Clebert calls 'Gypsy legends'. This material is intermixed with historical references to Gypsies that portray them emerging from various exotic locations. He commentates on a process wherein almost anyone of a travelling ilk, looking the least bit foreign, was described as having an affinity to Gypsies.[213] In the course of this exercise he notes how Indian scholars, 'show an awkward tendency to name *all* nomads as Gypsies'.[214] Clebert[215] presents a catalogue of historical references to various nomadic peoples/tribes. He defines most of them as Gypsies on the strength that 'Gypsies were never given a name except by the natives of the countries'.[216] These are then placed in a chronological and geographical order. The result of collation is presented as the progress of the Gypsy exodus. For Clebert the 'clear connection between the basic Gypsy language' and the dialects of northern India, mark the start of the 'Gypsy exodus from India' that took the form of a sudden scattering of Gypsies over the East.[217] This analysis represents the extreme of the kind of romanticism found in the literature. The work includes all the excesses of this tendency that many academics have, to a greater or lesser extent, replicated.

The Gypsy diaspora

The concept of diaspora, although rarely used in the literature relating to Travellers, has become part of the discourse on ethnicity and identity,[218] but the contention of an Indian origin followed by a dispersal means that the notion has an underlying presence in the analysis of Traveller identity. At the same time the function and meaning of diaspora are distinctly romantic. For Stuart Hall, the peoples of diaspora are:

> products of hybridity. They bear the traces of particular cultures, traditions, languages, systems or belief, texts and histories which have shaped them ... They are not and never will be unified in the old sense, because they are inevitable products of several interlocking histories and cultures, belonging at the same time to several 'homes' – and thus to no one, particular home.[219]

To this extent, the notion of a Gypsy diaspora from a direct or pure Indian origin is unrealistic. Hall, in seeing the diaspora as a composite of sentiment and subjectivity confirms the basis of Cornell and Hartmann's position that diasporas are characteristic of the modern world, an effect of the developing importance of identity. Within this feelings of affinity to the locations where the supposedly diasporic populations find themselves are undermined. Where people happen to live becomes merely the setting of identity that has origins elsewhere. This may not be a geographical locale but could be an imagined centre of awareness and/ or experience, more of a narrative of diaspora than an actual place.[220]

This suggests that the notion of diaspora is essentially a means of explanation of people's feelings about and affiliation to the locality in which they were born and/or live. It has been used as a tool by theorists and academics and this may have done much for the proliferation of the concept over recent times. The reality of diasporic notions is that they are somewhat abstract, often having mythological elements, which have the potential to fuse minority groups together around ethnic or nationalistic enterprises.[221] Thus the romanticism of the diasporic notion is evident, but the concept of diaspora also has a narrative force, primised on a level of exclusion or separateness.[222] It may be argued that these phenomena are prime generators of diasporic feelings. For the moment it can be understood that the notion of diaspora is applicable to the understanding of the development of Gypsy and Traveller identity within the literature. The analysis is circular:

1   Travellers are seen as set in diaspora (Indian origin).
2   Travellers are understood to be an oppressed, widely dispersed, yet distinctive group that maintain cultural and ethnic links.
3   Travellers are portrayed as having origins beyond their place of residence and little cause for affinity to 'host' communities.
4   Writers and theorists have thus sought confirmation of the diasporic heritage in an idealized, foreign, relatively exotic origin and noted what they see as arcane, archaic traditions and preserved language traits.
5   This is the perception of Gypsies that underlies Traveller identity as presented in the literature.
6   Travellers are seen as set in diaspora (romantic, exotic, alien, foreign, otherness).

Clebert[223] exemplifies this process and his example is replicated throughout the literature. He focuses on Gypsies on a country-by-country basis. He systematically chronicles their oppression and interaction with alleged host-populations. Very little space is given to possible recruitment to the Traveller population from non-Gypsy sources, this would undermine the romantic, diasporic narrative by the use of mundane empirical material to expose routine social causation.

Pseudo-sociology

Clebert does say that many British Travellers 'are not pure Gypsies',[224] but what would constitute a pure Gypsy is never established in any definite sense. This kind of empty dichotomy is taken on to establish a blood stratification or order in the 'Supplementary Notes on British and American Gypsies by the Translator'. Here the British Traveller population is broken down as follows:

1   Romanies: about 10,000 – these are true Roms.
2   Posh-rats: about 10,000 – half-bloods.
3   Didikois: about 10,000 – mixed, less than half-blood.
4   Travellers: about 20,000 – no Gypsy blood.

It is made clear that these are not official figures but 'careful and conservative estimates' made by 'Mr Derek Tipler' who Clebert describes as 'an enthusiastic amateur' and someone who was 'deeply interested in these people and, failing any official figures, decided to make his own census, which is probably not far wrong'.[225] This kind of pseudo-sociology is typical of the genre, as exemplified in Willems.[226]

For Clebert, assimilation into the Gypsy population seems almost impossible. Marriage to 'a Gypsy woman' is the least that needs to be done, although according to Clebert this is disapproved of (it is not clearly stated who does the disapproving). For Clebert this disapproval will most often result in exclusion 'from the tribe', the 'outlaw no longer has the right to the name of Gypsy (whether it be a man or woman who weds in an unrighteous marriage)'.[227] No concrete evidence of this allegedly Gypsy propensity is provided.

In his detailing of the Gypsy lineage of persecution, the central unifying element of what he sees as the Gypsy race, Clebert fails to consider the possibility that any problematic group might be called/reported as being Gypsy (again this would disturb the romantic/diasporic narrative) for the sake of political convenience/expedience. For example, he cites an incident of 1782,[228] involving the Hungarian military driving Gypsies, Poligari, in to dangerous swamps (he sees this as the origin of that people's 'phobia for wet places'). According to Clebert, this group (the Poligari) were seen as Godless heathens, cannibals and child abductors. Who would be more deserving of persecution than such people? Of course, if the group driven into the swamp had been benign, even devout wanderers or landless labourers, such treatment would have been unacceptable but what came first, the label Gypsy or the alleged antisocial behaviour?

Within this analysis it is possible to identify much use of the imagination but little empirical evidence. There is movement from a historical record of an attack against a group of people to an assumption that this fits into a pattern of Gypsy persecution:

Historical reference	*The possible contemporary analogy*
1 This group was Poligari (nothing else).	The group are itinerant (nothing else).
2 The Poligari were child abductors, etc.	The itinerants are layabouts/ spongers.
3 The Poligari were/are Gypsies.	The Gypsies were moved on.
4 Gypsies are phobic of wet places.	Gypsies are anti-authority.

Alternative theory	
i The group were poor peasants – not able to pay taxes.	The group were homeless.
ii Because of their poverty they were perceived as a threat.	The group contradicted the housing norm; conventional (psychological) forms of social control could not be applied.
iii The group had to be labelled as evil/subhuman (else the military/ the King could be seen to be evil/inhumane).	The group had to be labelled as inherently corrupt (else the system could be seen to be operating in the interests of the market).
iv The group were murdered.	The group were harassed.
v Poor peasants fear tax collectors.	The homeless are alienated.

Much of the literature, which concentrates on Gypsy experience,[229] views the situation of Travellers from what might be thought of as behind the barricades;

the position of Gypsies and Travellers as part of a social context is not established. Clebert's romantic focus on the Hungarian Army versus the Gypsies is
typical of this propensity. The act he refers to cannot be understood or decoded
without the context of events attached to the murder of the alleged Poligari
(Gypsies). Thus, Clebert's claim for a Gypsy race or ethnicity can be seen to be
perilously tangential. It is based mostly on legend, or myth; it is a prime exemplum
of romantic narrative set within the fable of a Gypsy diaspora. A real, racially
pure, Gypsy is identified by a complex code of behaviour, not entirely articulated, that may relate or correspond more or less to perceived patterns observed
or translated elsewhere by 'deeply interested' or entranced amateurs like Mr
Tipler. Other aspects of this theoretical position include ideas about an inherited
language, set within a community of blood, that cannot be transgressed, infiltrated or polluted by outside influences. These elements of a Gypsy ethnic paradigm are questionable indicators of origin. Clebert[230] does not see this and as
such provides little substantive evidence concerning Traveller origins.

Fraser[231] (illustrating how the above form of analysis has infused the literature
relating to Gypsies) is also seemingly distracted by the romantic, diasporic narrative. He moves unproblematically from the observation of itinerant groups to
the certitude of ancient origins, removed from current conditions and modern
considerations. Fraser's work is an exhaustive, world-wide study of the records
relating to the appearance, practices, traditions, language and cultures of a
diverse number of itinerant groups, tribes and communities, which Fraser places
together under the label of the Gypsies.

Apart from the rather fragile reliance on language, which he concedes is an
unreliable indicator of ethnic origin,[232] Fraser provides no definite rationale
to explain why these very different peoples, which appear at different times
and places, should be placed in a single category, other than their itinerant
background/life-style. He gives little consideration to the possibility that these
groups may not be of like origin. Neither does he feel the need to address the
effect the process of industrialization or modernity may have had on the Traveller
population. Fraser states that from such divisions around 20 'principal tribes'
have been isolated in what was Yugoslavia and that a number of these might be
subdivided. Each might be seen to have their own territory, subculture, occupations, dialect and marriage rites.[233]

In a similar way to other writers,[234] Fraser is not able to establish who is a pure
Romany. Unlike Fraser, Dodds cites influences, other than simple heritage, as
adding to the Gypsy population. He mentions the Irish potato famine and the
depopulation of the Scottish Highlands. Dodds also makes the point that when
discussing Gypsies we are referring to 'Britain's outcasts and refugees'.[235] This
provides some hope that his analysis will include definite consideration of social
influences on the Traveller population, but Dodds, like other writers, subscribes
to the idea that Travellers have northern Indian origins[236] and really does not
take the matter any further. This is surprising given Dodds' energetic contribution to Gypsy affairs. Although he does make the point that, 'There are plenty
of romantic books about the life of Gypsies . . . there is nothing at all about the

human problem',[237] at no time does he connect the post-Second World War housing crisis with the seeming growth in the numbers of people, who became visible after 1945, resorting to caravan-dwelling, that is, fundamentally, a form of temporary shelter.

The problem of seeming continuity

Much of the literature focusing on the social experience and history of Travellers assumes that there is a continuity of treatment or discrimination in respect of this population. Clebert[238] is followed by Acton,[239] Fraser,[240] Kenrick and Clark[241] and others in deciphering historical events, attitudes and circumstances as if modern human taxonomies have been constant throughout time. However, concepts such as ethnicity, race, nation and a people are relatively recent forms of categorization, whilst ideas about self, difference and even skin colour are historically specific terms.[242] As Stuart Hall points out:

> There have been many significantly different racisms – each historically specific and articulated in a different way with the societies in which they appear. Racism is always historically specific in this way, whatever common features it may appear to share with similar social phenomena.[243]

Even this statement is specific to a historical period wherein race is a recognized form of distinction. There could be no racism in a social environment wherein no concept of race existed.

Unreliable chronology: written records

Fraser traces the progress of the movement of what he sees as the 'original Gypsies' mostly through written evidence; some accounts are hundreds of years old. He unproblematically connects these writings with contemporary understandings of ethnicity and culture. Out of this a notion of Gypsy diaspora, the path of Gypsy migration, is traced. However, Fraser like others before him[244] gives no consideration to the possibility that the written record might have been produced after the physical arrival of what are taken to be itinerant tribes. This time-span (between arrival and recording of the same) is likely to differ over time and place. This factor would disturb the seeming chronological process Fraser presents. At the same time he does not consider the likelihood that itinerant groups would have conscripted/recruited people of other origins on their travels,[245] whilst losing personnel through assimilation and integration into host cultures. Neither does Fraser contemplate that the groups labelled as Gypsies (or alternative titles) could have been other (non-Gypsy) groups who were simply unrecognized or misrepresented. Any group in his analysis could have been the target of false description to justify maliciousness towards an offending community or minority. In the same vein the depiction of strange, exotic types entering an area could have been used to create a diversion from misrule through pogrom.[246] This myopia preserves the romantic, diasporic narrative but the cost of this is that Fraser's theoretical conclusions lack the necessary rigour needed to accurately discern definite ethnic origins.

Pseudo-science

Guy identifies similar weaknesses in Clebert, when he points out that Clebert may be appointing himself as the protector of bona fide Traveller culture as he understands it rather than as a historian chosen by Roms experiencing the actuality of Traveller life-style.[247]

Guy goes on to point out that how Roms are depicted is the fundamental problem that confronts those involved in Gypsy studies and issues.[248] He sees that researchers are confused:

> especially social anthropologists who have pursued an inconclusive search for definitive objective criteria of the ethnic group. Fredrik Barth has recently attacked this whole approach, arguing that the ascriptive aspect is logically prior to any objective characteristics of the ethnic group . . .[249]

This kind of weak analysis limits the value of Fraser's work in terms of establishing Traveller identity or the probable make-up of the Traveller community. Fraser moves the reader away from possible social and political explanations of the Traveller population towards an argument that portrays Travellers as a definite ethnic type that has a kind of victim relationship with the rest of society. Whilst there may be what might be understood as trace archaeological credence and interest in the debate that Fraser promotes, it fails to explain the current position and make-up of the Traveller population. Fraser offers a limited perspective, the analysis could be understood as representing the 'pseudo-science' that Okely refers to:

> Another critique is based on a pseudo-scientific theory of race which equates to social groups of Gypsies with distinct genetic groups . . . outside observers use blood and so-called 'genetic inheritance' more as metaphors for their own social categories . . . The 'real' Gypsy is identified by selective cultural traits which appear most exotic or picturesque . . .[250]

Fraser seeks to give archaic racial, what in another time and place might be called 'volk', myths some kind of analytical/factual validity. In the process he creates a kind of clinical separation of peoples, unsullied by social, economic or political factors. This borders on the fantastic given the nature of modern society and the events and situations that gave rise to the same.

Distinctiveness and mysterious continuity

Acton[251] experiences something of the same set of problems. He sets the scene for his book with the subtitle: 'The Development of Ethnic Ideology and Pressure

Politics among British Gypsies from Victorian Reformism to Romany National-ism'. Like Fraser and many of his predecessors and successors, Acton's work is devoted to the romantic, even heroic notions of the type embedded in the subtitle, the phraseology of which perhaps gives away an aspiration emerging out of Guevaraist symbolism, embodying a kind of reshaped Gypsy romanticism, moulded out of the middle-class student rebelliousness of the 1960s. What makes Acton a little different are these radical undertones, related to 'pressure politics' and 'nationalism'.

Acton seems to want to include everything that has ever been said about Gypsies in his analysis.[252] As such, the work is confusing. It is difficult to extract any clear or consistent line of thought. He makes a case for 'change as continu-ity'.[253] This seems to be based on a notion of maintenance of role inviting a continuity of response. In short, this predisposition prevents the incursion of wider society into the continuance of Gypsy culture, although Acton states that it would be unrealistic to see Travellers cut-off, or separate from, outside influ-ences. Again, like other writers, it seems that he wishes to promote the idea of Gypsy separateness; an ability to remain relatively untouched as a cultural entity by the surrounding society, even though the need to state the likelihood of incursion cannot be resisted. What is being suggested is that the distinctiveness of Gypsies sustains a mysterious continuity. This is perhaps a symptom of the nature of Acton's focus. In a similar manner to Fraser,[254] Acton views the world from a standpoint of a minority life-style, and calls upon a strange mixture of research, including folklore, but he also uses a rather dense sociology of ethnicity and nineteenth-century lay anthropology. The work is not quite able to conceive of the experience of Travellers in the context of the wider social realm; the analysis seems to be cut off at the borders of its subject.[255]

The problems with this stance are partly addressed by Liegeois who states that, in the case of Gypsies, it is:

> arbitrary – and often sociologically, politically, anthropologically and cul-turally irrelevant – to separate groups of Indian from those of indigenous origin (and sometimes even impossible to do so). They interact both locally (contacts between family groups; inter-marriage) and more widely (in inter-national Gypsy political organizations) and they occupy identical positions in an environment that treats them all the same.[256]

This argument is enforced by the existence of other major migrations through-out the last 150 years from Romania, Ireland, Yugoslavia and Portugal. For Liegeois, Gypsies, having constantly interacted with each other, non-Travellers and other divergent nomadic and itinerant groups, hold a huge diversity of cultural and linguistic traditions and represent a wide and varied mixture of people. Liegeois, when looking at the theories of Gypsy origin, suggests that ideas relating to the subject can owe more to imagination than substantiated facts, and may be 'spiced with romanticism'. He states that a single characteristic that might be more of less indicative of a particular travelling group can become the basis of a whole theoretical framework and that supposed facts, that may support forms of prejudice and stereotyping, seem to become prevalent more swiftly than research findings.[257]

Liegeois defines the idea of Indian origins applied to all Gypsies as largely the stuff of legend:[258] 'random structures are concocted out of wholly gratuitous assertions of myths that have nothing to do with Gypsies at all. Most of the hypotheses are no less fabulous than the legends'.[259] However, he argues that trace elements of Hindi having been identified in Romany languages, although classic studies of the language used by Gypsies in Wales have also established Welsh, Greek, Slav, Iranian, Romanian, German and French influences, may indicate that contemporary Gypsies have a connection with ancient migrations of people from India to the West. This movement is characterized by Liegeois as a continuous flow of nomadic peoples.[260] For all this, he indicates that those seen as Egyptians, a favoured medieval expression for mysterious Travellers thought to be of eastern Mediterranean origin, need not have been of exotic origin, understanding that even highwaymen and criminals were referred to as Egyptians. He argues that since the beginnings of the Gypsy presence in Europe they have been 'lumped together' in law and record with 'vagabonds and vagrants'.[261]

Added to this complication of terminology, according to Liegeois, the ancestors of migrants may well have been absorbed by indigenous Travellers.[262] As such, Gypsy culture can be understood to reflect a mixture of a number of origins.[263] He states that: 'Recent migrations merged with communities that had been criss-crossing all Europe since the fifteenth and sixteenth century.'[264]

Liegeois notes that the answer to the problems that host communities have in connection with this wide and complex group of itinerants has traditionally been banishment. He does not, however, see the possibility that such a practice may have obliged the continuance of an itinerant existence and/or be part of the social generation of a category of travelling people. He is not able to conceive of a process that could lead to a historical merging of individuals and groups, the outcasts of society, who for a range of social, political and religious reasons, have been obliged to wander. The likely intermingling of the socially peripatetic, the rootless of history, is problematic in terms of the proposal for the notion of a distinct Gypsy lineage and a Gypsy diaspora.

Perhaps Liegeois is caught in the same trap as other writers. Okely[265] points out, in the opening chapter, 'Historical Categories and Representations', that non-Gypsies have written Traveller history. The paradox of this is obvious, but her coverage of the Traveller in history is amongst the most balanced in the literature. This is exemplified by her useful critique of the Gypsiologists and their interest in identifying racial categories, couched in a tendency to seek out and perpetuate, what Okely calls, exotic origins. She pulls the two sides of this critique together when she points out that the claim to Indian origins was not introduced by Travellers. Okely sees all roles ascribed to Gypsies by non-Gypsies, 'trickster, exotic or victim', as carrying the 'risk of self-degradation and a dangerous sense of unreality'.[266] However, this is not expanded upon. In fact Okely contradicts herself by claiming that the ethnic boundary of Gypsyhood is based on pollution beliefs, founded on the practice of inner purity.[267] This demonstrates a level of romanticism in her analysis, although, as pointed out earlier in this chapter, she contests the grand notion of an Indian origin.

Okely suggests that the bringing together of varied and heterogeneous groups under the title of Gypsy, is perhaps a questionable pursuit. She states that she was able to 'crack the code' of 'historical and folklorist data'[268] through co-existence with Travellers. This re-energizes the very exotic, sentimentalist and romantic interpretations that she criticizes. This to some extent is unavoidable, given her ambition to justify an ethnic paradigm.

Okely[269] argues that for Gypsies the best opportunities may be found in occupations that others are unwilling to undertake.[270] This is a somewhat vague assertion, and suggests that Gypsies take on a sort of scavenger role in terms of work. Again, this need to ascribe definite modes and characteristics to behaviour is indicative of the anthropological perspective. General statements of the type that Okely makes about the 'economic niche' of Gypsies offer only a stereotypical view of Travellers, very much akin to the Gypsiologists Okely attacks. Neither does it sit well with a later assertion that Gypsies 'denounce the dominant wage labour system'.[271] This implies choice rather than an inherent propensity, via ethnic position, to undertake the work that non-Gypsies reject.

Okely's claim to be free of the misinterpretations of others because she lived amongst Gypsies is tempered by Rehfisch and Rehfisch who provide a very wide-ranging and probably one of the most rigorous anthropological/sociological studies of Traveller culture throughout the world, including examinations of Traveller communities in the USA, Britain, France, Germany, Switzerland, Spain, Czecho-slovakia, Ireland and Norway. Most of the contributors demonstrate the same useful scepticism that Rehfisch and Rehfisch exhibit in their opening remarks when they identify a propensity amongst Travellers to offer elaborate and heavily embroidered explanations regarding customs and life-style, as these often elicit greater rewards than more realistic interpretations. They go on to suggest that previous studies of Traveller groups have been unreliable due to this and other reasons connected with the attitudes and dispositions of those involved in research.[272]

In the same book Okely gives an example of how ethnicity can be generated by anthropological wish fulfilment. Although she goes on to make the case for an ethnic identity by pointing out that nineteenth-century family names attributed to Gypsies can still be found amongst current Travellers in southern England, she points out that her research demonstrates that Gypsy family trees almost invariably include non-Gypsies.[273] This position appears to indicate a definite scepticism about concrete notions of Traveller identity based on the literature. This is emphasized when Okely states that those who have taken up a Traveller life-style from a non-Traveller background, are denigrated. This would make the claim of a non-Gypsy heritage or origin less likely (to avoid 'denigration' one would claim to be a 'true Gypsy'). This, together with her contention that stereotypes have been exploited by Travellers,[274] confirms the Rehfischs' point regarding the contortion of Traveller traditions and identity for the ears of interested non-Travellers.

Guy points out, when working with Gypsies, 'one encounters deep ambivalence towards their identity', and that they are, 'Righteously angry at the hostile stereotype others hold of them.'[275] This would, perhaps, be a useful reply to most of the conclusions about Traveller identity. It does seem to be the case that much of Gypsy identity is in the eye of the beholder who, looking for Gypsyness, finds it.

Barnes seems to typify this approach. For her Irish Travellers, being mainly of Celtic origin, are different from the 'Gypsies' that 'hail from India'.[276] Not only does this conveniently neglect the historical antecedents of the Celts, that have been claimed to be sub-continental/Asia Minorian,[277] but also she moves from contemporary Traveller life-style to an ancient people who arrived in the geographical area thousands of years ago. This is like saying that the current occupants of southern England are Jutes, or the present residents of Rome go back to the first days of the Caesuras. Barnes creates a Traveller lineage by simply stating it and then she moves on as if this has in some way been established or confirmed. Given the migrations to and from Ireland and the incursions by Vikings, Normans, Puritans, Presbyterians and Elizabethans, the claim of Celtic origins for all Irish Travellers is doubtful. That Tinkers could be a population group consistently energized and modified by the historically constant social, economic, agricultural, religious, political and industrial upheavals in Ireland, Scotland and England is not considered. Yet this, what might be termed, development model would seem much more credible than the 'hygienic heritage' model suggested by Barnes. But of course, the former would imply connection rather than separation, and become more the province of sociology than anthropology. It would also depart from the conventional romantic narrative. It is perhaps more attractive to be the ancestor of a Celtic Prince than a grocer from Lanark.

Sandford provides a similar type of analysis to Barnes.[278] He presents a collection of 16 Traveller biographies and anecdotal material that fit with Sandford's general view, which he makes clear from the start, referring to his subject as 'Gypsy citizens'.[279] The first part of the book is littered with sweeping, unsubstantiated contentions about the character of Travellers; this includes claims that there are about 25,000 Gypsies living in houses, that some intermarry with non-Gypsies, that they speak English with a 'sprinkling of Romany' and that 'India is the place from which their ancestors came'.[280]

For Sandford, 'Gypsies have rejected much of our culture . . .' (whatever our culture is) 'not in an intellectual way but instinctively . . .'.[281] Within the literature on the meaning and motivation in Traveller culture, one often discovers an ill-defined concept of the natural. In Sandford's case some of the material he presents gives this position a glint of validity, where informants provide a mixture of the idyllic, nostalgic, romantic, sentimental and tragic. Traveller life is portrayed as a kind of drama, or soap opera. The respondents claim Gypsy or Romany identity, but this is not elaborated in terms of genealogy or other corroborative material. Typical is the statement made in the final anecdotal section, 'Water Gypsies'. The informant claims to be a 'dark person', the same as 'Gypsies', even though the life-style described is very overtly that of a barge-dwelling family: the bald statement or claim of identity is made and Sandford proceeds as if the fact of identity has been established. In this way identity/ethnicity is invented within the pages of the book; it is not referring to definite external or neutral markers, the Gypsy is generated by a wish to see Gypsies. It seems for Sandford one could find oneself in almost any situation and claim a Gypsy lineage. This has been the tradition of Gypsy studies.[282]

The final section of Sandford is concerned with legislative matters and informal politics, but it is still blighted by sweeping, unsupported statements. For example, when referring to the attitude of Gypsies that have moved into housing he states that:

> They will tell you, when you knock at their door, with pride, that they are Gypsies. Not for them the uncertainties of some Gypsies on the road who will deny being Gypsies or ask you to refer to them by euphemisms.[283]

Throughout the book Traveller identity or culture and the motivation to travel, seem to be based on a way of life or a rather loose notion of image.[284] However, none of Sandford's respondents demonstrate more than two or three of the image facets referred to, such as the use of slang, an interest in horses and 'The gathering and selling of wild flowers' ('the travelling Gypsy is a born naturalist'). These, essentially behavioural, traits are for no apparent reason connected with 'Gypsy blood'.[285]

Sandford is part of a writing tradition within the 'Gypsy genre' that picks up on the romantic tradition, but swaths it in a technique that looks scientific, using popularist sociological/anthropological language, together with references to legislation and welfare rights. This is not an accusation of dishonesty on the part of the likes of Sandford, but it is pointing out that such material is based on well-meaning assumption and myopic enthusiasm, rather than rigorous research and disciplined analysis. As with much of this type of literature, Sandford does not leave the reader very much wiser in terms of the nature of Traveller identity and the formation of the ethnic category of Gypsy.

Formal Gypsy organizations

Throughout this book I argue that the production of Gypsy identity is significantly affected by academic activity, the literature concerned with Traveller affairs and legislation interacting with social and economic factors. However, this interaction produces interest groups and organizations that arise out of defensive reactions, political motives and expressions of inter-cultural and cross-cultural solidarity, that complement and confirm the situation from which they sprang. There are a huge number of these organizations that also play a part in defining Traveller culture, identity and ethnicity in Britain. An illustrative selection is outlined below to provide a map of the formal Gypsy organizations that claim insight into the history of, support, politically represent and/or promote Traveller interests and culture.[286] Some others are included in Appendix Two. This material was gleaned from Internet research and approaches made to 50 organizations and groups whose central concern are Travellers.

In terms of function, there is a great deal of overlap within and between nearly all organizations, institutions and groups specializing in Traveller interests. Although there appear to be distinct areas of primary interest, for example education, professional, political, welfare, rights, publication and research, any one organization can encompass a number of these concerns. For instance, 'The National Association of Health Workers with Travellers' (NAHWT) is straightforwardly a professional association. However, this group's concern for Traveller health will cause them to adopt a position on welfare issues in respect of this group. The NAHWT seeks to:

1   Recognize Gypsy/Travellers as an ethnic minority group.
2   Promote appropriate and non-discriminatory health-care provision in order to reduce inequalities.

The NAHTW is based at the Birmingham Specialist Community Health NHS Trust. It aims to provide clinically effective services of a high quality for the communities it serves. It also aims to make these services fair and accessible. As such, the NAHTW can be seen to have a political standpoint. Health is also related to the condition of sites, hence the NAHWT is an organization not only concerned with rights but it also has some interest in health education and research.

Given this, it would be futile to attempt to categorize these organizations by a single concern or issue interest. This being the case I will present them in a random order.

The Advisory Council for the Education of Romany and other Travellers (ACERT)

ACERT was established in 1973, with Lady Plowden as its president. It was one of the first agencies in Britain to promote good practice in the education of Traveller children. It has had an ongoing involvement in developing Traveller education and research.[287] ACERT works for:

- equal access to education for Gypsies and Travellers
- safe and secure accommodation for Gypsy and Traveller families
- equal access to health and other community services for Gypsies and Travellers
- good community relations, endeavouring to eliminate discrimination against Gypsies and Travellers on racial or other grounds
- equal opportunities for Gypsies and Travellers

It provides advice and information on Gypsy and Traveller traditions and rights and publishes a newsletter, reports and books focusing on Traveller issues. ACERT has assisted Travellers with planning problems and appeals and is setting up an advocacy and advisory help-line.

The European Federation for the Education of Children of Occupational Travellers (EFECOT)

EFECOT was founded in 1989 with the aim to improve educational provision for children and young people from the families of occupational Travellers and children with an itinerant life-style. This was based on the assumption that fairground and circus people, bargees and season workers, having no fixed abode for at least part of the year, often have to overcome major hurdles to access continuous schooling.

EFECOT undertakes activities and projects to provide and optimize education and training for occupational Travellers all over Europe. With the support of European partners it seeks to create and promote educational provisions adapted to the particular needs of travelling people and to prevent 'them falling through the regular educational net'.

The Interface Collection, based at the Gypsy Research Centre at the Université René Descartes, Paris

The Gypsy Research Centre at the Université René Descartes, Paris, functions through the activity of international teams and working groups of experts. It sees itself as the main institutional influence on the understanding and awareness of Gypsy culture. It claims to have established this through research publications (in Britain via the University of Hertfordshire Press) and the monthly journal *Interface*.

Established in co-operation with the European Community and the Council of Europe in the early 1980s, the Gypsy Research Centre sees its work as principally focused on: 'ensuring the systematic implementation of measures geared towards improving the living conditions of Gypsy communities, by way of the dissemination of information, training, documentation, publication and coordination etc.'[288] This is premised on 'research axes' in the fields 'of sociology, history, linguistics, social and cultural anthropology . . . .'[289]

Overview of Gypsy organizations

The above organizations and those referred to in Appendix Two by their very purpose can be understood as being the arbiters of a self-confirming analysis. For example the Gypsy Research Centre sets out to justify the view of Gypsy culture and history as exemplified in what might be called the traditional theoretical canon in terms of the literature concerned with Traveller identity. Its *Interface* publications, some of which have been critiqued above, are part of this.

Collectively, perhaps with the exception of EFECOT, the organizations detailed make the assumption, unproblematically, that a Gypsy ethnic group or human typology exists. They do not, in any overt or forceful manner, consider the effects of social or economic considerations in the development of the Traveller population. Thus it can be argued that these organizations, alongside the literature focusing on Traveller issues, are involved in a process of reinforcing a partial and flawed perception of the Traveller population. This is perhaps not surprising in that, as suggested at the start of this section, as well as helping to sustain this incoherent perception, these organizations are products of the same limited perspective.

Conclusion

In this chapter I have looked to critique the notion of Gypsy and Traveller ethnicity as developed in the literature focusing on Traveller identity. I have pointed out the limitations of the literature, highlighting the overall failure to consider the social and economic context within which the Traveller population has developed. I have also identified the propensity within theory surrounding Gypsies and Travellers to present Traveller identity within a paradigm of romanticism and a biological/hereditary nexus. Out of this framework emerges the contradictory proposal that travelling people are a homogeneous population made up of heterogeneous groups. I have shown that although this constructed homogeneity has been challenged in recent times[290] it continues to dominate the discourse around Traveller identity and is the foundation on which the claim of difference and the assumption of Traveller ethnicity is premised.

I have further illustrated that Traveller ethnicity is based upon particular ethnic markers all of which I have demonstrated to be tenuous and vague. I have also shown that the contention of Gypsy and Traveller ethnicity and difference is reinforced by organizations that exist to promote the interests of Gypsies and Travellers.

Overall, I have suggested that the Traveller population or constituent proportions of this group cannot be accurately understood as a hygienic continuity of blood, race, ethnicity or hereditary factors. Considering the position of New Age Travellers, research looking at the identity of other Travellers and historical data relating to Gypsy and Traveller groups, I have begun to build a position that suggests that social and economic considerations need to be included in the analysis of Traveller identity in order to produce a more precise analysis of the Gypsy and Traveller population.

I will now go on to demonstrate the contemporary position of Travellers in England. In the chapters that follow I will further develop the argument that Traveller ethnicity is, to a significant extent, socially generated and go on to show how legislative activity affecting Travellers is connected to the promotion of State and market norms.

2 What is ethnicity?

Introduction

Within the literature relating to Gypsies and Travellers there is sympathy for the notion of a Traveller ethnicity.[1] Notions of blood, hereditary, race and theories of origin or lineage[2] are central within the discourse surrounding Traveller identity. However, Hall has argued that cultural diversity is a factor of the modern world and as such ethnic absolutism is a regressive characteristic of late modernity. For him forms of cultural identity that attempt to secure identity by the adoption of closed versions of culture or community arise from the refusal to deal with cultural difference.[3] According to Hall, 'the boundaries of difference are continually repositioned in relation to different reference points'.[4]

Traveller identity seems, in the main, to be established on the basis of lifestyle[5] and self-ascription.[6] Traveller identity or ethnicity can thus, it seems, be culturally adopted. The resulting confusion within the collective analysis of Traveller identity is compounded by its lack of consideration for the role of economic, social, inter-group and interpersonal factors within the development of the ethnic paradigm of Traveller identity.

This chapter explores the notion of ethnicity, in particular relating to Traveller identity. This is necessary in order to critically examine the character of Traveller identity as an ethnicity, but also to understand, in the context of the contemporary explanations about individuals, groups and society. The chapter argues that ethnic categories are socially constructed, adopted and ascribed. It examines the social purpose, maintenance and relevance of ethnic categories in contemporary society. As Stuart Hall has pointed out, the issue of race provides an important insight into the history and functioning of society.[7] I will suggest, using a Weberian perspective, that social action contributes to the process of ethnic categorization. The analysis includes an exploration of the confusion surrounding Traveller ethnicity and identity and the reductionist position that portrays Travellers arising out of what might be called a blood nexus, which describes Gypsy identity via a discourse relating to hereditary and diasporic factors. This obviates the importance of an examination of the social, economic, inter-group and interpersonal factors impacting on the development of Traveller identity and ethnicity. There is a need to understand what this categorization means for the travelling population and society in general.

The theme throughout this chapter echoes Stuart Hall's hagiography for cultural studies which emphasizes fractures rather than continuity:

> In serious, critical intellectual work, there are no 'absolute beginnings' and few unbroken continuities . . . What we find, instead, is an untidy but characteristic unevenness of development. What is important are the significant breaks – where old lines of thought are disrupted, older constellations displaced, and elements, old and new, are regrouped around a different set of premises and themes . . .[8]

From race to ethnicity

Banton[9] argues that the idea of race has moved from a pre-eighteenth-century interpretation of an expression of decent to a nineteenth-century concept, based in an erroneous scientific movement, relating to human types.[10] This construct was to be discredited in the twentieth century, confining the language of race to fringe political activity. In everyday discourse the seemingly less biologically determinist notion of ethnicity replaced race as the defining category of human taxonomy.[11] However, the notions of race and ethnicity have both been deployed as distinctive forms of categorization.

This emphasizes the social nature of ethnic categorization. As such ethnicity can be understood as a product of social interaction, although Malik[12] points out that there is no consensus about the meaning of ethnicity and argues that race and ethnicity have no objective reality.[13] This appears to hold true in relation to Travellers who are portrayed in the literature as essentially a consistent, natural, real, eternal, stable and static phenomenon, who are the victims of a host community beyond themselves. It is hard to understand why discourse surrounding Travellers and the general debate relating to ethnicity should be so moribund, but as Sollors states, 'Assimilation is the foe of ethnicity'. He argues that there are numerous polemics against melting pot, mainstream and majority culture that result in an 'isolationist, group-by-group approach that emphasizes "authenticity" and cultural heritage within the individual, somewhat idealized group'. This undermines the view that social conditions are the product of broad historical conditions, cultural mores and social interaction.[14]

Why ethnicity?

The requirement for separateness and authenticity runs through the literature relating to Gypsies and Travellers.[15] However, Sollors questions this seemingly taken for granted attitude in relation to the ethnicity, seeing ethnic groups as a product of the historical process and modern nationalism. He suggests that there is a pretence that ethnic groups are eternal and essential, but in reality these flexible, unstable and constantly changing and redefined groupings are products of contemporary times.[16] Contemporary situations give rise to ethnic formulations that complement and are necessary to these situations. Sollors suggests that the literature betrays a certain ancestry seeing 'the formulas of "originality" and "authenticity" in ethnic discourse a palpable legacy of European romanticism . . . .'[17]

It was not until 1953[18] that ethnicity really came into general usage. Malik[19] argues that '"Ethnicity" is a peculiarly post-war word.' He cites Huxley and Haddon as being the first to suggest that the concept of race should be replaced by the notion of ethnic groups. This allowed for the study of social difference without the political connotations evoked by ideas relating to race which are elaborated by McLoughlin.[20] Malik argues that the term ethnicity, like race, is used in a somewhat wanton manner, but there is little agreement as to the meaning of the word. Although he makes the case that, in the main, race refers to differences arising out of ascribed biological divisions, whilst ethnic categories are based on perceived cultural differences, Malik sees the definition of ethnicity as tautological, in that an ethnic group is that which is defined as an ethnic group. However, it is this that allows academics, politicians and other social commentators to segment humanity into distinct categories without suffering the accusation of racism.

The term ethnicity could be seen as useful because it avoids objective, biological categories, but it does this by introducing subjective distinctions. Malik[21] argues that in usage, the concept of ethnicity cannot be discerned from that of race. He[22] sees ethnicity as race with the biology expunged and argues that ethnicity includes the biological ideas of race as a factor in identity. For Malik, ethnicity merges the social distinctions inherent in the concepts of race and culture. Ethnic differences in British society are expressed via values and behaviour[23] so instead of going from the starting point of racial differentiation to the cultural differences inherent to that race, the analysis moves from cultural differentiation to the racial end point. The sum of both processes is the same – racial differentiation and ethnic groups retaining an essentialist/homogeneous identity. This gives credence to the idea of multiculturalism, which overestimates the autonomy and homogeneity of ethnic groupings whilst underestimating the amount of interdependence of cultural forms.

Culture, for Malik, has taken on the role of race, being something that one is regarded as having been born into. As a consequence, a cultural history includes the power of biology. Culture represents an exclusivity set in a common past that includes some and excludes others. The past is made teleological and determinist. It has power over the present through notions of roots and tradition.[24] For Malik[25] culture is used to refer to a connecting factor that links generations. This continuity is founded on kinship and intermarriage, but is reliant on a common consciousness of shared descent. This gives rise to a legacy of heritage that takes the form of and operates through particular attributes that are passed on by immediate ancestors to progeny. This is a wholly biological inheritance, not a social process.

For Malik, the stripping away of biology from the concept of race, seeing through the focus of cultural inheritance, has created a new discourse of race amenable to the post-Nazi period. Cultural debate has reincarnated the assumptions of racial thought but in a guise that can accommodate the cultural exclusivists and help them to deny their racism. This analysis argues that the notions of culture, ethnicity and race are interchangeable as analytical notions. However, for the purposes of analysis I will explore the notion of ethnicity, because in contemporary social discourse it seems to be the most prevalent of the terms used to categorize/separate human beings into discreet types. However, this opens ethnicity and culture up to the same accusation made against race by Montagu,[26] who asserts it is 'Man's most dangerous myth'. It appears that the notions of culture and ethnicity are, like the concept of race, problematical taxonomies. For all this, the persistence of the social propensity to ethnically/ racially/culturally categorize continues. This might be seen to arise out of a drive to cleanse, or equalize, a desire to celebrate difference or oppress those who are deemed to be different by a dominant or host society. The moment a distinction is made it can be used in both positive and negative ways, but it is making difference an aspect of notoriety that starts the ball of categorization rolling.

What is ethnicity?

According to Lee[27], over the last 40 years there have been three main approaches to examining the nature of ethnicity:

- The primordialist view
- The circumstantialist or constructivist view
- The oppositional view

The primordialist view

The primordialist perspective sees ethnic identity as incorporating shared blood, speech, customs and so on that are experienced as, at times, having an irresistible power.[28] From this standpoint ethnicity is, a priori, inexpressible and effective. Within the notion of Gypsy identity the idea of Indian origins and the perseverance of Romani culture, align with the primordialist view. For example, Reid[29] argues that there are three dominant theories relating to the origin of Scottish Travellers, which he refers to as indigenous, Indian and fusionist theories. The Indian theory, according to Reid, argues that Travellers are immigrants, with ancestral origins in northwest India.

Lapage[30] relates to this tradition in the literature seeing that the definition of Gypsy identity was generated against a backdrop of a resurgence of the Romantic movement. She argues that this was part of a 'desperate search for a special culture of the Gypsies', an effort to 'salvage the culture and identity of a group' that was 'believed to be disappearing'. This perspective 'maintained that the Gypsy people of Britain were a "pure race"'. For Lapage this amounted to an argument 'for separateness of a minority group based on a stereotype of appearance, dress, customs and so on'.[31]

The circumstantialist or constructivist view

This perspective argues that ethnic identity is a product of social interaction and does not have any necessary foundation. However, it can be argued that there is an element of the primordialist perspective in this position in that it can still situate origins in a vague and mystical past. For Reid there is something of the circumstantialist in the indigenous theory, relating to Travellers the belief that this group were not immigrants like 'pure Gypsies' but 'aboriginal people'. Reid suggests that this indigenous theory was summed up by Tim Neat in 'The Summer Walkers', a BBC documentary, made in 1971, that portrayed Travellers as the descendants of a pre-Christian era caste of nomadic metalworkers of 'high Celtic society', or the ancestors of 'aboriginal hunter-gathers who were pushed into northern Europe in the Neolithic period'.[32]

Mayall takes a circumstantialist stance when he points out problems with the romantic notions of Traveller identity highlighted by Lapage.[33] For Mayall, what is of concern is not whether customs were adhered to by the majority or some Travellers, but the ambition to attach these to racial analysis. Mayall[34] questions the perception of the Traveller as an image of Rousseau's noble savage. He argues that given the likelihood that Travellers married non-Travellers[35] it is difficult to hold with notions of purity, or a Gypsy culture not impinged upon by outside influences. This equates to what Reid calls the fusionist theory.[36] This approach proposes a fusion has occurred amongst the indigenous people and immigrant groups from the sixteenth century on. Reid argues that those who adhere to the indigenous theory are obliged to concede that, 'there was undoubtedly a certain degree of socio-biological fusion'.[37] Acton[38] also adopts a more constructivist stance when he suggests that Travellers, from the earliest times[39] would have been 'mixing culturally, linguistically and genetically with local populations'. As such Gypsies can be understood to be a separate group, but as having an identity founded on cultural considerations more than a racial analysis.[40]

This is congruent with Barth's contention that it is 'the ethnic boundary which defines the group, not the cultural stuff which it encloses'. This boundary requires 'continual expression and validation'.[41] It was Barth who 'emphasized the mutually reinforcing inclusionary and exclusionary processes involved in the separation of groups'.[42] For Barth, the nature of such boundaries might be understood through their comparative opaqueness/transparency, that is, to what extent 'the degree to which the characteristics beyond the boundary can be seen . . . the relative proportions of these dimensions will determine the strength and functioning of the boundary'.[43] These boundaries are fabricated within the process of human interaction, economic, social and psychological. For Barth, it is not blood ties that hold Gypsies together as a distinct group. For him Gypsy solidarity arises mainly out of their shared experience of travelling, following on from a history of serf bondage and their rejection of 'puritan ethics of responsibility, toil and morality'.[44] Thus, according to Lee, 'any ethnic attachment is based on continual construction, modification, reinforcement and validation of identity'.[45] This is likely to occur in the light of social and economic factors.

The oppositional view

Spicer[46] attempted to bring the primordial and circumstantial perspectives together. For him, 'some groups of people with some effective attachments to cultural symbols have persisted, under different conditions, for long periods'.[47] Spicer called these groups 'persistent identity systems'. They had:

1 Out-lived several types of State organization.
2 Experienced pressure for assimilation or incorporation.
3 Successfully resisted such pressures.
4 Developed well-defined symbols of identity.

Spicer saw 'continued opposition' as a crucial factor in explaining a persistent identity system. For him these are formed by, maintained in and related to, the conditions of opposition within the conflict between these groups and those involved in the extension of social control.[48]

Jenkins[49] proposes another form of oppositionalism. He sees externally located categorization, as Mann put it, 'a class whose nature and composition is decided by the person who defines the category'[50], as being critical in the production and reproduction of social identity. For Jenkins the experience of categorization can strengthen group identity through resistance and reaction. As such, categorization may foster group identity. At the same time group identification is confirmed though categorizing others.[51]

Ubiquitous oppositionalism

Lee argues that all the above approaches assume a level of opposition to explain why ethnic identity exits. The circumstantialist position relies on boundary maintenance and the separation that is implicit in this and the primordialist analysis and is dependent on an opposition between 'coercive congruities'[52] that differentiate one identity from another.

A variation on these perspectives is supplied by Castells[53] in what he calls 'legitimizing identity'. This is engendered by those who control society to extend and justify their domination by manipulation of groups that make up society. This interpretation is central to Sennett's theory[54] of authority and domination, but can also be seen in operation within theories of nationalism. This perspective might explain why much of the discourse surrounding Travellers[55] sympathizes with an ethnic understanding of this group. However, the element of oppositionalism is clear.

Ethnicity: a social construction

A consistent feature in this analysis is that ethnicity is best understood as a socially constructed phenomenon. This is even the case within the primordialist position, which seems to be the least tenable but at the same time the most imbrued with notions of heredity and biological categorization. This position is affirmed by the conclusions of many theorists; for example for Smith[56] ethnic identity is generated through the contemporary social situation and is 'not archaeologically salvaged from the disappearing past'. This fits with Gilroy's outlook that sees identity in a constant state of flux, regeneration and reformation and he expresses enthusiasm for the idea that, 'it ain't where you're from, it's where you're at', as it gives a precedence to the present, expressing a view of identity as an organic process of 'self-making' at a time when 'myths of origins' are so prevalent.[57]

The problem of ethnic identity is that no single heuristic device is able to explain the whole phenomenon. Overall ethnic and cultural differences can be understood as a function of groupness, they appear as forms of distinction and opposition as part of a process of discrimination. However, the existence of a group is not necessarily a reflection of cultural difference. The existence of an ethnic group implies ethnic relations and these logically involve two main collective parties, they are not unilateral. Identity is a matter of inputs and outputs. This goes along with the social constructionist and oppositionist models of ethnicity, that ethnic groups are what people believe or think them to be; cultural differences mark groupness, they do not cause it (or indelibly characterize it); ethnic identification arises out of and within interaction between groups. Jenkins exemplifies this approach, describing the basic social anthropological model of ethnicity as being:

- about cultural differentiation; identity is a dialectic between similarity and difference;
- concerned with culture, shared meaning and is based in, and the outcome of, social interaction;
- no more fixed or unchanging than the culture it is part of or the situations in which it is generated;
- as a social identity, collective and individual, expressed in social interaction and internalized in self-identification.

On the basis of this Jenkins argues that culture and ethnicity are not things that people have, or to which they belong. They are complicated structures that people use and within which they build a developing idea of themselves and those around them.[58]

Weber sees the adoption or implication of a race or ethnicity as a kind of secondary response to other social phenomena:

> race creates a 'group' only when it is subjectively perceived as a common trait: this happens only when a neighbourhood or the mere proximity of racially different persons is the basis of joint (mostly political) action, or conversely, when some common experiences of members of the same race are linked to some antagonism against its members of an *obviously* different group.[59]

And further:

> ethnic membership does not constitute a group; it only facilitates group
> formation of any kind, particularly in the political sphere. On the other
> hand, it is primarily the political community, no matter how artificially
> organized, that inspires the belief in common ethnicity.[60]

As such, for Weber, ethnicity does not, in itself, have the cohesive power to
combine individuals into discreet groups. However, potentially it is a binding
factor in particular political situations. This being the case, for Weber, the ethnic
group is fundamentally a political collective that in a circular manner motivates
the conviction that the group arising out of political conditions has a shared
ethnicity. It seems to be, for those who follow the Weberian/social constructionist
analysis,[61] that ethnicity is the product of inter-group agitation/dissatisfaction.
This is exemplified in Weber's notion of social closure, which can be seen as an
elaboration of oppositionalism.

Ethnicity and social closure

For Weber[62] social closure is a means by which certain social groupings mono-
polize particular resources. Access to these resources is reliant upon the possession of prescribed social or physical circumstances, be these of a negative or
positive nature. Those to whom access is denied form a category (or categories)
that is outside: they occupy an area of exclusion in terms of economic or social
opportunities, relative to those who exist above the plimsoll line of closure. In
terms of the generation of an ethnic identity, a justification for exclusion by the
excluders can be founded on the premise of race or ethnicity, as in the colonial
situation or the treatment of the Jews in Nazi Germany.

Parkin[63] refines and enlarges on Weber's theory and considers the deployment
of closure strategies on the part of those who have been defined as ineligible, in
order to resist the dominance of the excluders. For Parkin, this amounts to a
response to the power exercised in a downward direction from the excluders by
power projected upwards by the excluded in order to gain greater access to
resources. So, in terms of racial/ethnic categorization, the likes of the Black
Panthers and Rastafari can, by their exclusion of whites, be understood to be
excluding the included.

As such this process can be seen to facilitate the development of ethnic labels
by the included excluding and the excluded excluding the included. The provision of sites is[64] justified within this social discourse. The Traveller site might be
understood as a concrete example of housing exclusion. At the same time the
expressed wish on the part of Travellers to be placed on a site could be interpreted as a means to exclude the included.

For Parkin, the attainment of qualifications and the institutions of property
constitute the apparatus of exclusion in capitalist society. According to him, it
is these mechanisms that act as the gatekeepers to resources. As such, exclusion is

at the heart of the social and legal structures of modern, Western society. Ethnicity can be an extraordinary form of qualification or property. We have already seen that it is not reliant on birth, but is adopted by way of a plethora of signs and symbolic references. Even when an individual inherits definite physical, ethnic traits such as colour, this, in itself, does not disqualify movement through the exclusionary apparatus. Indeed, the physical identification of ethnicity can in itself be used (by both excluders and excluded) as a type of qualification. It is possible to argue that Travellers are excluded by economic, social and legal considerations from certain types of housing property. The pressure of law to remain itinerant given the lack of legal sites or social housing provision heightens the incidence of poverty and affects their potential for social inclusion by way of property. At present, an itinerant way of life restricts educational opportunities[65] and health-care,[66] so limiting opportunities to gain qualifications.

Ethnicity and race are bound up in the legal system through equal opportunities and the various race relations legislation. In respect of Travellers, legal power of an elite excludes them from access to the means of life and labour, including work, welfare, health provision and housing. A Gypsy is not excluded and cannot, in law, be excluded from the same legal rights as a non-Gypsy because s/he is a Gypsy. However, Gypsies, who do not live in houses, are excluded because their access to the means of life and labour is limited via their social position: even legal sites deny residents certain basic domestic facilities and the type of social acceptance housing provides.[67] This undermines the hopes that the creation of legitimate sites, as formulated in the Traveller Law Reform Bill 2002,[68] will have dramatically equalizing effects in terms of those living on sites and the rest of society.

This demonstrates that ethnicity, of itself, does not necessarily prevent inclusion. The inability to gain access to social resources is at the hub of exclusion, but also, at the same time, has the power to create the mirage of the ethnic group. The grouping together of excluded individuals, some of whom might carry the label Traveller, can be seen as a symptom of social closure and a form of legitimization. This being the case, it can be seen that Barth[69] can be vindicated when he asserts that, 'the ascriptive aspect is logically prior to any objective characteristics of the ethnic group'.[70] The social context can thus be understood to generate Traveller identity and that social closure is a generator of ethnicity.

Fanon, colonialism and the Gypsies

The colonial situation places one group in the role of the oppressed and another group in a dominating position. This deeply influences the lives of those bound up in the colonial situation. Traveller ethnicity might be understood to exist within a broader colonial situation of this type. Franz Fanon argues that the colonized are defined by and dependent on the definition of the colonizer. He discusses the way in which a group of people become defined by another (an outsider group) to the extent that their whole idea of self and understanding of their humanity is dependent on that definition. Fanon points out that once people become dependent on this definition from another – from the outsider – they begin to live in order to fulfil that definition; they become as the oppressor would have them be.[71]

Fanon[72] outlines an analysis of the 'colonial neurosis', what might be thought of as a colonial mentality. For Fanon,

> The central idea is that the confrontation of 'civilized' and 'primitive' men creates a special situation – the colonial situation – and brings about the emergence of a mass of illusions and misunderstandings that only a psychological analysis can place and define.[73]

According to Fanon colonialism establishes a relationship between oppressor and oppressed that is founded on an assumption of the inferiority of the oppressed group and superiority of those who make up the oppressing elite.[74] He argues that this relationship becomes part of the mentality of the oppressed to the extent that they are only able to perceive themselves as they are portrayed or understood to be by the oppressing group. It can be seen to be the case that this analysis is applicable to Travellers who define themselves according to official, academic and/or popular/romantic stereotypes. According to Fanon, the oppressed become trapped in this definition of their self. Fanon argues that this is a dehumanizing process, the oppressed are not regarded as fully human, by themselves or the oppressor; they define themselves and are defined as 'the other'. Only the oppressor is wholly human.

This is the fundamental problem with calling someone a Gypsy or a Traveller. The identity as a human then takes on a secondary status; one is first a Gypsy; a type with traits of that type that differentiates and alienates the individual from the whole. The only way out of this situation is to move back into the mainstream through forms of social compliance and conformity to particular norms. Fanon argues that the mechanisms of adaptation and imitation within the colonial relationship are often very subtle. Certain 'norms' are established and imposed with which the oppressed group are then required by law to conform. Assimilation is an example of this kind of imitation imposed by the colonial elite; the proposals in the Traveller Law Reform Bill 2002[75] might be seen as imposition of this type. For Fanon these mechanisms can also be overt and deliberately instituted, with sanctions stipulated by the oppressing group, in the case of Travellers the 1994 Criminal Justice and Public Order Act for example.[76]

Whilst the first example of imitation (subtle) seems spontaneous the second (overt) is induced. For Fanon,

> The arrival of the white man in Madagascar shattered not only its horizons but its psychological mechanisms . . . An island like Madagascar invaded overnight by 'pioneers of civilization,' even if those pioneers conducted themselves as well as they knew how, suffered the loss of its basic structure . . . The landing of the white man on Madagascar inflicted injury without measure.

The consequences of the interruption of Europeans onto Madagascar were not psychological alone, since, every authority has observed, there are inner relationships between consciousness and the social context.[77]

This process is not too far from that experience within the relationship between Travellers and the State. The invasion of Traveller life-style, by the means of social pressure and force of law, is undertaken in order to oblige Travellers to comply with housing market-norms.[78] Unless the Traveller conforms s/he will remain confined within the characterization of the Traveller and suffer the consequences. Fanon sees the individual's experience of being colonized as corresponding to the level to which they are discriminated against by the colonizer. This is a process in which the person at the focus of the colonization procedure is robbed of their individuality and, as such, their self-worth. They are defined as being parasitical and, in order to address this, conform as much and as swiftly as possible to the norms of colonial society.[79]

According to Fanon the drive to become like the oppressor (White) and as such cultured, leads the acculturated colonial subject to despise those less fortunate in his society. This might be understood in the Gypsy context as being similar to the negative feelings so-called pure Gypsies are said to have towards other travelling groups, in particular New Age Travellers.[80] Thus Travellers can be seen to be bound-up in a colonial narrative that can only be compounded by the notion of Gypsy ethnicity. The means to address this situation seem to lie in the development of a more accurate, rational understanding of the nature of the travelling population, that is not based on conventional/traditional romanticism or contemporary notions of ethnicity. The Gypsy persona as the 'other' needs to be challenged by an analysis that can accommodate the means by which the Traveller population arises out of the social and economic fabric of the State. As far as Gypsies are concerned this amounts to a discourse of decolonization. I will look to undertake such an analysis in the next chapter.

Conclusion

In this chapter I have deployed a theoretical analysis of the nature of ethnicity to show that this is primarily a social construct.[81] This position is in opposition to the dominant paradigm found in the literature focusing on Traveller identity, which argues for what might be understood as the transference of identity by means of blood. This, in effect, proposes a hereditary ethnicity that is not easily distinguishable from a racial categorization.

Continuing with the effort to demonstrate how ethnicity is socially constructed, I went on to look at the workings of social closure.[82] This analysis suggested that the distribution of social resources can be seen to energize the generation and maintenance of ethnic identity. I then complemented this essentially structuralist point of view using a Fanonian[83] analysis to construct a theory of a colonial narrative of Gypsy ethnicity. This again demonstrated the ethnicity-generating forces arising out of economic and social relations.

This combined analysis provides an alternative view, relative to the fundamentally racial model found in the literature, of how Traveller ethnicity might be developed and maintained. I have argued that ethnicity is a notion rather than an indisputable, concrete phenomenon. I have suggested that, at least in part, Traveller identity has arisen and develops out of social action, interaction and the general socio-economic environment. Ethnicity then can be understood as being defined by the self in relation with other selves, importantly within historically and socially specific terms of reference.

Following this chapter ethnicity can now be recognized as an ethnic narrative. This can be used to analyse the meaning of ethnicity; why and how the notion of ethnicity is deployed and maintained within general social discourse. This is the task I will address in the following chapters. In the next chapter I will look more concretely at how Traveller identity is produced through social and economic situations and circumstances. I will examine family and social factors that function to maintain, adopt, combine and abandon a travelling life-style and identity. I will also explore the relationship between housing and caravan-dwelling in order to illustrate the defining force that social resources exert in terms of Traveller identity.

3 The social generation of the Traveller population

Introduction

The first part of this chapter explores the possible links between social phenomena and the generation of the travelling population of England, through a qualitative assessment of some of the social patterns of, and motivations to adopt, a Traveller life-style. The purpose of this is to illustrate the pressures on individuals and groups to adopt a Traveller identity. In the process some of the problems and contradictions inherent in describing someone as a Traveller will become apparent. An examination of the state of housing provision since the Second World War is included. I have also provided a comparative analysis between the Dutch and English situation with regard to legislation affecting caravan-dwellers, demonstrating the potential that legislation has to generate an ideology of identity.

On the basis of the analysis, in the chapter I argue that some of those whom society recognizes as Travellers or Gypsies may be a product of social phenomena, such as employment or, in particular, housing needs. This leads to a contention that a proportion of the travelling population has adopted this way of life, or come from families who have a history of caravan-dwelling no longer than a few generations. As such, I suggest that a significant percentage of those seen by many as ethnic Gypsies may not be connected to an itinerant life-style through a cultural or ethnic tradition or inheritance. This position does not look to preclude what might be called traditional Travellers from the Traveller population, neither does it discount hereditary considerations as part of the explanation for the continuance of a Traveller way of life. The material that follows provides a reassessment of the influence of social trends on the profile of the Traveller population. At the same time, this part of the book offers a critique of the social response to Travellers as a wholly or mostly ethnically generated group.

Research and Travellers

My own background and contacts within the travelling population proved useful in terms of establishing access and trust in the development of the appropriate research methods needed to undertake social research into the diverse groups referred to as Travellers and Gypsies. However, the method of data collection was inspired by Okely,[1] but was informed by a qualitative ethnographic approach towards the research subjects. Cottle[2] maintains that people need the opportunity to speak freely if their intentions and the meaning of their words are to be understood. For full details of the research methodology see Appendix One.

The Traveller population and homelessness before 1978

What follows shows specifically how social interaction and conditions might contribute to the development and expansion of the Traveller population. I have exemplified this by looking at this group alongside the development of homelessness since the Second World War.

After 1978 the task of establishing an estimate of the number of families living in caravans and identifying a trend in homelessness was made more straightforward by the publication of the figures for households claiming homelessness and the twice yearly caravan counts. However, trying to put together a picture of the nature of these groups or the possible links between these populations before 1978 is difficult. Although Adams *et al.*[3] state that a considerable number of non-nomadic people had taken to caravans, and Okely blames the housing shortage for a rise in the numbers of people resorting to caravans, whilst the Hampshire Association of Parish Councils in 1960 noted that the Gypsy population had been 'infiltrated by poor whites'.[4]

According to Greve,[5] homelessness in Britain 'is not a new or transient phenomenon'. The state of housing provision was in crisis from the post-Second World War period right up to the early/late 1970s. Greve *et al.*[6] demonstrate a sharp increase in the number of homeless people in temporary accommodation in London from 1949 to the early 1970s. This region was found to be the most densely populated area in terms of Travellers by the early 1980s; over 60 per cent of known British Travellers were to be found in this area.[7] At this point the housing situation was critical on a nation-wide scale.[8]

The estimates in Table 1 are of homelessness in the 1960s and 1970s. They demonstrated a continued growth in homelessness, although definitions are unclear and likely to refer only to those living in registered hostels and other limited local authority provision.

Table 1 Number of families living in temporary accommodation provided by London Boroughs, 1966–70. (Adapted from Greve *et al.* (1971) *Homelessness in London*, p. 66.)

Year	Inner and Outer London	Per cent Increase	Per cent
1966	1,573	1966–67	8.8
1967	1,711	1967–68	16.9
1968	2,001	1968–69	14.6
1969	2,293	1969–70	21.5
1970	2,787	1966–70	77.1
Increase 1966–70	1,214		

Table 2 Homelessness, 1970–6 (Central Statistical Office, HMSO 1974 and 1977.)

	Greater London	*Rest of England and Wales*	*Total*
1970	3,193	3,351	6,544
1973	3,446	5,106	8,552
1974	11,360	Not available	Not available
1975	12,610	21,100	33,710
1976	12,400	21,280	33,680

Table 3 Local Authority loans, 1945–55 (Adapted from Manby, *Pamphlet 188*, p. 7.)

Local Authority Loans	Number of Dwellings (000s)	Amount Lent Per Dwelling (£s)	Amount Lent (£s)
1945–51	46	848	39
1951–52	23	1,086	25
1953–54	27	1,185	32
1954–55	41	1,293	53

Greve goes on to say that after the Second World War there was a huge rise in homelessness in Britain, particularly in London and other cities that had suffered substantial bomb damage. The homelessness problem was also heightened by the demobilization of millions of people and evacuees and war-workers returning to the cities. A complete halt to new building from the start of the war and huge problems in terms of repair and maintenance did not help matters. Although the problem was to some extent ameliorated during the early 1950s, in the immediate post-war years a shortage of one and a quarter million dwellings existed. There were over two million dwellings more than one hundred years old and land prices became highly inflated in the most popular living areas as a response to higher demand. The cost of a new house had risen from £1,380 in 1948 to £1,956 in 1956 (a 30 per cent increase). Interest rates had risen by 3 per cent to 6 per cent during the same period.[9]

It can be seen from Table 3 that the late 1940s and early 1950s were relatively slack years in terms of local authority loans compared to the 1954–5 period. At the same time the cost per unit (represented in amount lent) rose steeply. Price and demand were growing together, a trend that was to continue with the growth in private home ownership.[10] The rise in land prices and demand created a whole new situation in the housing market, wherein owner occupation was quickly to become the major tenure, but it is plain that this was an option that was getting beyond the reach of the poorest sections of the population.

The housing available for rent by local authorities did not match the type of demand that existed nor their own selection procedures, which favoured families with three or more children. In 1976, 17 per cent[11] of local authority stock had only one bedroom. Twenty-nine per cent had two bedrooms, 51 per cent had three bedrooms.[12] Only 3 per cent had four or more bedrooms. Thus council housing had the largest overcrowding problems of all tenures. At that time 55 per cent of council-dwellings built after 1891[13] were in need of major repairs. The number of unfit-dwellings in England and Wales reached an all-time high by 1967, 1,836,000 dwellings were considered to be unfit for human habitation at this time compared to 820,000 in 1965 and 622,000 in 1960.[14] The 1967 figure represented 11.7 per cent of the total housing stock. At the same time 2,371,000 dwellings lacked at least one basic amenity.[15] By 1981 there were still over 1.2 million dwellings unfit for human habitation in England and Wales.[16]

From the late 1950s, to the early 1960s, the trend in homelessness was on a definite upward curve. Initially, and most clearly, this could be seen in London, but soon this phenomenon became evident in other parts of the country. As the 1960s went on there was a recognition, on a national scale, that there was a crisis in housing.[17] It was during the later part of this period that the Traveller population began to be the subject of national debate. Adams *et al.*[18] point out that Travellers up to this time had been given relatively little significance in terms of Parliamentary activity. Up to 1961 the numbers of caravan-dwellers were not included in the national housing census.[19] However the 1961 census revealed that 183,688 persons were living in caravans from 75,373 households.[20] This group had been seemingly invisible before 1961, presumably because it had been too insignificant for inclusion in the census returns. This 'new visibility' has been attributed to birth-rate alone.[21] But an estimated growth in the population of 20,000 over the ten years between 1951 and 1961[22] from, in the early 1950s, around 60,000 Traveller families, cannot serve as an adequate explanation for the apparent rise in numbers of people resorting to caravan-dwelling.[23] However, the 1961 census followed hard on the impact of the 1960 Caravan Sites Act,[24] that had the effect of bringing the numbers of people resorting to caravan-dwelling down. This is borne out by successive census figures. By 1971 the number of people living in caravans had fallen to 168,320 individuals from 72,105 households.[25] At first sight this does not appear to be a dramatic fall, the effects of the 1960 and 1968 Acts considered. However, this situation needs more consideration.

1   The post-war housing shortage had carried over into the 1960s.
2   Up to 1961 the caravan-dwelling population did not seem to be significant.
3   By the early 1960s the size of the Traveller/caravan-dwelling population warranted attention (census, legislation).
4   Throughout the 1960s the Traveller population would have grown via birth-rate, but it would have been diminished by the effects of legislation.
5   By the early 1970s there was still a housing shortage.
6   There continued to be a significant number of caravan-dwelling households, enough to warrant inclusion in census returns.

On the basis of these considerations it is possible to suggest that there was a great deal of movement within the caravan-dwelling population between the

Table 4 The caravan-dwelling population, 1961–81 (Adapted from Census Information, HMSO.)

Year	No. of people in caravans	No. of hsehlds in caravans	People in caravans % decrease over 10 yrs	Hsehlds in caravans % decrease over 10 yrs	People in caravans % decrease over 20 yrs	Hsehlds in caravans % decrease over 20 yrs
1961	183,688	75,373				
1971	168,320	72,105	8.4	4.3		
1981	93,180	42,202	44.6	41.5	49.3	44

early 1960s and the start of the 1970s. The housing crisis would have made caravan-dwelling an option for many poorer families, whilst the Caravan Sites Acts would have driven significant numbers of caravan-dwellers[26] with the appropriate resources, to move into private housing. The 1981 census revealed that 93,180 people from 42,208 households were living in trailers.[27]

This seems an impressive demise, but it has to be considered in the light of its context. The impact of the 1960 and 1968 Caravan Sites Acts would be expected to have perhaps an even bigger effect, particularly the 1968 Act, that effectively outlawed a nomadic way of life in England.[28] It is likely that the 1981 figure included what might be called a central group[29] of caravan-dwellers, those who could not, or would not resort to other forms of housing. Not all of those included in the census material could be described as Travellers. People living on some recognized residential sites for instance would have been included.[30] However, it is unlikely that many people in this situation would have been seriously affected by the legislation of the 1960s and this section of the caravan-dwelling population would be a fairly static, small minority of the entire population.

Thus, by the early 1980s there was a situation of high housing demand alongside a problem of supply, linked to the price of home ownership. At the same time there was a relative lack of suitable rented accommodation: the share of permanent dwellings completed for local authority rent in 1968 was 44.1 per cent[31]; this proportion had fallen to 19.7 per cent in 1983.[32]

It is possible to suggest that the option to take up caravan-dwelling might have become a popular resort for poorer families in such circumstances. The average size of caravan households seems to be consistent with those least likely to be near the top of the housing lists; single persons, childless couples and families with two or fewer children.[33] Whilst many of what might be thought of as traditional Traveller families might have been obliged to give up a travelling or caravan-dwelling life-style, it would be surprising if the numbers resorting to trailers were not bolstered by some of those who were not amenable to housing provision. As such, it would seem reasonable to conclude, given the hostility to a travelling life-style encapsulated in the Caravan Sites Acts[34] that those living in Caravans after 1970 included many without options outside of trailer-dwelling.

Indeed, it is plausible to suggest that by the early 1980s the Traveller population was made up less by those who might be understood to be traditional Travellers and more by people who had moved from a conventional housing background to a caravan-based life-style. At the very least, in the closing years of the twentieth century it would seem likely that the travelling population of England was an heterogeneous group, very much a product of social and economic forces, rather than a hygienically closed ethnic homogeneity, cemented by blood, rite and/or culture.

Homelessness: the current situation

According to Greve,[35] the homeless have consistently looked to rented accommodation for a solution to their housing difficulties. This in effect means they have had to approach housing associations and local authorities as housing provision by landlords had fallen from more than 90 per cent after the First World War to just 7 per cent in England at the time when Greve was writing. However, local authority housing stock has been diminishing throughout the last part of the twentieth century following:

1   the sharp fall in council house-building between the early 1970s and the 1990s[36] and
2   the sale of council housing.

Greve pointed out that privately rented accommodation, in the main, targeted, 'students, young salary earners or higher income tenants'.[37] This left homeless families with very restricted options.

For Greve, as housing provision became more and more reliant on the private housing market, the market gap between low incomes and the price of housing remained an essential feature of homelessness. He points out that this continued despite owner-occupation making up 70 per cent of dwellings in England and Wales, although homelessness among house purchasers had risen dramatically in the last part of the twentieth century.[38] According to the Council of Mortgage Lenders, 49,410 properties were repossessed in 1995. In the same year 75,258 possession orders were made against homeowners in England and Wales. Before the start of 1996, 389,780 homeowners were in mortgage arrears of three months or more.[39]

The data relating to those claiming homelessness in England, as can be seen from the graphs included in the second part of this chapter, reflect the situation described above; a general rise from the late 1970s to the early/mid-1990s. More recent figures do show some signs of a decrease, but this could have as much to do with the perceived uselessness of registering as homeless at that time as anything else.[40] Over the same period in most areas of England there seemed to be a complementary rise in the number of caravans according to the biannual caravan counts. As suggested below, this implies that these populations, although maybe distinct and mutually exclusive, are subject to similar social phenomena.

This is reiterated in the general pattern of both the homelessness and caravan-dwelling trends produced by graphical representation.[41]

The link between housing shortages and official anxiety about the travelling population continues up to the present time. The current concern with South-East house prices[42] and governmental action to provide housing in this area, in particular for service workers, coincides with the Traveller Law Reform Bill 2002.[43]

Travellers and social interaction

Patterns of employment and movement

John Moris owned a very successful tobacco pipe factory in Pentonville in 1823. He became a Warden of the Guild of Tobacco Pipe Makers of the City of London and Westminster. He had been a soldier in the Napoleonic wars. By 1839, his son, Thomas William, had set up another outlet in Wapping. In 1861 the site of his business had moved to Barking. Edward John, John's grandson, following the demise of the clay-pipe industry that was heralded by the more varied supply of tobacco-related products, became an apprentice sail-maker in Barking with William Morgan in 1859.

Barking declined as a fishing port by 1865, following the extension of the railways to east-coast ports nearer the fishing grounds. The trawlers moved to Yarmouth and Gorleston in Norfolk. The last fishing vessel left Barking in 1898. Edward John moved with the fleet and married the daughter of a Barking fisherman, Sarah Ann Jones, in Gorleston in 1870. At this time he was a fisherman. Come 1888 he had returned to London, working as a labourer in a malt factory in the newly built industrial area of Silver Town, some seven miles from his former Barking home. It is likely that family connections, together with sea haulage links, had led to this move. In 1913 he became a watchman. Before his death in Plaistow, East London in 1923 (aged 76), he had found a role in the expanding railway network as a stationary engine driver.

Walter Moris, one of Edward's eight children, was born in West Ham in 1888. By 1913 he was working for H. B. Warmsley, Malt-Roasters, as a labourer. Following his demobilization from the Army in 1918, being twice decorated for bravery, he went back to the same job. Warmsley's moved to Bromley-by-Bow in 1926. In 1940 he was sweeping the roads for the Borough of West Ham and also worked as a part-time watchmaker.

Walter junior, born in 1918, first worked as a cellar-boy in the West End. In 1930 he was employed as a loader for a coal merchant. He had a string of jobs including builder, labourer in a cement factory, caustic tank cleaner, case repairer in a glass factory, before starting a 24-year stint with the West Ham/Newham council as a labourer in 1956.

Walter married Violet Neal in 1952 at St. Mathias Church, Plaistow. Violet's father, William, came from a Traveller background. He had obtained work as a stevedore in the King George V docks after the First World War.

Walter's son, Peter, started working life as an apprentice carpenter with the same local authority as his father in 1974. Over the last 25 years he has had a succession of semi-skilled and unskilled jobs interspersed with one long period of unemployment. During this period Peter married and divorced one of two daughters of a woman from Irish Traveller and east London extraction. They had two children who attend school in Newham. Walter's daughter, after initially working in offices, factories and shops has been a career civil servant for the last 25 years and is now a higher executive officer, having successfully completed a postgraduate qualification in Management Studies.

This movement around, in the main, one specific geographical area, through strata of employment, with the odd wider migration to follow work, is not an uncommon experience amongst working-class families. Comparatively few families remain tied to the exactly the same locality or line of work over more than two or three generations. We cannot say for instance that John Moris' lineage has been one set in any one area or job framework. There has been much movement over a few generations. We cannot say that the above family tree reflects a picture of a stable, unchanging working-class or even East End background. Given the huge social, economic and political upheavals that have accompanied development in such areas, this is perhaps not surprising.

Through using the biographical approach it is possible to question and criticize notions of traditional modes of life, cultural affinities and assertions of ethnicity. This does not mean the invention of an alternative aetiology of Traveller origins based on personal experiences/background. However, it does represent an effort, on the basis of lives lived, to look critically on some of the more fantastic theoretical musings of academics with a professional interest in propagating an ethnic narrative in relation to Travellers.

Social origins

There is a long history of large numbers of rovers or wayfarers in Britain,[44] including out-of-bond peasants, performers, peddlers, pilgrims, mendicant friars and preachers. The literature relating to Travellers acknowledges the presence of Tinkers before any records relating to Gypsies (or 'Egyptians') appeared.[45] Shakespeare's *Henry IV* refers to Tinkers and the word 'Tinker' was around as a sur/trade name in the 1300s.[46] Groups of people, who were taken to be of foreign origins, were recorded as earning a living from anything from casual agricultural labour to fortune-telling from the twelfth century onwards, long before they were seen to be of a specific type or group.[47] In the mid-1300s there was a growing number of rovers, a wandering class of serfs or escaped villains.[48] However, at the same time there was wide-ranging legislation prohibiting people from leaving their home areas, perhaps a direct result of landowners needing a supply of day and wage labourers.[49] This might be understood as an early manifestation of the type of concerns expressed in contemporary/modern legislation.[50]

By the fifteenth century, Europe had a relatively massive itinerant population who could be considered as part of the root of the modern proletariat. Okely[51] suggests that some might also have been the 'ancestors of many Gypsies' – those who were not bound as serfs or assimilated into guilds or trades. These people, in common with the escaped villains and rovers, sold their labour at a daily or hourly rate.[52] As Okely states, Marx suggests another origin of the modern proletariat that could also have some relationship to the contemporary Gypsy population – a section of the population that spurned wage labour:

> The prelude of the revolution that laid the foundation of the capitalist mode of production, was played in the last third of the 15th and first decade of the 16th century. A mass of free proletarians was hurled on the labour market by the breaking up of the bands of feudal retainers.[53]

Former clerks, servants to the feudal nobility, became wandering beggars. Dispossessed peasants may also have added to the groups that were to be called Gypsies when their land had been taken out of agricultural cultivation and turned into grazing for sheep during the growth in the wool industry.[54]

It does not seem at all incredible that many from these groups, that amounted to a mass of free labour, may have by association and marriage become known as, or for various of social or economic reasons called themselves, Egyptians and eventually Gypsies. Throughout Europe, as Clebert[55] notes, the appearance of exotic travelling groups coincided with the establishment of the *corporations de gueuserie*, the 'guilds of beggars'. It may have been the case that these groups were distinct, but they could also have been manifestations of the same phenomenon. Even if not, people may have moved between such groups without undermining the ascribed and organizational boundaries.[56] Okely points out that these itinerant groups, made up mainly of indigenous, disenfranchised individuals, may well have come together for reasons of survival. They could have 'adopted an exotic nomenclature, parts of a second secret "language"'.[57] This may have had advantages in terms of gaining certain types of work or even being given access to income as entertainers/travelling performers. This being the case, the project to formulate a substantial concept of Gypsy or Traveller roots, set in the notion of blood or heritage, can be seen to be deeply problematic.

Cultural complexity: values, attitudes, sentiments and families

This section explores the similarities and difference between some case studies, focusing on values, attitudes, sentiments and families. The data derives from *Itchy Feet*[58] and an interview with a New Age Traveller.

Mel and Michael McDonough were introduced as 'Irish Travellers' and 'part of the estimated eight million Gypsies in Europe'.

Mel: The first house, number one, is my eldest brother. So my eldest brother Christy, his wife and their five children live in that house. Myself, Michael and our five children live in number two. Then we have the trailers. One is my nephew's.

Maclean (presenter): For the McDonoughs a journey is more than just moving from place to place. Travel to them, with its changes and cycles and seasons is as fundamental to their identity as is home to the rest of us.

Michael: A Traveller is a person that belongs to the community of people, that is not necessarily a person that's moving from a to b. I live in a house, I'm very much a Traveller. I know lots of settled people that live in caravans but that doesn't make them Travellers. What Travellers are is what you think about life, like, I'll give you an example. If you ask most people who or what they are, people normally respond with their profession. They say 'I'm a producer', 'I'm a doctor' or 'a teacher', whatever their profession is. But when you ask a Traveller who and what are they, they normally respond that 'I'm a McDonough', 'I'm a Collins', 'I'm a Joyce'. They respond with a family name, more so than with an occupation. Because what occupation you're involved in, it necessarily doesn't matter that one should be able to survive and make a living from it. So you adapt and change. Movement is also very important to your occupation but it's not the sole reason for it.

Mel: The most prized possession we have as Travellers is our ability to know that we can move. To settled people, to people who have for generations – the only amount of travelling they've ever done is maybe to go away for two weeks' holidays, and this is done with precise detail because this is so exhausting to them and people come back wrecked from going camping or their holidays because they've spent a year planning for it. It's the opposite with us. It's the most natural thing to us.

Michael: You move for many different reasons. Because of economic reasons to get employment and get work. Also social reasons. Very much like, our whole social organization and the way the whole network of families is made up, you must try and keep contact with your whole family network. The reasons for trying to keep contact with your family network is the support mechanisms that are in there. And also the whole prospects of marriage. Like among Travellers the whole matched marriage still exists. So the whole potential partners that exist out there. So you must move around within your family, so that matches can be prepared and you can meet with people and keep up the contacts.

One of the big things for moving was to meet people, but the other thing was to also to avoid people. And that's a really important thing. And one of the things you would have done, you'd had a dispute between a family, you would move on. So not to allow it to escalate. Movement and travel actually allows you to relax. I've talked to many teachers and children that have been all through the Summer, have not moved, when they come back to school in September they are restless. Whereas families that have gone out and left their area and travelled around the country, met with other members of their family, they're all refreshed and ready for work.

Mel: When daddy got a house here, about ten years ago . . . he actually got physically sick. He was physically sick for weeks and weeks on end, because he felt as if he was anchored. He was tied down, he couldn't move. It didn't mean before this, before he got the house, that he was moving every second day of the week, but he knew he could do it if he wanted to. Whereas now their house gave them a permanency that he didn't want.

Michael: Like the road is no stranger. So you don't have to make massive preparations to move. It's that, like sometimes you feel, like you haven't got enough money, oh God now, wouldn't it be lovely just to get up and go.

Mel: That's the whole thing about being a Traveller again, about how we can adapt, so readily and so easily to different situations. We can adapt to situations where you could have to survive on one can of water for three or four days. And that's today, that's in the 90s. You survive with what you have.

Michael: Time's not a master. And it shouldn't be our master. So you shouldn't have to live by the tick of a clock.

Mel: I think maybe 'em, part of what we're looking for, I don't think that it's anything to do with the physical beauty, I don't think it's got anything to do with what's happening in that town, I think it was who was there belong to us. It's our past. It's our link with our past.

Michael: It's the whole, getting there, is important. Like it's not just arriving on the scene, like. I think there is an old saying of Native Americans. Walk a mile in someone's moccasins to get to know them. I think that's really important, because, you know, if you walk with somebody, and one thing you might hear Travellers saying is one thing is to shorten the road, and to shorten the road actually means to tell a story. Now I'm not trying to glorify or trying to recapture a past, or live in a fantasy situation, that's not what I'm trying to say. But it was the whole sort of experience of actually

	moving with people and sharing a life with people and going somewhere with a purpose, but the purpose not only reaching your destination, but what happened in between. And, I think that's the most important part of it. It's like a process and a product. Your products are very important, but how you go about getting that product is every bit as important.
Mel:	Now, unfortunately the only means, way of travelling, now is to go by van and by motor cars. Years ago, if you have a horse, you could travel the length and breath of Ireland for nothing. Only by the horse eating the grass and the side of the road. Unfortunately that's gone now and you need petrol. But that's all. But people say, 'oh' like, 'you need this and you need lots of money and capital wealth to live and to be Travellers'. No you don't need that. You need strength and pride in who you are and a desire to get on and to move. And once you have that you have everything.
Michael:	How do you know when it's time to move? I think when the realization comes about that you're becoming too permanent. I think then is the time to move. We can stay here, for as long as we realize we can go.
Mel:	Last Sunday it was a beautiful day here. It was a grand warm morning. And I was hanging out clothes on the line and Michael was there cutting the grass or doing something. He was getting ready to clean out the garden. And I just says to him, I says, 'you know' I said, 'God be with the days of the Travellers'. It really hit home to me that we were becoming, we were doing things that settled people do. If we were camping on a camp on that day, we'd have a big fire lit outside, and we'd be all round chatting around the fire. But here, we in a two storey little house, hanging out clothes, getting the garden ready to clean out. That hit home to me that I think we are being forced to settle. We are being forced by the people waving the card at us that our children need education. I think the most important thing is education for life. And you know if it comes that we have to give up absolutely everything of our travelling history our travelling being, just to be accepted, it's time now to move.

It is useful to compare this picture of Traveller motivation/sentiment with the situation of someone who sees himself defined as a New Age Traveller. At the time I made contact with Sparrow he had been travelling for six years. He told me he was 29 years of age. The recording below was taken from an interview as conversation at the 1996 Glastonbury festival. Sparrow agreed to the interview as a result of preliminary conversations, which detailed my own Traveller connections, so as to allow him to speak freely as possible. Originally Sparrow comes from Bristol. He has a degree in economics. Both his parents work in banking.

Sparrow: As you learn to travel, or part of learning to travel is, adapting to environments. If you have to live on vegetables that's no big deal, you just do. Most people who don't travel couldn't do that. We do not serve the clock. I don't even have a clock! That's difficult for people who don't travel. I'm not too interested in time. Day's for waking, night's for sleeping.

BB: Why do you travel?

Sparrow: Why travel? Why not? People have always travelled. Most of human history has involved nomadism. It's a bridge with the people of the past. Life itself is a journey. We are all leaving and arriving. The Aboriginal peoples in Australia, the Native Indians in America. They are spiritually connected to movement and the earth. Our lives are like tales of travel. It's not where you're going that matters, it's the way you go, and where you're at. You don't ask where a stream or a river is going you just connect with its flow. You need nothing to travel. That's good. What you need comes to you. It's amazing how if you just ask someone for something, they will often just give it to you. I asked a guy for some diesel the other day. 'Sure' he said. I offered to do his horoscope, but he was a Christian or something. Everything you need is in the journey see.

I never feel permanent. I never did. As soon as we've had enough we just leave. I've stayed in places for months though. I was in a squat for nearly a year a couple of years ago. But I was still a Traveller, travelling. On my way somewhere. Sometimes it's just enough to know that you can just go. You move to the cycles and seasons of the earth. She becomes your identity. I'm not a job, or where I live. I am what I feel. The family I am with are 'The Good Intent'. I tell people that and that says a lot about who I am, more than if someone tells you that they work in Marks and Spencer or something. We sometimes go places because we know that we fulfil a need.

BB: Do you get much work?

Sparrow: Well yeah, but that's not the only reason. You move for different purposes. For work, but social connections as well. To link up with other groups and families. Collectivity is our strength. We are part of a spiritual whole. We need to mingle, take lovers, partners to travel the road with you. Travel is a mellowing thing. Or maybe not travelling just winds you up. I've got two kids with other families and they are so mellow compared to kids who don't travel. They go to schools and they don't like it compared to the travelling schools. They find kids who don't travel very aggressive and immature.

The following was taken from the same BBC *Itchy Feet* programme referred to above.

Tamanny Baker (Bristol photographer): I've always been a keen Traveller. On one of my trips over to the Far East I returned on the Trans-Siberian, and I passed through Russia, and as I did so, I felt something strange inside me. And basically what it was is complete fascination and captivation by the country and its people, as I was passing through. This was about eight years ago, and since then I've been through university, I did a degree in psychology, and then left university and decided to be a photographer.

About three years ago, I was having a chat with my mother, and she told me about my Russian roots. And my great-grandfather was a Russian photographer . . . which I hadn't known before. And, that moment I think I suddenly felt that there was some kind of quest for me to return and to find out more about this. Because for me it was like fitting a part into an unknown story for me. What I did was I went round all my relatives in England, my long-lost relatives, I didn't know any of my father's relatives whatsoever, who know more about the Russian ancestry. And in that process I've been gathering Russian documents, copies of Russian documents, photographs, anecdotal evidence, and been pulling together those different strands from all the separated fragments of the family.

I went out last year. And I took all the Russian documents I had with me and a friend out there translated them quite well. The documents talked about the various places that he lived in . . . I took the overnight train down from Moscow and just spent six hours in this town . . . where he came from. They told me he lived in this little village that was about 40 kilometres away . . . I told them I wanted to go and they were surprised. They said 'Why do you want to go? There's nothing there.' I said, 'I just want to be there' . . . It felt like a home from home . . . it was like filling in that gap inside. Looking at my images from that trip, they're very different kinds of pictures, more from my heart than from my head. Pictures of what I felt deep down.

All of these people relate to links with the past, family, the desire to travel and a range of deep, inner feelings. Discourses on freedom are enigmatically blended with ideas relating to set, internal, natural identities, kinship and communal attachments and pulls. Each of the respondents refer to a powerful biological drive to travel. This is a type of reductionism that seems to explain the inexplicable, mystic and ephemeral urge to move on or travel. It seems that the urge or desire for movement, whether brought about by biological determinism, personal expression, social orientation, spiritual or psychological disposition (or a combination of all or any of these) is not confined to one ethnic or cultural niche. Indeed, in Radio Five's *Twenty-First Century Vox* of 5 June 2000, which looked at the hobby of caravanning, there were examples of many people, from sedentary, non-Gypsy backgrounds, who had met and eventually married whilst involved in the Junior Caravan Club, their families being members of The Caravan Club of Great Britain. Examples of whole family and social networks generated through The Caravan Club of Great Britain were given. One woman spoke of her feelings of depression and 'claustrophobia' when unable to take to her caravan for a while.

Many of the claims made and information given in the interview with Mel and Michael reflect and repeat Michael's position in McLoughlin[59] and it has to be said that his status[60] as National Coordinator for Accommodation for Travellers for the National Council for Travelling People may well have coloured his opinions. However, Mel and Michael talk a lot about the family. An individual's name is of central importance in terms of defining identity and it is seen as more important than life-style or occupation. To be in close proximity to one's closest relatives also appears to be significant. This kinship factor is linked to being a Traveller, there is an expressed pride in a collective history and a need to maintain links with the past, yet, somewhat paradoxically, clock-time seems to be regarded as oppressive. The sense of belonging or community is valued above living in a trailer in terms of identity. Mel and Michael exhibit a taken-for-granted solidarity and distinction played out, with some difficulty, within what they see as a different or alien cultural setting, but in slight contradiction to this, the ability to cope with change and adapt is equally important. Movement, not necessarily collective, avoidance of family is part of the rationale involved in at least a part-time itinerancy, is motivated by occupational needs but also involves sentimental and recuperative considerations. The potential to be able to travel is valued and a level of itinerancy is understood to be natural, even essential to one's health.

A pattern of identity emerges out of Mel and Michael's conversation that appears to be responding to institutional pressures and norms, feelings of attachment and a discourse on freedom and control. All this is set in a kind of underlying sense of primal diaspora. Michael talks of the importance of stories and Sparrow relates to 'tales'. It can be seen that there does not seem to be a great deal of difference between the feelings voiced by Mel and Michael and those expressed by Sparrow, even though their connection with a travelling way of life might be seen to differ. Mel and Michael carry an ethnic/cultural identity whereas Sparrow has made a choice of life-style, but all three share sentiments and motivations that are practically identical. They all have moments in their lives when they settle, even taking up the option of conventional housing. Unlike Mel and Michael, Sparrow was not born into what might been seen as a travelling culture, with social influences and pressures to conform to the same. If anything, he might see himself departing from convention. But, in a similar fashion to Mel and Michael, Sparrow dismisses 'clock-time', but incongruously connects his own travelling experience with a global and historical continuity of migration. He seems to see himself as a representative of a timeless culture that he sets within a naturalistic and therapeutic narrative; like Michael he makes reference to indigenous people as a source of inspiration (both interviews refer to Native Americans). For Sparrow, travelling is an intellectual and empathetic conversion; it is an adopted life-style – he talks about 'learning to travel'. It connects him to everything else yet sets him apart. Like Mel and Michael, Sparrow sees his travelling self as arising out of nature; he is what he is, not definable by occupation. He also, again echoing Mel and Michael, sees the ability to adapt and the potential for movement as important. Sparrow concurred with Mel and

Michael's view that travelling could be connected to work, but that it was also part of wider social, cultural and emotional considerations.

The feelings expressed by Tamanny Baker are very much akin to some of those put across by Mel, Michael and Sparrow. Like Sparrow and Mel and Michael she suggests that she is pulled by forces set in her own nature, an internal feeling or drive. Not too dissimilar to Mel and Michael, but unlike Sparrow, who although he relates to a familial connection, Tamanny's position points to a basis for her travel in blood kinship. Her journeys in Russia have direct family influences. She is involved in a search for some continuity with the past, alluding to roots, that together with a family history of migration, her own potential for travel and shared profession with an ancestor propose a lineage. This energizes a kind of pilgrimage of attachment. Again, unlike Sparrow and more overtly than Mel and Michael, Tamanny has a strong sense of being part of a diaspora or even hybridism. She does not conform to social pressures in the same way as Mel and Michael. She does not have the same family/kinship/cultural influences. Neither does her motivation seem strongly connected to Sparrow's seeming rebellion, which oddly related to conformity with natural force. However, she may well be understood to be conforming to current trends linked to establishing exotic/foreign identities.

From the feelings and opinions expressed by Mel and Michael, Sparrow and Tamanny Baker[61] it appears that travelling or itinerant ways of life are constructed from a diversity of social, psychological, spiritual, familial and economic considerations. However, these considerations seem to not only generate particular types of Traveller, they seem to play a part in the development of the travelling population as a whole, that is, as a consequence, made up of people from a range of backgrounds and origins. Other sources confirm this:

> One of my earliest memories was when I myself was about three and a half years old. My brothers Paddy and James and myself were living with my grandfather and mother in their house.[62]

> I lived in a house and was born in a house.[63]

> I remember when I was a year old . . . I was at my granny's house.[64]

From the cultural and biographical complexity discussed it is possible to see the diverse social influences both within the Traveller population and between Travellers and non-Travellers. It would seem that the personal histories of Travellers move across distinct borders and categories. This contrasts with the general portrayal of Gypsy culture in the literature that in effect separates Travellers into definite categories. For example, Earle *et al.*[65] argue for five categories of Traveller outlined by the National Gypsy Council (NGC), see Table 5.

It would be difficult to claim that the groups identified within Table 5 have stayed pure, and the NGC does note possible admixtures of Travellers and infiltration of the non-travelling community. However, other categories of

Table 5 The five categories of Traveller outlined by the National Gypsy Council (NGC) (Adapted from Earle *et al.*, *A Time to Travel.*)

Tinkers	From Ancient Roman descent, skilled metalworkers with particular specialization in tools such as knives. The Industrial Revolution limited this trade and many tinkers moved on to scrap dealing.
Peddlers	Travelling salespeople providing any commodity required by outlying communities. Wares were also sold at fairs and markets, especially as the pottery industry expanded, so diversifying the range of goods.
Romanies	Probably descended from Indian nomadic tribes travelling across Europe in the fifteenth century. Although the language and nationality of the host country may have been superficially adopted, their culture remained separate. The Romany language, rooted in Sanskrit, is their own.
Irish tinkers	People whose families travelled for centuries throughout Ireland, many of whom have been driven from the country by eviction, famine and poverty. Their language is Gaelic based and called Shelta or Gammon. They have been joined recently by migrant Irishmen seeking construction work.
Scottish tinkers	Probably descended from Celtic metalworkers, and originally called tinkers. Their numbers were swelled by the massive Highland clearance campaigns of the nineteenth and early twentieth centuries. They are still more likely than other Travellers to use bender tents as homes.

Traveller have been mooted; 'Push-rats', 'Mumplies', 'Pikies',[66] 'Didakais'[67] and 'Drovers'.[68] The Dublin Travellers Education and Development Group, although seeking to identify a distinct Traveller culture, demonstrate the difficulties in establishing cultural purity, or definite distinctiveness, arguing that customs, beliefs and superstitions are much the same as those of settled people to the extent that it is sometimes impossible to identify the root of particular cultural practices.[69]

Noonan also confirms the probable complex nature of the development of the Irish Traveller population, suggesting that Travellers may be seen as the descendants of people driven to the roads during the economic and political upheavals in the seventeenth and nineteenth centuries. He goes on to point out that the various theories regarding Travellers' origins all lack conclusive evidence to support them.[70]

The social generation of the travelling population

The material selected below relates to what might be called a social generation of a section of the Traveller population and arises out of the research outlined in Appendix One. It must be said that most people when asked about how they became involved in Traveller life relate to a tradition or culture (although these particular words are hardly ever used by respondents), the beginnings of which often seem to be lost in time. For example, 'I was born a Gypsy. Me father was

Table 6 Housing experience (Okely, 'Gypsies Travelling in Southern England', p. 63.)

Main upbringing in a house	8.8 per cent
Some experience of housing	15.8
Never lived in a house	75.4

a Gypsy as was his father. Both were born on the wagon.'[71] During the research this kind of response was given in approximately 70 per cent of first contacts. This does not seem to be unusual. Okely[72] obtained the figures presented in Table 6 when looking at the housing experience of Travellers.

Even though the figures presented in Table 6 showed that almost a quarter of the sample had some experience of housing, this might not be the whole picture. Jimmy, a youth worker in Minster at the time of the research commented:

> The more one tries to find out what a true Gypsy is, the more evident the very mixed heritage of the Traveller becomes. As you get to know people more the question becomes more and more futile. Two families in the Minster area have been identified as having taken up travelling from a previously settled background. Most of the young Travellers I have come into contact with were born into trailer-dwelling. Many of their parents had a similar experience. However, from this point it is hard to define a Traveller lineage.

It seems as soon as you ask questions relating to Gypsy lineage the complexity of the situation is made manifest. For example 'My granddad was a farmer, but my grandmother was a Gypsy',[73] and:

> There is a lot of resentment towards 'New Age' Travellers. They are often seen as being little more than trouble to the so-called 'true' Travellers. This negative feeling is often voiced by young Travellers, who are aware that one or both of their grandparents took up travelling from a previously settled life-style.[74]

During the research I came into contact with David Ward. His initial story of his lineage (see above) emphasized a strong Traveller lineage. After working with his family and other families on the same unofficial encampment throughout one summer quite a different set of circumstances emerged. David stated:

> Me father was on the buildings in Dublin. When I was a boy we moved up to Belfast for the work, but what with the family being Catholic and coming from the South, it was hard to get a house. Me uncles had put themselves in trailers, and the trailer was better than what housing there was. Me Brother got some work in England on the roads. The firm he was with put him in a trailer by the site. As they made the road so they moved along with it. He

got me in on this and I was going backward and forward between here and there as the work turned up. But after a while it was easier to stay in England what with the kids and all. So I do bits and pieces between any work I could get. But the work got less and less until now there's no casual stuff at all. I've gone back to Ireland, but things are worse there.

David Ward's story illustrates one of the many paths to Traveller life. At the time of the interview his first priority was to get onto an official site. This would enable him to access better welfare benefits and get his children into education. For him, his best course of action was to claim 'a Gypsy's right' to such provision. Once on an official site he could press for housing and this would make him more likely to be able to obtain regular, decently paid work.

In David's case, the search for work, housing provision and sectarianism all seem to play a part in him finding himself and his family living in a caravan. Whilst those who do not inherit a travelling way of life, like David Ward, seem to take up caravan-dwelling for a range of reasons, broadly speaking, this group seem to be generated by the following social phenomena:

1   Unemployment
2   Homelessness
3   Marriage

A fourth motive is a kind of psychological or spiritual rejection of conventional housing. This is often associated with so-called New Age Travellers[75] but the same type of reasons are shared by many of those who would not usually be categorized or thought of as New Age. This being the case I will look at these four areas of social generation separately but, as can be seen from the example given by David Ward, the reasons for taking up a travelling way of life are often complex and overlapping. The four areas of social generation, marriage, homelessness, unemployment and the search for an alternative life-style, will be elaborated with data from my own research and data derived from previous academic studies on Travellers.

Wedded to travel

Originally I come from Hackney, the Wick. My Dad was at sea, like his Dad before him. Me Mother done factory work, her Father had been a carpenter, but he'd died before she left school. TB. She was always dead scared I'd get it. I was about 15 when I met the wife. She was camped up by the marshes for most of the winter. Come the spring I just jumped on the back of the wagon. After we was married I took up the booths. I was about 20. 'The Fighting Gypsy' they called me. That's how I got into fairground work.

This personal story, of the start of a travelling way of life, is typical of many of the recollections I have come across. It can be seen as indicative of the historical overlapping between cultures and diverse groups as pointed out by Noonan.[76] The research provides some evidence that this has been constant over recent decades. For example, Earle *et al.* illustrate that the above biographical reference is not an uncommon experience when they point out that 'a house-dweller may start a relationship with a Traveller and join that partner'.[77] Further examples are not hard to find:

> My earliest memory was when we were living in a very old house beside the cathedral . . . In Ireland I always lived in a house. So when I got married I had to move into a trailer.[78]

> My father was born in Athlone and my mother was born in Kilkenny. My father lived in a house in Athlone. My mother told me they used to travel all over Ireland and that was how she met my father. He would come to the camp on a bike to chat with mammy.[79]

> The Old Girl was a proper 'Gypo'. Her Mum and Dad were darker than her even. They looked like Pakistanis. Anyway, the Old Man wouldn't leave her alone. He would bike down from Canning Town to the site at Bonny Downs every day. She told him to piss off, but he wouldn't take no for an answer. When they got married they moved into flats on the Isle of Dogs. He had a fist fight on the cobbles with a great big Irish bloke for that. They got into a house in Churchill Road, Custom House. When that was bombed Mum found Samson Street empty and we moved in there.[80]

It is impossible to say how many people have moved in and out of a travelling life-style by way of marriage or whether there has been a net loss or gain in respect of the Traveller population. Okely found that over 26 per cent of couples with whom she had close contact included at least one non-Traveller. More than a quarter of these couples had no Traveller background at all. This was based on fieldwork between 1970 and 1972, a time of relatively low unemployment and homelessness.[81]

What seems certain is that there has been an appreciable intermingling between the settled population and caravan-dwellers. This would seem almost unavoidable given the common pursuit of casual labour on the part of many Travellers and sections of the non-travelling working class.

> Ivy lived in King Street, Canning Town. She met the feller down hopping, in Yalding. He'd been called up. They got married in Yalding. He owned a caravan. She moved in and he went to war. When his people moved off, Ivy went with them.

> I met our Rose working in Lyon's Corner House. She lived on a local site. We became good friends. That's how she met Harry, my brother. They moved in with my Mum in Beatrice Street.[82]

Recent years have given rise to other considerations around life-style:

> I've lived with Rod for nearly three years. He was part of a Grunge group. My Ma was horrified when we took off in an old bus. I think we paid about 40 quid for it. Rod has been travelling since he was a kid on and off. All we had was a few bits of food and an old mattress. There was about a dozen of us at first, but we were the only ones left last winter. We've only had the trailer for about six months. We bought it off Ted and Joan. I think it's better for Dale (her two-year-old son). They live on this site. We're respectable Gypsies now (she laughed). We're still a bit hippie though. Rod says we're 'Gypie-hippies', but everyone on the site is okay.[83]

Given the current problems in housing provision for poorer groups in society, and the possible meeting points of Travellers with the non-travelling population (around working-class institutional, employment and cultural activity), it seems more likely that the Traveller population would be added to by way of immigration from the non-travelling community. Although such a conclusion cannot be in any way definitive, my research indicates that it would be more difficult to argue for a movement in the opposite direction.[84]

Homelessness

> At first it was just a case of not being able to find decent rented accommodation and not being able to afford a mortgage. I have always worked one way and another, so I had nothing to lose by going into a trailer. It was either that or moving in with her parents and neither of us fancied that.[85]

Whilst it is likely, given the plethora of legislation that impinges on a travelling way of life[86] that many Travellers have been obliged to move away from caravan-dwelling, my research provides evidence that caravan-dwelling has been an option for many homeless individuals and families and those for whom the lowest quality of housing would be the only other choice:

> There are also a lot of negative reasons for travelling . . . The current housing crisis is a major factor in many peoples' decisions. With the recent rent rises, changes in the law regarding squatters, it is possible that more will be forced onto the road. High rents and constant bills can be traded for a cheap mobile home and few bills. In some cases, the accommodation available is so poor that it does not seem worth paying £50 per week in a shared house, which compares unfavourably with a £200 trailer.

> The Government's 'back to basics' campaign makes housing unavailable to young people, forcing them to live with friends and relatives . . . or wherever they can . . . rented accommodation is unavailable to those with limited finances.

> I couldn't pay the mortgage on a flat in Essex . . .[87]

The following data is taken from an interview with George, a settled Traveller who gave up caravan-dwelling in the late 1970s.

BB: When did you start travelling?

G: We went on the road proper around 1950. During the war I'd been back and forward a couple of times with the evacuation, in between mum, my brother and me had lived with my gran. When dad first got back we got a place but it was in a right state, although it wasn't just that. Dad really couldn't settle. He'd seen a lot in the Far East and he really wanted to get away from the town. At first we just got involved with summer work, fruit-picking and the like, going up to the end of the hop season to the start of the autumn, that meant we could stay in the shelters provided, hopping huts and that. For two or three years we went back to London in the winter, but when dad bought an old van we were moving around full time. By then I'd finished my schooling.

BB: How did you live?

G: Well, apart from the picking there was plenty of labouring work, we did a bit of totting too. Scrap got quite big for a while and I suppose we made a good living. By the sixties me and my brother had brand new vans and we had time for the lurchers and a bit of horse-trading. We got quite good at that sort of thing, for city boys anyway.

BB: Were there any other Travellers in your family?

G: No, I don't think so, although my daughter is married to a Gypsy lad. He isn't on the road anymore. They live near Basildon. No, we were the first as far as I know. I think if we could have had a decent home mum and dad would not have taken up travelling. He would have settled down eventually. But what we had was not all that, and when he first came home, probably because of the work he chose to do, he never got round to saving up enough to put down on a house. By the time he had that kind of cash we had got used to being on the move. He never did settle.

BB: Why did you stop travelling?

G: It was a case of no longer having to. I was able to do me business from one place. I always saw meself settling down eventually, although my brother still travels in the summer.

It seems that there is some indication of a consistent link between homelessness and caravan-dwelling. As pointed out in the last section, Adams *et al.*[88] identify that a considerable number of 'non-nomadic' people had taken to caravans, whilst Okely[89] saw the housing shortage resulting in a rise in the numbers of people resorting to caravans. Part of George Orwell's *Road to Wigan Pier*[90] reinforces this point by showing that the connection between homelessness and caravan-dwelling existed during the inter-war period of the 1930s. A substantial quote from Orwell appears below as it contains crucial aspects that are relevant to the discussion throughout this chapter including the institutional pressures on Travellers, the problematical dichotomy between 'real' and 'New Age' Travellers, but in particular the social and economic links between caravan-dwelling and homelessness. However, the overarching impact is the conditions and privations imposed by caravan-dwelling. Whilst the living environment Orwell describes below might not be typical of caravan-dwelling today, some of the conditions he writes of can still be identified on many present day unofficial and some official sites.

> Anyone who wants to see the effects of the housing shortage at their very worst should visit the dreadful caravan-dwellings that exist in numbers in many of the northern towns. Ever since the war, in the complete impossibility of getting houses, parts of the population have overflowed into supposedly temporary quarters in fixed caravans.

Immediately the reader is confronted with the fact that this example of a caravan-dwelling group has been generated as a result of housing shortages and poverty. It should be noted that Orwell describes the caravans as 'fixed'. Many legal sites today are made up of non-mobile caravans, sometimes cemented to the ground, without wheels.

> Wigan, for instance, with a population of about 85,000, has round about 200 caravan-dwellings with a family in each – perhaps somewhere near 1,000 people in all. How many of these caravan-colonies exist throughout the industrial areas it would be difficult to discover with any accuracy. The local authorities are reticent about them and the census report of 1931 seems to have decided to ignore them. But so far as I can discover by enquiry they are to be found in most of the larger towns in Lancashire and Yorkshire, and perhaps further north as well. The probability is that throughout the north of England there are some thousands, perhaps tens of thousands of families (not individuals) who have no home except a fixed caravan.

It seems that the problem of establishing anything other than a very rough approximation of the numbers of people living in caravans is not a contemporary aberration, but Orwell's educated guess puts the number something in excess of 1 per cent of the population at a period of extreme housing shortage and poverty.

> But the word 'caravan' is very misleading. It calls up a picture of a cosy Gypsy-encampment (in fine weather, of course) with wood fires crackling and children picking blackberries and many-coloured washing fluttering on the lines. The caravan-colonies in Wigan and Sheffield are not like that. I had a look at several of them. I inspected those in Wigan with considerable care, and I have never seen comparable squalor except in the Far East. Indeed when I saw them I was immediately reminded of the filthy kennels in which I have seen Indian coolies living in Burma. But, as a matter of fact, nothing in the East could ever be quite as bad, for in the East you haven't our clammy, penetrating cold to contend with, and the sun is a disinfectant.

Orwell conveys a traditional romantic view of Gypsies, at the same time he cannot grasp the possible connections between the people he is describing and those he thinks of as 'Gypsies'. For all this, he begins to highlight some of the conditions of caravan-dwelling life, not least the constant battle against the weather and being 'sited' largely on low quality land. Orwell also draws attention to what might be thought of as the progenitors of the ad hoc dwellings inhabited by contemporary New Age Travellers:

> Along the banks of Wigan's miry canal are patches of waste ground on which the caravans have been dumped like rubbish shot out of a bucket. Some of them are actually Gypsy caravans, but very old ones and in bad repair. The majority are old single-decker buses (the rather smaller buses of ten years ago) which have been taken off their wheels and propped up with struts of wood. Some are simply wagons with semi-circular slats on top, over which canvas is stretched, so that the people inside have nothing but canvas between them and the outer air. Inside, these places are usually about five feet wide by six high (I could not stand quite upright in any of them) and anything from six to fifteen feet long.

Although the caravans Orwell is describing were a mixture of what are seen as traditional van and bow-top vehicles, the overall dimensions of these dwellings are not inconsistent with the living space many Travellers are obliged to make do with currently.

> Some, I suppose, are inhabited by only one person, and some of them contained large families. One, for instance, measuring fourteen feet long, had seven people in it – seven people in about 450 cubic feet of space; which is to say that each person had for his entire dwelling a space a good deal smaller than one compartment of a public lavatory. The dirt and congestion of these places is such that you cannot well imagine it unless you have tested it with your own eyes and more particularly your nose. Each contains a tiny cottage kitcheners and such furniture as can be crammed in – sometimes two beds, more usually one, into which the whole family have to huddle as best they can. It is almost impossible to sleep on the floor, because the damp soaks up from below. I was shown mattresses which were still wringing wet at eleven in the morning. In winter it is so cold that the kitcheners have to be kept burning day and night, and the windows, needless to say, are never opened.

General structural problems with caravans have not essentially changed over the last 70 years or so. Whilst a new trailer will be adequately insulated the life of a caravan is, relative to conventional housing, very short. Within a few years even the most modern of caravans, with constant wear and tear, will begin to spring leaks and develop faults that inflict all the problems associated with condensation and the incursion of damp, giving inhabitants little choice other than to keep trailers constantly heated. Many poorer travelling people, often relatively large families, are obliged to purchase older, second-hand caravans that have seen better days, being in the twilight of their usefulness as homes.

> Water is got from a hydrant common to the whole colony, some of the caravan-dwellers having to walk 150 or 200 yards for every bucket of water. There are no sanitary arrangements at all. Most of the people construct a little hut to serve as a lavatory on the tiny patch of ground surrounding their caravan, and once a week dig a deep hole in which to bury the refuse. All the people I saw in these places, especially the children, were unspeakably dirty, and I do not doubt that they were lousy as well. They could not possibly be otherwise. The thought that haunted me as I went from caravan to caravan was, 'What can happen in those cramped interiors when anybody dies?' But that, of course, is the kind of question you hardly care to ask.

Contemporary Travellers resorting to unofficial or illegal sites are unlikely to have ready access to water or toilets. Many official sites offer little more provision in terms of access to fresh water than that described by Orwell.

> Some of the people have been in their caravans for many years. Theoretically the Corporation are doing away with the caravan-colonies and getting the inhabitants out into houses; but as the houses don't get built, the caravans remain standing. Most of the people I talked to had given up the idea of ever getting a decent habitation again. They were all out of work, and a job and a house seemed to them about equally remote and impossible. Some hardly seemed to care; others realized quite clearly in what misery they were living.

Given that housing shortages continued right through the 1930s and long after the Second World War, it might well be speculated that many of those currently labelled as Gypsies in contemporary society have their roots not in India but in the 'caravan-colonies' Orwell wrote about. However, these people living in caravans are no longer seen, at least in the literature, as culturally amenable to conventional housing. Now they *belong* on the site.

> One woman's face stays by me, a worn skull-like face on which was a look of intolerable misery and degradation. I gathered that in that dreadful pigsty, struggling to keep her large brood of children clean, she felt as I should feel if I were coated all with dung. One must remember that these people are not Gypsies; they are decent English people who have all, except the children born there, had homes of their own in their day; besides, their caravans are greatly inferior to those of Gypsies and they have not the great advantage of being on the move.

Here again Orwell slips into the assumptions of his time. First, he conforms to the idea that there is a discernible difference between 'Gypsies' and non-Gypsies; as we have seen, this notion continues in contemporary academic analysis. Second, he implies that 'English people' are more 'decent' than 'Gypsies'. However, his point about the advantages of itinerancy relative to being bounded within the confines of the site would still make sense to many Travellers.

> No doubt there are still middle-class people who think that the Lower Orders don't mind that kind of thing and who, if they had happened to pass a caravan-colony in the train, would immediately assume that the people lived there from choice. I never argue nowadays with that kind of person.

This is another point that has poignancy today. The literature focusing on Travellers rarely considers that caravan-dwelling might not be a matter of culture, choice, tradition or something 'in the blood'. It fails to understand that for many people living in a caravan is neither a matter of desire nor culture and may be experienced as an unpalatable necessity or the best of a limited number of unattractive alternatives.

> But it is worth noticing that the caravan-dwellers don't even save money by living there, for they are paying about the same rents as they would for houses. I could not hear of any rent lower than five shillings a week (five shillings for 200 cubic feet of space!) and there are even cases where the rent is as high as ten shillings. Somebody must be making a good thing out of these caravans!

The danger of the effective deregulation following the demise of the Caravan Sites legislation of the 1960s with the coming of the 1994 Criminal Justice and Public Order Act is that those obliged to resort to caravan-dwelling might well be subject to a range of abuse. The proposals contained in the Traveller Law Reform Bill 2002 might well curb some of the worst types of exploitation, but this relies on the system working and government (and future governments) keeping funding at an appropriate level. As Orwell points out, there is profit to be made from the continuing problems in terms of access to conventional housing provision, and the omnipresence of economic imperatives and the notion of 'Best Value' throughout the Traveller Law Reform Bill shows that Orwell's warning still has relevance.

> But clearly their continued existence is due to the housing shortage and not directly to poverty.

The above quote connects a visible and substantial group of caravan-dwellers to homelessness/housing shortages. It demonstrates that the connection between homelessness and caravan dwelling has a concrete precedent and a place in the social and economic history of the modern British State. As such, caravan-dwelling can be understood as much of an accompaniment to the capitalist system as the housing market.[91] Indeed, caravan-dwelling could be seen as an unavoidable consequence of the housing market in that all markets include those that can buy into them and exclude those who are unable to afford entry. However, the latter group cannot be allowed to exist outside the market economy; this would, after all, contradict the logic of market economics. As Orwell shows, those who cannot gain entry to the conventional housing market will be assigned or conscripted to another market that is separate from, but complementary to, the market they have been excluded from.

Unemployment

The search for work has traditionally involved people adopting an itinerant life-style.[92] Indeed, mass itinerancy has a history at least going back to the enclosure movement of the late eighteenth/early nineteenth centuries.[93] As the livelihood of the 'Chapman', the 'Trampers', Drovers and others gradually diminished so they slowly took up supplementary trades and activities.

> My Great-uncle came from drover stock in Wales. They'd drive anything. Cattle, geese, turkeys, anything with legs. The trade didn't die overnight though. There was still some short-range work before the first war. But they had to take other things up. Any kind of farm labouring, round-ups, even tinkering. Gradually that's all there was and a lot of folk turned it in. But I reckon most of those travelling in Wales have drover blood.[94]

> We're the people who got on our bikes and got on with our lives . . . We got on our bikes and looked for work . . .[95]

> The high level of unemployment has influenced many to become nomadic. In some cases it is to look for work and be able to live wherever work is . . .[96]

During the research caravan-dwelling and occasionally (but not always) the site, often seemed to be related necessities connected to other considerations. Likewise a straightforward need to move was just one of a number of reasons given for the taking up and continuance of an itinerant life-style. Frequently, the need for a site and the decision to move were connected to economic considerations. Peter is a young man who lived on a tolerated site in Minster:

Interviewer: Have you got your name down for the new site yet?
Peter: Yeah. A man came round a bit ago and took some names.
Interviewer: Would you stop on it long if you got on it?
Peter: I don't know. I like to get around. I've just come back from Black-pool.
Interviewer: What's it like over there, any good?
Peter: Yeah. There's plenty of work. Plenty of scrap and gardening work.

Interviewer: Are you going back?

Peter: Yeah. If I don't get on the site. If I did I don't know how long I'd stop on it.

Given the literature's constant reiteration of the simplistic need for sites and tolerance for those wishing to live in caravans it seems important to note that few of the research respondents expressed a straightforward desire to live in a caravan on a site. When respondents did express a wish to live on a site this did not necessarily equate to an aspiration to live on a permanent or even long-term site. Preference for any form of caravan-dwelling was rarely unconnected to other life-style wants or necessities.

Search for alternative life-styles

The rejection of social conventions and the search for alternative life-styles have led many to take up a travelling way of life. The contemporary manifestation of this may be seen as the New Age Travellers,[97] but the 'New Age' can be traced back at least as far as the end of the Second World War.[98] Indeed, it is hard to draw a definite line between 'New Age' and 'Old Age' and discern to what level people rejecting 'modern' life or seeking to create a 'new' life have merged with 'traditional' Travellers.

Another side of the social generation of Travellers is the socio-psychological disposition to travelling. This motivating force seems as powerful as the self-categorization of Travellerhood. A conversation between a female youth worker and two young Traveller women, Karen aged 17, and Val who is 15 years old, in Minster, demonstrates the complex feelings about and background to a travelling life-style. What is illustrated is a much more intricate pattern of ideas about choice and opportunities than often portrayed when referring to Traveller expectations and origins and how parental experience of a non-travelling life-style can impinge on choice. The youth worker describes the situation:

Val has recently started using the club again, initially attending up to the age of 13. Karen and Val used to be something of a handful, always questioning and disputing issues with the workers and each other.

Youth Worker: What have you been doing since I last saw you?

C: Nowt.

Youth Worker: That must be boring.

C: Not really. I help me Mam.

Youth Worker: What do you do?

C: Clean the trailer with her.

Youth Worker: Have you always lived in a trailer?

C: I never been in a house.

Youth Worker: What, never?

C: Only to door.

Youth Worker:	Do you think you will always live in a trailer or would you like to try a house some time?
C:	Never been in one so don't know if I'd like it. I like it where I am.
Youth Worker:	What, with your parents?
C:	No. In a trailer. It's all I've ever known. Me Dad lived in a house once but not me Mam.
Youth Worker:	Does your dad want to stay in a trailer or go back to a house ever?
C:	He told me he was trapped in a house and he can't remember it much. It wasn't for long.
Youth Worker:	Are you happy?
C:	I'm bored here!
V:	I've lived in a house.
Youth Worker:	Where, in Minster?
V:	In Arfom, Criton, Rangly.
Youth Worker:	Why so many areas?
V:	We didn't settle. I don't know really.
Youth Worker:	Did you like it?
V:	No.
Youth Worker:	Why not?
V:	I don't know.
Youth Worker:	Would you ever go back in a house?
V:	No.
Youth Worker:	What if you had no choice?
V:	Everyone has a choice.
Youth Worker:	Well, sometimes the choice is taken away from you and people get forced to do things they would rather not do.
V:	Me Mam and Dad wouldn't go in a house again. They like it in a trailer.

It is quite difficult from this conversation to establish just what these two young women want in terms of accommodation. Both are keen to present a challenge to youth workers. The questioning worker is a non-Traveller. Given what is known about these two young women, it seems unlikely that they will indicate that their life-style is in some way less preferable to the life-style of the adult worker. Ostensibly, they come down in favour of trailer-living, but neither can say exactly why. Val seems really to have no other experience to draw on in terms of making a choice. Karen appears to be unable or unwilling to say why she feels that housing is not for her (apart from family preferences). This may be based on negative experience of housing. Poor quality provision, problems with finance, difficulties with neighbours, amongst other considerations, may all have contributed to her feelings or have been transmitted to her via her family.

It may be the case that Karen felt unable or unwilling to talk about her reasons for rejecting housing. Responses concerning family preferences need to be understood in the context of the cultural milieu in which they are made. The

Traveller community, in common with other working-class groups, are not always ready to be perceived as being obliged to live the life they are living. What is portrayed to outsiders and within the community as a choice could well be an authentic response. However, this could equally be an attempt to transmit a view of self as autonomous and an ambition to be understood as a person who is in control of their own destiny. Karen's final responses may indicate the possible presence of such an attitude.

What is also evident from the above and throughout this chapter is just how difficult it is to bring together substantial, reliable data about Travellers. It is clear that evidence can only be useful when based upon long-term association, trust, understanding and a general feeling of acceptance of the researcher by the informant. But it also poses a question about choice. Both Karen and Val have parental connections with non-trailer living, but do they have a housing option beyond the site?

This cultural complexity issue is considered by another youth worker interviewed in the Minster area. Steve commented on and offers insight into an individual Traveller youth called Jack:

> You often hear people talking about Travellers settling in houses. It is often taken for granted that this would be quite a simplistic transition, this assumption is implicit in the Criminal Justice Act.
>
> Jack has, for a long time, been talking about moving into a house. To be independent of his family, 'It's time I got a place of my own', is the kind of phrase he often used. Some time ago I rented a three bedroomed house. I offered to rent Jack one of the rooms. On 13th June he moved in. At the end of July he had returned to his family home.
>
> Jack had developed something of an idyllic view of independent living; doing what he wanted, coming and going as he pleased, staying out late at night, lying in bed all morning if he wished. The reality was somewhat different.
>
> Jack had little idea of how to live with someone who is not prepared to look after him. He was unable to plan his finances, do his own shopping or clean up after himself. Sharing a bathroom was an anathema. I found myself wiping up his urine, the consequence of him missing the bowl. Jack was also relatively ignorant about the preparation of food. For example he would attempt to fry chips starting with cold oil and left frozen food out to be eaten days later.
>
> Jack is a Traveller and has never been exposed to life in a house. This could be seen to be the reason for his ineptitude in terms of domestic necessities. However, the caravan does not offer the same opportunities to develop the skills inherent in the housed situation. Traditional divisions of labour according to gender and the need for disciplined domestic roles, given limitations of space and continued movement (a bit like the division of labour found in the barge community or even aboard ship) have their impact. It must also be remembered that many young people, who have

perhaps been restricted by parental practices (spoilt) or held in comparative ignorance in institutional settings, often experience similar difficulties in terms of social and or domestic skills.

Jack also found the comparative isolation of life off the site difficult. He told me, 'It's the loneliness that gets to me. Not having people around me. At home, in the trailer, you've someone there all the time.' Again, young people who have spent time in institutional settings have similar feelings, as do those who start single living having come from a large family home. Jack also found 'architectural' differences. He reminisced about caravan-dwelling, 'The windows are low so you can see what's going on.' His problems with the physical environment of the house led to him feeling isolated and lonely.

Jack's difficulty in adjusting was instructive. I did not have time to help with his acclimatization and his family had little to offer in the way of advice or support. Jack told me that his family could not understand why he had moved out. They appeared to find it amusing that he was sharing a house with a man (this of course would not help with his adjustment). There were also comments within the club environment. Members asked questions like, 'Are you bumming him?' However, the membership exhibited a deal of interest in the situation. Why did Jack want to do it? What was it like? When they heard that Jack was moving out it seemed to confirm their prejudices – 'it just don't work'. Jack was somewhat low about moving out. He thought that he had failed.

This example shows how a travelling/caravan-dwelling way of life can be habituated. It also suggests that it may be very difficult, once obliged to take up caravan-dwelling, for successive generations to give it up or feel part of, or contemplate any life away from the site. Professional activity can also conscript individuals to a Gypsy/Traveller identity. Roy, a youth worker with young Travellers in Minster states:

We had talked at great length about his views on being a Traveller. He talked about his dark skin and black hair. He saw this as evidence of his Italian origins. To me this is fine. People can claim to come from where they want, but why? This interests me. When I first told him that the travelling people originally came from India he said, 'I'm not Indian!' I went on to explain that this was something like a thousand years ago, and that their passage through Europe took a long time, so he might have some Mediterranean blood in him. I also said that he might just have a dark complexion. I lent him a book called 'Surviving Peoples, Gypsies'. It was a brief history of travelling people. It was the first book he had read.

This young person's perception of himself has been redefined through the worker's formed definition of his identity. How was his Gypsyness identified? How does anyone know that he is the progeny of those groups, who have travelled continuously since the earliest times[99] to Europe from the Indian sub-continent? Why should this young person have more Gypsy 'blood' than any other person? What is the significance of blood? If it is because he happens to live in a trailer, is this the defining factor of Traveller identity? Where does this leave those who Orwell[100] describes?

Throughout this chapter I have presented data in terms of biography and interviews, which suggest that the fact that one lives in a caravan may be little indication of being part of a Traveller heritage. What the above example illustrates is that identity can be socially ascribed or culturally adopted. Roy, a youth worker with Travellers in Minster reflects:

> I was talking to a youth worker who is employed in the Minster area. This person has a ten-year-old child who has a disability and attends a school that specializes in special needs education. I asked if she knew of any young Travellers with disabilities. She replied:
>
> 'In the clubs we run in Minster I don't know of any, but at my son's school there is a lad from a travelling family.'
>
> I asked if she knew the family, she said that they come from the Criton site, but she didn't know them very well. She had spoken to the mother outside the school. 'Come to think of it, I'm the only one who does', she added. I asked why she thought no one else talked to this woman. She said:
>
> 'Well, you can see they're Travellers. They turn up in a pick-up and you know how people in Minster are. They're gypo's.'
>
> I asked if she knew of any groups in the Minster area that worked with young people with disabilities from the travelling community. She said she didn't, but said that they would be welcome at the clubs she was involved with. She added that no one actually worked on sites.
>
> Then she told me of a recent incident:
>
> 'My son loves this WWF wrestling. We took him to see it when it was on at the Leisure Centre. While we were having a drink in the bar, before we went in, my son said, "Look, there's Tom". This is the travelling lad in my son's school. We pushed James over to where Tom and his family were. As I talked to Tom's mother I noticed the looks we were getting. Now I'm used to getting looks, but this was different.'
>
> I asked about this difference.
>
> 'We were with the Travellers. That's why we were getting looked at. I felt very uncomfortable. Not for me but for the family.'

It seems that dominant visual clues take precedence over what become secondary characteristics. For example, the youth worker with a son who has a disability, the primary characteristic, in terms of contact with the Traveller family might well involve dress or general life-style. For those with less exposure to the experience of disability it may be likely that the presence of disability takes up the main perceptual preoccupation.

What this example illustrates is that discrimination is not necessarily based on concrete, factual premises, but is sometimes founded upon incomplete pictures and assumptions – prejudice. These manifestations of prejudice will rely on individual and group consciousness about particular categorizations. Hence, if a Traveller type is to the fore in personal or local consciousness, then any-one fitting that typology will be designated Traveller. In Germany the Nazi treatment of Gypsies, like the Jews, in the 1930s and 1940s was based on such discriminatory/prejudicial phenomena.[101] This demonstrates a process of social ascription.

Another example of this in the Minster context was noted during a prominent Racing Festival. A local pub landlord, Kevin, having recruited regulars to cater for the traditional influx of Travellers at this time, briefed his temporary recruits thus:

> You'll know the Travellers because they spend money like water. Don't worry about the change you give, they haven't got a clue. You can tell the men by their smell and the women by the mud on the heels of their shoes.[102]

These 'conscripting' statements or episodes are important because they repres-ent the closure of non-Traveller society to those designated as Travellers. This exclusion can, as shown with Val and Karen above, cause a rejection of alterna-tive options. This would be consistent with Weber's ideas on social closure.[103] In themselves they do not contribute to the Traveller population, but they can play a part in the maintenance of the same and this needs to be acknowledged as a powerful contributor to the development of Traveller identity.

People can be drawn in to the Traveller community from any one or combina-tions of the considerations outlined above. As the Minster research indicates, a well-developed Traveller group will demonstrate the 'cross-pollination' that exists between Traveller and non-Traveller populations. Using a biographical approach, if we look at one Traveller family, it seems to confirm that the social contributions to the Traveller population outlined above can each cause infil-trations into this population group. At the same time, it seems significant that Travellers should be understood as contributing to wider cultural formations.

A biographical perspective

Jimmy Stone was a Gypsy whose family took up residence on Bonny Downs, a tolerated site in Barking, Essex, sometime in the eighteenth century. In 1914 the 'Gypsy Boys' were recruited from the site as a group, similar to the street recruit-ment of housed civilians. Jimmy, alongside many of the men and boys from Bonny Downs never returned to the site. Jimmy was killed in 1916. All that came back to Catherine, his wife, was a blood-stained silk card.

Catherine now had to look for some way to support her three young children, Celia, Eleanor and Jim. Like many women of her class at this time, she was obliged to find a husband. She bore another child, Clara, by her second husband who was also lost to the battlefields of Europe.

After the war, Catherine married a widowed seaman, Bill Battles, to whom she bore Doris and Vera. Bill brought his only child Mary to the family. The young Jim Stone, after playing a part in the liberation of Europe, including a number of concentration camps, became a toolmaker. Eleanor married James Edward Belton, a stoker in the gasworks at Beckton. James saw active service throughout the Second World War as a Royal Engineer. In the early 1950s, alongside his son, James junior, he set up a number of small businesses that prospered during the 1960s and early 1970s.

Before becoming a bankrupt, the consequence of drug and gambling related problems, James junior married Joyce, the daughter of a Poplar Fireman and active local socialist politician. Young Jim and Joyce had two sons. The extended family followed many, what are often thought of as, East End and Traveller traditions, hop-picking, collecting china and annual visits to the regional horse fair at Horsmonden, Kent. Eleanor died in the mid-1980s, about ten years after her husband. Like her sister and her mother she was a victim of asbestosis, contracted from the notorious Barking asbestos factory.

James junior retired from his job as a local authority dog-handler in the late 1980s. His eldest son, after studying as a draughtsman, became a Police Officer. He married Susan, the daughter of a works foreman, employed at the Silver Town Tate and Lyall's site in East London. They had three children. One daughter became a teacher, the other works in the City, whilst the youngest child, the son, is looking to be involved with the performing arts. Jim and Joyce's younger son, during a dynamic career as a member of West Ham United's roving army of adolescent storm-troopers of the early 1970s, had a string of jobs and took up working with young people. Following professional training he became a youth worker. He went on to gain a good B.Sc. degree and was able to achieve a Master's degree whilst employed as a lecturer in higher education. He went on to write a novel and string of books on a wide range of subjects. He gained his doctorate at the dawn of the twenty-first century. With Rosy, a former North London, Arsenal-supporting, self-ascribed rag-a-muffin, child of immigrants (Irish and Belgian), who is now a National Inspector of Further Education, he has a nine-year-old son who celebrates his East End, Gypsy, Gaelic, Flemish ancestry with a deal of pride and humour, but most people know him simply as Christian, an eccentric, loving, sensitive and intelligent little boy, a developing human being with a budding and interesting personality. Interested in the world around him, his dog, medieval history, the meaning of words, Poke'mon, Bey Blades, Warhammers and the Simpsons. That is who he mostly and really is; *that* is *his* identity. The huge maternal influence of Eleanor persists. The interior of the family home still looks like a caravan.

This example of Gypsy lineage illustrates that the perception of an uninterrupted and unmediated consistency of blood, given the influences of modern existence, is somewhat limited. This background will be familiar to many who have been connected with travelling and Gypsy life-styles. Alongside the other stories and elucidations of lives lived given in this chapter it reveals the cultural complexity of individual biographies and is the defining feature of the social generation of Travellers.

Genetic v. social generation

The social generation of Traveller identity is reinforced by Kalaydjieva. She examined the parallels between the social and genetic history of Gypsies through a large study of three independent Gypsy groups. According to her: 'These three groups do not intermarry and have well defined and distinct group identity, yet all three share a rare gene mutation, suggesting at some point in their history these groups have shared a common gene pool.'[104] She explained:

> I thought of Gypsies in the ignorant way typical of most outsiders, that is a single population which is socially and genetically uniform. Gradually, I have come to realize that what we describe with the generic category of 'Gypsies', is in fact a very complicated stratified hierarchical structure.[105]

Although Kalaydjieva's work was primarily focused on genetic disease from a medical standpoint, she concluded that the basic unit of social organization is the Gypsy group, the identity of which is founded on historical migrations, trade, tradition, language, and in some instances 'organs of self-rule'.[106] However, she has concluded that, '. . . the overall structure is not static and has been described as fluid mosaic where splits and merges between different groups have occurred many times in history'.[107] The study has involved leading geneticists and Gypsy ethnologists from all over the world. According to Kalaydjieva:

> The most amazing finding is the extent to which they have diverged geneti-cally – these three Gypsy groups are at present more different to each other than the classical outlier populations of Europe (the Finns, the Basques and the Sardinians) which no geneticist would dream of pooling together. This despite the fact that they live in close proximity to each other, sometimes in the same villages, and is obviously based on differences in culture and tradi-tion of whose existence we are totally ignorant.[108]

For Kalaydjieva, these findings are relevant in terms of future genetic research in so far as they indicate that, 'important differences may and do exist between Gypsy groups and that pooling patients from different groups together may have a strong confounding effect'.[109]

This analysis, that has been developed and broadened[110], demonstrates that the idea of a homogeneous Gypsy ethnic identity has doubtful biological basis. This contradicts the characteristic academic perspective. For example, according to Okely: 'No one could simply take to the road and become a Traveller – he or she could gain some acceptance through marriage, but only the offspring could claim full ethnic identity.'[111] Also, 'A person has to have at least one Traveller or Gypsy parent to claim membership. The children of a mixed marriage between Traveller and gorgio . . . can claim rights of membership through descent.[112]

Comparative situations

To conclude this section of the chapter it is useful to provide a comparison with other studies on Travellers undertaken in the European context. There have been other studies that have suggested that Traveller populations have emerged from host populations and question the idea of distinct foreign origins. Heymowski,[113] for example, traced how the thinking about Swedish Travellers, or Taters (Tarrare) developed and the ways they differed from the host population. Looking at traditions, customs and language he concluded that there were not significant anthropological distinctions between Travellers and non-Travellers, but there were sociological variations. They had their own notion of belonging to a different group, but more decisive in terms of the creation and maintenance of a Traveller identity was that this was complemented and reinforced by the majority population.

Cottaar points out that Dutch authors depict the caravan-dwellers of Holland as having 'a distinctive tale of origin from the majority of Dutch people'[114] and that as soon as people in Holland started to take to caravan-dwelling in the second half of the nineteenth century, within Dutch society they were categorized as a separate group. According to Cottaar this gave rise to the current situation wherein people residing in a caravan are regarded as caravan-dwellers. She argues that the form of housing one adopted began to be closely linked to identity.[115]

Cottaar goes on to illustrate the dramatic rise in caravan-dwelling that occurred alongside the industrialization of Holland and the development of the road network.[116] See Table 7 and Table 8.

As one can see from Tables 7 and 8, caravan-dwelling grew quickly up to the Second World War. As Cottaar[117] points out, the totals of 1911 and 1918 may have been unreliable, as they were carried out at a time of year when movement was at its peak. Due to people giving up caravan-dwelling just before and during the Second World War the upward trend was halted from 1938, but it had clearly resumed by 1960, showing an increase of 84 per cent between 1948 and 1960. Cottaar argues that the growth of the caravan-dwelling population before

Table 7 Number of caravans in the Netherlands, 1879–1960 (Adapted from Cottaar, 'Dutch Travellers', p. 183.)

1879	1889	1899	1909	1911	1918	1920	1930	1938	1942	1947	1948	1960
16	93	429	817	584	988	1,418	2,261	2,722	2,719	2,696	2,631	5,616

Table 8 Number of caravan-dwellers in the Netherlands, 1879–60 (Adapted from Cottaar, 'Dutch Travellers', p. 183.)

1879	1889	1899	1909	1911	1918	1920	1930	1938	1942	1947	1948	1960
–	326	2,189	3,984	2,800	4,884	7,391	10,795	12,071	11,457	11,955	11,651	21,403

and after the Second World War cannot be explained by birth-rate. Her research revealed that many families and individuals had moved from conventional housing to caravan-dwelling and that rural caravan-dwellers have roots in the area they resided in going back generations. In the urban context she concludes that the relatively recent arrival of caravan-dwellers can be understood as part of a general migration from rural districts that started in the mid-1800s as a response to the pressure of the economic situation. This involved industrialization and patterns of work, for example labourers who needed mobile homes because they were employed in road-building, land reclamation or dredging. However the move to caravan-dwelling was also motivated by the shortage of affordable housing in cities in the period before the Second World War.

For Cottaar, the heritage of Dutch caravan-dwellers can be traced back to their settled past, a time when they were agricultural workers. She also argues that this population has hereditary links with trades and show people and that less than 20 per cent of caravan-dwellers in Holland have a long family history of travelling. According to Cottaar, the lineage of Dutch caravan-dwellers includes people from beyond the borders of Holland. Given this varied and cosmopolitan make-up of Dutch Travellers, Cottaar suggests that each historical period has produced its own Travellers. She found that people moved from a sedentary to a travelling way of life as a consequence of economic changes in agriculture or industry.

What Cottaar demonstrates is that the travelling population of Holland is not a fixed or permanent group. In her research into urban caravan-dwellers in The Hague she found that respondents had spent an average of 16 years as caravan-dwellers, 'with extremes ranging from less than a full year to up to 59 years'. She gives evidence not only of movement between caravans and houses/houses and caravans but also between caravan and houseboat. Cottaar concludes that caravan-dwellers do not come from a closed group and that this population has been subject to a continued migration from and to conventional housing.[118]

According to Cottaar it is legislation, significantly after 1968, in Holland that has now caused caravan-dwellers to become a closed group. She states:

> the heterogeneity of the pre-Second World War caravan-dwelling population became a thing of the past . . . After more than a century of stigmatizing government policy and actual segregation, the Dutch caravan-dwelling population is now, of its own volition, closing ranks.[119]

Whilst one cannot assert that the Dutch situation with regard to caravan-dwellers or Swedish Taters is a direct reflection of the experience of Travellers in England, Dutch and British society are close enough geographically, economically and socially to suggest that the social and economic circumstances that affected caravan-dwelling in Holland may have had similar consequences in England. As such, it would be fitting to argue in the light of Cottaar's findings and the research presented in this book, that similar conditions of internal migration resulting from industrialization and housing shortages have had a significant impact on the travelling population of England. It would also be appropriate to suggest that this population has a strongly heterogeneous background, that became closed over recent times following legislation that has marginalized and segregated Travellers, causing a self-labelling that in fact constitutes a defensive closing of ranks rather than an ethnic homogeneity.

What this short analysis looks to reinforce is the argument that social-historical and economic considerations cannot be left out of an analysis of populations whilst ephemeral biological distinctions, and mythical, abstract notions of tradition are placed to the fore.

Legislation as a generator of ethnicity

The next chapter will show how the pressurizing power of the legislation affecting Travellers can act as a separating force. Its impact can marginalize caravan-dwellers, creating lines of demarcation between Travellers and non-Travellers. The consequence of this is the development of defensive movements[120] that themselves emphasize the dichotomies erected through the legislation. This process, of abstraction via oppressive legislation and defensive solidarity in the face of the same, can be seen to energize ethnic categorization: it operates as a form of social closure. This situation has been noted by Cottaar[121] as an effect of Dutch legislative activity referring to caravan-dwellers. She argues that this group has been transformed into an ethnic category by the effects of legislation.

Indigenous foreigners

Cottaar points out that since 1980 the Dutch government has pursued a special policy towards ethnic minorities, a term covering groups of socially disadvantaged people of foreign origin who maintain their own culture. However, caravan-dwellers, who are primarily of indigenous descent, are embraced by this policy. According to Cottaar, the decision to include caravan-dwellers in this process was made not because of their distinctive form of housing, but because of their 'socially backward position'[122] in terms of employment, housing and education. Compared to the British attitude towards Traveller identity the Dutch situation is relatively transparent, the notion of Traveller identity having always been somewhat mystical and abstract in the British social experience. However, since the Second World War, as in Holland, the Traveller in the English context, as may be evidenced in Chapter One, has been associated with a similar socially backward position and seen as being part of English society but at the same time being 'foreign'. For Cottaar the government was responding to public opinion when it defined Travellers as a distinct group. However, caravan-dwellers themselves, at the same time, claimed that they were different from typical Dutch people, having a distinct culture of their own. Unlike other western European states, the Dutch government has traditionally distinguished between caravan-dwellers and Gypsies, the term Gypsy being reserved for itinerant caravan or tent dwelling people of foreign origin.[123]

As can be seen from previous chapters of this book, this situation is not too far from the English experience. Travellers have developed a definite profile in legal, media and academic spheres and this has been accompanied by the generation of groups and organizations gelling around the resulting identity. Whilst of late, with the marked arrival of East European refugees and migrants, the term 'Gypsy' has regained much of its significance as a metaphor of threat and foreignness alongside parasitical connotations, authorities and writers on Gypsy issues have consistently avoided the possibility of indigenous roots. This has made the recently developed ethnic label less problematic to apply. However, in the Dutch context Cottaar states:

> At a certain moment a wagon with a wood cabin on top offered people whose way of earning a living required travel the chance to take their family with them on the road. After 1900 we see people using these wagons to an increasing degree, not only to travel, but also to live in. They offered, especially in the cities, an alternative in an era plagued by a shortage of housing. Urban caravan-dwellers have always confused the government because they were not supposed to live in caravans.[124]

Cottaar makes the point that at the beginning of the twentieth century a separate, homogeneous group of caravan-dwellers did not exist. She argues that this group came from diverse origins and vocational backgrounds and as such there were 'significant differences'[125] between various groups of caravan-dwellers, whilst there were numerous overall similarities with the sedentary population in terms of work and life-style. According to Cottaar an itinerant way of life and their chosen form of housing were the main features that marked out caravan-dwellers as different from the settled population. As argued in previous chapters, it is this view that is neglected in the overall analysis of the English Traveller population together with the transforming nature of legislation that has effectively marked out a distinct population based on a form of housing and itinerancy.

'Ethnocizing' via legislation

Cottaar argues that before the First World War municipal authorities in Holland had a record of socially excluding caravan-dwellers[126] and pressuring for State legislation to place restrictions on this group.[127] This led to the 1918 Caravan

Act that required municipalities to provide sites for caravan-dwellers. For Cottaar this aided minority formation through segregation, but at the same time caused an apparent increase in caravan-dwelling. This, according to Cottaar, was the very opposite of what was expected from the Act, the legislation having the covert aim of deterring caravan-dwelling. The answer to this rise in numbers was to place these sites in undesirable locations, near rubbish dumps and graveyards etc., with limited facilities. Cottaar suggests that alongside this the municipal authorities promoted the idea that the caravan-dwellers themselves were responsible for the poor upkeep of the sites.[128]

For Cottaar the segregating effect of the 1918 legislation was made worse under German occupation. In 1943 the freedom of movement traditionally enjoyed by caravan-dwellers was prevented by the enforced movement to assembly camps.[129] Although freedom of movement was restored after 1945, the occupation, according to Cottaar, had created a new awareness amongst Dutch administrators, the consequence of which was the insistence of the Ministry of Justice for a revision of the Caravan Act responding to the large numbers of people who began to live in caravans after the Second World War. It was proposed to divide the caravan-dwelling population into sedentary and non-sedentary categories. The sedentary group included the homeless, who were thought to deserve housing. The non-sedentary, itinerant caravan-dwellers were to be subject to a more resolute and rationalized application of existing law. Road builders were not covered by the legislation, nor were show people mentioned in the proposal.[130]

This led to the Dutch 1968 Caravan Act that was, Cottaar argues, 'intended to promote caravan-dwellers' adaptation to sedentary society'.[131] The 1968 Act set up regional sites and although caravan-dwellers kept their right to move about they were not allowed to station their homes anywhere outside a regional camp, and official permission was required to move from camp to camp.

As exemplified in previous and subsequent chapters of this book, the response to Travellers in the English post-war period reflects much the same pattern as the Dutch experience after 1918. The response of English local authorities to the legislation of the 1960s was similar to the reaction of Dutch municipalities from the post-First World War period on, whilst the Dutch and English legislation of 1968 mirrored each other in effect.[132] This, for Cottaar, amounted to spatial segregation. However, the legislation in Holland also regulated the caravan population through the principle of descent: one had no right to take up caravan-dwelling unless one married a caravan-dweller and only offspring of caravan-dwellers retained the right to live in a caravan on condition a stand was available. Whilst this kind of blood transference of rights was not replicated in the English context via legislation, as we have seen, it has been evident in the literature. Cottaar argues that this further energized minority formation. She contends that in Holland segregation was enforced spatially and legally. For Cottaar the official activity of the Dutch government generated a negative image of caravan-dwellers. House dwellers began to perceive caravan-dwellers as deviant and, given their housing and way of life, alien.[133] As the size of the Dutch caravan-dwelling population grew or became more visible, so stigmatization became more prevalent.[134] This analysis can be equally applied in the English context, particularly following the 1994 Criminal Justice and Public Order Act and, although from a seemingly more positive perspective, the Traveller Law Reform Bill 2002.[135]

Cottaar points out that one of the effects of the Dutch response to caravan-dwellers was to curtail their traditional forms of employment. This led caravan-dwelling families to be more dependent on State welfare.[136] The effective curtailment of itinerancy in England would logically have similar effects. Travelling life-styles are dependent on geographical cycles of employment/income, in recent years the door-to-door selling of carpets for example. Once an area has been canvassed and the selling market exhausted there is a need to move on to pastures new.

The contemporary prevention of itinerancy in England means that Travellers who have developed life-styles that incorporate employment with family movement are likely to look increasingly to State welfare for support as, according to Cottaar, is the case with their Dutch counterparts. This again emphasizes the ethnic categorization both through social backwardness and marginalization.

The 'Balkanization' of Travellers

Cottaar points out that Dutch show-people, from the start of the twentieth century, portrayed themselves as different from caravan-dwellers in an attempt to safe-guard their own social position, although they had not traditionally lived in a separate sphere, sharing camping grounds and, for Cottaar, having 'unmistakable ties' with caravan-dwellers through employment and kinship.[137] She argues that similar responses occurred in Germany and England. In 1889 the Showmen's Guild was set up in Britain. A decade later Ons Belang[138] was formed in Holland. The purpose of these organizations was to draw distinctions between show-people and Gypsies. The point was to deny common origin in order to avoid the effects of proposed legislation focusing on those living in caravans; in Britain the Moveable Dwellings Bill was similar in effect to the Dutch Act of 1918. For Cottaar this also had consequences for the general process of group formation, emphasizing as it did human typologies based on origin or race,[139] but it can also be understood as the beginning of what might be thought of as the Balkanization of the travelling population that has continued up to the contemporary period, wherein legislation and academic activity focusing on Travellers develop distinctions between New Age Travellers, Gypsies, show-people, Tinkers and others, the latest of which are economic migrants.

Cottaar suggests that caravan-dwellers have derived a culture based on travel and an emotive connection with a link between itinerancy and freedom, but this has been effectively curtailed.[140] This and negative feelings towards the State that restricted their freedom can be understood to have created ideology based on identity, that needs to defend itself against the rest of Dutch society. For Cottaar the Dutch Caravan Act of 1968 saw to it that: 'the population group of caravan-dwellers was sealed off from "outsiders" . . . In combination with a century of negative stereotyping and stigmatizing policy minority formation has turned out to be the inevitable outcome.'[141] Thus two distinct but complementary motivations for the adoption of an ethnic label has been generated. In the first instance the enactment of legislation has made caravan-dwelling an unattractive option, but it has also marked out what might be called an incorrigible group who exist on the margins of society, within a different realm of society, the culture of which becomes a series of ethnic markers. Second, in defence, the group so marginalized use the product of their marginality, Traveller/caravan-dweller ethnicity, the only weapon the State and society provides them with, as a means to gain or achieve rights (a more favourable share of social resources). The Traveller Law Reform Bill 2002 might be understood as a practical manifestation of such a process. As such, it can be seen that legislation has played a part in creating an ethnic Traveller identity and obliged the adoption of the same.[142] I would suggest that much of the effect in this Dutch context reflects and replicates the impact of legislation and attitude in the English situation.

The Traveller population

In the final part of the chapter I suggest that social and economic forces, pertaining to the provision of/access to housing, may have a part in the generation of the caravan-dwelling population. This argument will be utilized to demonstrate the contribution of social and economic considerations to the maintenance and development of the Traveller population.

Statistical comparison between homelessness and caravan-dwelling

In what follows I highlight the similarities between the population profiles of those living in caravans, through a comparison of the biannual caravan counts, and households claiming homelessness, from the figures compiled by the Chartered Institute of Public Finance and Accountancy, in the annual *Homeless Statistics Actuals*.[143] The analysis will encompass a period of over 20 years, from the initial presentation of these figures up to the contemporary period, stopping at the point when the Criminal Justice Act 1994 began to take effect. This represents a quantitative analysis, involving a huge number of calculations of regional statistics. Such an exhaustive audit has not been undertaken before and as such represents an original and insightful contribution to the study of the Traveller population and homelessness. It examines the trends in homelessness and caravan-dwelling with the objective of suggesting potential links between these two populations.

It is understood that this exercise does not enable any definitive statement about the relationship between the Traveller population and the number of homeless people in England and Wales. However, the very similar patterns of development pertaining to homelessness and caravan-dwelling are illustrative of possible social connections between Travellers and other groups. This suggests that those identifying themselves as homeless may have been, and could continue to be affected by social and economic forces similar to those that cause individuals and groups to adopt or continue a travelling life-style.

Problems with the figures

There are a number of likely deficiencies in both the *Homelessness Statistics Actuals*, the means used to establish the numbers registering as homeless, and the biannual caravan counts as reflections of the Traveller population and the number of homeless people respectively. As Skellington points out: 'The real incidence of homelessness can be disguised by official definitions and categorizations, much of them embedded in complex legislation . . . Statistical data on homelessness is problematic and may only measure the tip of the iceberg.'[144]

Whilst there is no definitive proof that all homeless people do not present themselves to local authorities, it is unlikely that this is the case. Greve points out that the numbers of people recorded as homeless by official statistics relate only to those meeting local authority definitions. He goes on to point out that approximately twice as many people present themselves to local authorities as homeless but many do not bother.[145] Shelter reinforce Skellington's argument that the figures for those accepted as homeless 'are the tip of a very large iceberg'.[146] The households in the 'accepted as homeless' category, as presented in the *Homelessness Statistics Actuals*, are those who are defined as being in the 'priority need' for rehousing. I have sought to counter this to some extent by using the 'households claiming homelessness' figures; but they are unlikely to provide any more than an underlying trend in homelessness. The statistics include only those who see themselves as having an opportunity to register (be accepted) as homeless; those with some realistic hope of rehousing. This does not include the majority of single homeless people for example. The figures are also likely to exclude many couples and small families.

As Skellington[147] argues, the definition of homelessness has become an issue deeply set in the ideological context of 1980s Thatcherite Britain. This has continued under the New Labour Government of Tony Blair. The very blurred picture we have of homelessness is, to some extent, a product of the British political and social milieu of the period between the late 1970s and 1990s. There is and has been a political investment in minimizing the perceived level of homelessness, whilst emphasizing portrayals of the homeless as feckless or near pathological.[148] Importantly, during the 1990s the links with New Age Travellers as part of a youth culture style gave the appearance that homelessness was an intentional and identifiable international youth subculture. Blackman[149] states: 'For government and media this non-traditional lifestyle was portrayed as deliberately upholding values which were inappropriate to those of mainstream society.'

The perception of the Traveller population as being, as a whole, a natural caravan/site dwelling population[150] can be seen as part of the effort to marginalize homelessness as an issue. At the same time this contention of naturalism undermines the need to provide the choice of conventional housing to at least a section of the Traveller population.

Added to these considerations the figures produced by the caravan counts can only safely be thought of as representing trends in caravan-dwelling as:

1   there are significant differences in profiles for the January and July counts (the months when counts are carried out);
2   the population resorting to unofficial sites fluctuates much more than the caravan-dwelling population as a whole;
3   the counts are only carried out in England, they do not allow for movement into Wales, Scotland, Ireland or Europe (likely to be summer options);
4   the counts include no way of assessing the numbers of part-time caravan-dwellers that may retreat to housing provision particularly in the Winter months;[151]
5   all counts rely on 'known' sites; as such they will unavoidably miss more transient groups who might use encampments for no more than a few days at a time or perhaps just one night.

Because of these statistical variations and potential errors I have chosen to use both July and January counts to establish some notion of continuity and balance of analysis. However, it must be reiterated that because of the deficiencies, flaws and approximations inherent in the statistics, all that can be drawn from them are broad trends in caravan-dwelling and homelessness. For the purposes of this part of this chapter an insight into general trends will be sufficient, as I am restricting the analysis to a general comparison of two trends over almost 20 years. I am not seeking precision counts or figures, but relativity within each set of statistics – the number of caravans and those identifying themselves as homeless and between the respective overall patterns of development.

Homelessness/caravan count data generation

The Department of the Environment biannual caravan counts are restricted to England. This being the case these had to be matched with similar areas (Wales is excluded) from the *CIPFA Homelessness Statistics Actuals* returns for the Number of Households Claiming Homelessness (detailed in the *Homeless Statistics Actuals*). During the research the nine major regions of the caravan counts were compared to the same area's data from the *CIPFA Homelessness Statistics Actuals*. Combined data from South-East/London/East, East/West Midlands, North-West/ Yorks and Humberside/North, Metropolitan, Non-Metropolitan and England was also generated to provide further analysis.

I have limited the analysis from when both these sets of data were inaugurated, 1978, up to and including 1996, as at this point the effects of the 1994

Criminal Justice and Public Order Act would have begun to distort the overall perspective.[152]

The figures

In all 42 figures were produced for the research. In the main text I have reproduced the figures presenting the overall situation in England together with a brief analysis. A further three areas are analysed in Appendix Three.

Overall I have presented these figures to demonstrate a similar trend in the numbers registering as homeless and the numbers of caravans identified by the biannual counts in England from 1978 up to and including 1996. Each series of figures will be preceded by a short description of the comparison.

Figures generated from the caravan counts

Caravan counts have been undertaken in England in January and July each year since 1979 in the following regions: Greater London; the South-East; the East; the West Midlands; the East Midlands; the South; Yorkshire and Humberside; the North; the North-West. These are brought together as the count for England. Figures were generated for each of these regions for both January and July counts. Areas were also collectively represented. These included:

1   South-East/London/Eastern to give a collective view of the situation in the southeast of England.
2   East and West Midlands to provide a perspective of the caravan-dwelling population throughout the Midlands.
3   The North, North-West, Yorkshire and Humberside to provide an overview of the caravan-dwelling population in the north of England.

From the information given in the counts it was also possible to construct figures for Metropolitan and non-Metropolitan areas to replicate areas represented in the statistics gathered concerned with homelessness, for the purposes of comparative analysis.

Within every figure each of the years between 1979 and 1996 are individually represented by a column. The year of the count is detailed at the bottom of each column. The scale for the numbers of caravans can be found on the vertical axis of each figure. At the top of each yearly column the number of caravans counted is detailed (corresponding to the left-hand vertical axis).

Figures generated from the numbers registering as homeless

From the information given in the *CIPFA Homelessness Statistics Actuals* it was possible to generate figures representing the numbers of people registering as homeless in regions corresponding to those used in the caravan counts. For the purposes of comparative analysis, figures for the numbers registering as homeless were generated for the same areas wherein caravan counts are undertaken.

The figures can be read in much the same manner as the graphs concerned with the caravan counts. The years between 1979 and 1996 are individually represented by a column. The year of registration is detailed at the bottom of each column.

The scale for the numbers registering as homeless can be found on the vertical axis of each figure. At the top of each yearly column the number of those registering as homeless is detailed (corresponding to the left-hand vertical axis).

It should be noted that the numbers for 1979–80 did not include the 'registering as homeless' category used in all other years. As such, the numbers for 'accepted as homeless' were used in the 1979–80 bar. Strictly speaking, given the anomaly, the number for 1979–80 should not have been included. However the number appearing in this bar has been used to avoid confusion.

England

Early peaks in homelessness occur in 1984/5, 1986/7, these are matched in the caravan counts. The characteristic 'late peak' or 'upside down tick' profile is evident in both figures detailing the numbers of caravans and the figure showing the homelessness numbers. As such a relationship between the populations is suggested. Although they might not be said to depict the same group, it seems possible that both groups, caravan-dwellers and homeless, may be subject to similar effects of social phenomena. This being the case, it appears likely that

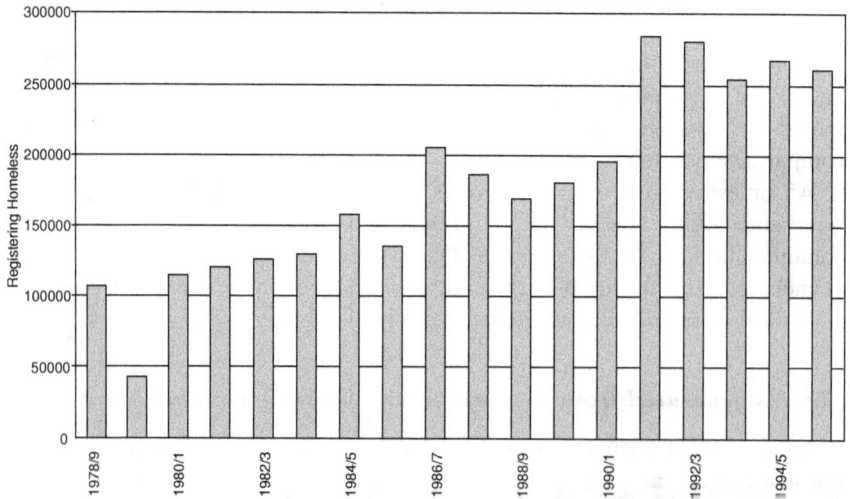

Figure 2 Homelessness – England, 1978/9–95/6.

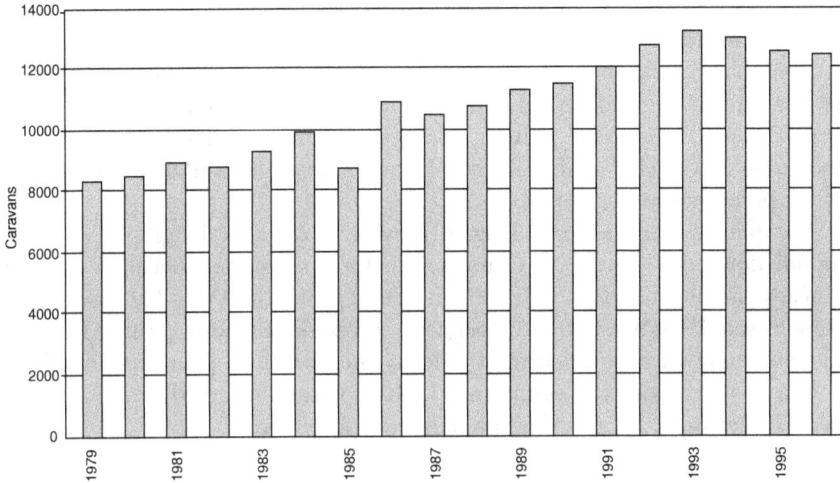

Figure 3 January caravan counts – England, 1979–96.

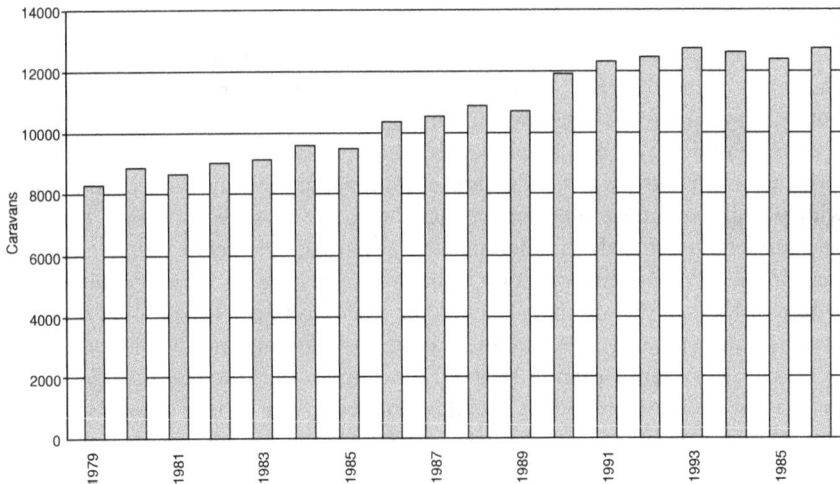

Figure 4 July caravan counts – England, 1979–96.

the groups have an affinity in social terms and that as such there are likely to be points of affiliation as well as instances of recruitment/conscription from one group to another. However, because of the difficulties accessing conventional housing from the point of caravan-dwelling, together with the relatively simplistic path from homelessness to caravan-dwelling (pre-1994), it seems likely that the number of people resorting to caravan-dwelling from the point of homelessness would be greater than those making the reverse trip.

Figures overall

The characteristic 'upside-down tick' or 'late peak' pattern, a gradual rise from 1979 until the mid–late 1990s, with a gradual downturn thereafter, occurred in 80 per cent of homelessness graphs; 12 out of 15. Two of the remaining three graphs had a 'twin peak' pattern, with high points in 1995/6, but they still showed a high level of conformity in relation to the profile found in the majority of the other graphs.

The January caravan counts again provided 12 out of 15 graphs with the 'upside-down tick'/'late peak' characteristic. One out of the other three showed a steady rise (no tail on the tick) with an overall peak in 1995/6. The July counts demonstrated that 9 out of 15 (60 per cent) corresponded to this profile. Three of the remaining six took the form of a steady rise, with high points in 1995/6.

Out of the 30 caravan count graphs, 21 took the form of the 'upside-down tick' (70 per cent). Four achieved a 'tail-less tick' pattern.

Figures conclusion

The sets of figures presented above and in Appendix Three, although not by any means a mirror of each other as a set, do indicate, overall, a consistent similarity in terms of trend. One could indulge in a deal of speculation about the details of the numbers presented above, the role of the Mental Health and Community Care Acts of recent years on the homelessness numbers for instance; this would not be in sympathy with the overall purpose of looking at the data. The aim has been to tentatively suggest a link between homelessness and caravan-dwelling in terms of response to social conditions, suggesting that they may be related groups, with possible affinities, allowing or facilitating for cross-recruitment. This has been undertaken in order to offer an alternative or supplementary explanation to that provided in the general body of literature relating to Travellers about the nature of the caravan-dwelling population; that it is partly the product of social and economic polices, in the main housing provision and not wholly or mainly of an ethnic or racial origin. As such, this implies that the so-called Traveller population needs to be thought of and responded to as a diverse group of people, with differing social and cultural backgrounds and individual needs.

Conclusion

Using the data in this chapter I have endeavoured to highlight, by the means of qualitative and quantitative methods, the very diverse social origin of the Traveller population.

This has included informal interviews, media material, family history and biography, literature relating to the housing situation since the Second World War and theory surrounding Traveller issues. I have also, in preparation for Chapter Four, developed a comparative model drawing on analysis of the caravan dwelling population in Holland, in order to illustrate how legislative activity can be understood to motivate the formation of a Traveller ethnicity through the identification and isolation of a marginalized group. This gives rise to the adoption of defence strategies by this population in the face of oppressive legislation. This demonstrates a duel process of ethnicity building that is generated by means of legislative conferment and defensive adoption. Finally I have provided a statistical analysis illustrating a similar pattern in relation to trends in homelessness and caravan-dwelling. This statistical exercise could not claim to produce definitive conclusions, but it does provide an illustrative analysis that allows greater consideration of the part of economic and social forces in the generation of Traveller identity/ethnicity.

The qualitative data included in this chapter is of a like character. Its subjective nature provides a demonstrative analysis, facilitating a deductive process. It does not provide concrete proof derived from objective factual examination of impartial survey results and/or findings from neutral questionnaires. However, when the different data sets presented in this chapter are considered as a whole they reinforce the argument that the generation of the Traveller population needs to be considered in the light of the social and economic environment.

Overall, the chapter has sought to demonstrate the role of social and economic phenomena in the generation of the Traveller population, including a tentative suggestion that there is a link, engendered by social circumstance, between homelessness and caravan-dwelling. This has been undertaken in order to offer an alternative or supplementary explanation to that provided in the general body of literature relating to Travellers about the nature of the caravan-dwelling population. The data suggests that the caravan-dwelling population is partly the product of social and economic factors. It has used the example of housing provision to exemplify this and argue that the Traveller population is not wholly or mainly of an ethnic or racial origin. This implies that the so-called Traveller population needs to be thought of and responded to as a diverse group of people, with differing social and cultural backgrounds and individual needs.

I have questioned the idea of an essentialist and homogeneous Traveller population, strongly built upon notions of ancestry, tradition, culture and genetics. I have also looked to heighten the awareness of, and the relationship between, social phenomena in the generation of this population, because there is so little attention given to this type of analysis in the literature. It could be argued that this omission from the literature plays an important part in the development of the position that 'the site' is a 'normal' or 'natural' habitat for Travellers. To this extent it is their ethnicity or race that dictates their living conditions and location. As Goldberg has pointed out: 'Race inscribes and circumscribes the experience of space and time, of geography and history, just as race itself acquires its specificity in terms of space-time correlates.'[153]

This discriminatory and stereotypical approach leads to an emphasis on the provision of sites for these categorized groups as alternative housing.[154]

In the next chapter I will look at a range of legislative activity that has affected Travellers. I will illustrate that this activity has a discernible line of evolution that can be seen as responsive to the development of homelessness and the Traveller population.

4 Legislative regulation of the Traveller population

Introduction

The 1960 and 1968 Caravan Sites Acts can be understood, in terms of their inception, as positive efforts to provide what Gypsies needed – sites with standards for minimum provisions.[1] The 1994 Criminal Justice and Public Order Act is seen to be out of step with these previous responses. This legislation was detrimental to site provision, in that it repealed part II of the 1968 Act, removing the duty on local authorities to provide sites, and abolished the government grant for constructing Gypsy caravan sites.[2] The Traveller Law Reform Bill 2002, as its very title suggests, apparently redresses some of the negative (in terms of Travellers) aspects of the 1994 Act. As such, there is a seeming discontinuity in English legislative activity.

However, these acts, together with the Traveller Law Reform Bill 2002, do have a continuity or logic in respect of their effect, or in the case of the latter, proposed effects. This chapter argues that law, up to the 1994 Act, has placed increasing pressure on those resorting to caravan-dwelling, who for the most part do not conform with traditional, sedentary forms of housing within the market system (rent/mortgages). This will demonstrate how an alternative to the housing market, informal caravan-dwelling, has been made increasingly less viable.

Despite all this government activity the caravan-dwelling population has continued to exist within and outside the law and to be seen as a problem. As such, legislation intended to address/control Travellers has not been successful. I will argue that the Traveller Law Reform Bill 2002 can be understood as a response to this fact and represents the official recognition of the desirability of widespread site provision that will in effect bring caravan-dwelling into the legitimate housing market and act as a means to absorb and reform those who at present take to the deviant housing resort of caravan-dwelling.

The post-war legislation affecting Travellers and its political context

The post-war legislation affecting Travellers has been framed within an environment of social policy starting in the 1960s, an era marked by the consensual politics that was based on the ambition to reform.[3] Whilst the policy relating to Travellers during the 1960s can be seen to have underlying control functions and regulatory elements, it was characterized by an apparent level of tolerance and accommodation of Traveller life-styles.[4] At face value the legislation contained provision that would encourage the integration of Travellers into life-styles more congruous to the sedentary norm.[5] Policy was founded on the implementation of activity that might improve the living standards of caravan-dwellers.

With the rise of what might be called an anti-collectivist Conservative ethos, from the early 1970s, following concerns about the extra-governmental influence of some left-wing local authorities and trade-unions,[6] the disciplinary mechanisms inherent within the policy affecting Travellers became more pronounced, in the first instance via the interpretation of legislation by many local authorities and subsequent action taken against Travellers at a local level.[7] By the mid–late 1980s, after State confrontation with the National Union of Mineworkers and other intermittent mass breaches of public order in response to racial harassment and the Poll Tax, the then existing policy focused on public order did not have the character or necessary mechanisms to serve State concerns. The perceived need for the strong regulation of the social, economic and political environment inevitably led to legislation directly concerned with profound and overt control, for example the 1986 Public Order Act. This encompassed the regulation of Travellers.[8] By the early–mid-1990s, following the Criminal Justice and Public Order Act 1994,[9] a move away from liberal ambitions and concerns had been effected, heralding a more control-orientated system wherein the State asserted its primacy over life-style and increased its level of intervention into political and social activity. This, in particular, was focused on alternative life-styles and protest activity outside of mainstream political organization.[10] From the mid-1990s, however, there was increasing concern with the results of this process on the travelling population[11] and this led to a specific response in the form of the Traveller Law Reform Bill 2002.

Pre-1960

The government report of 1967, 'Gypsies and other Travellers',[12] identifies various legislation before 1960 as making 'the Gypsy way of life' an unlawful pursuit. These included the Public Health Act 1936 and the 1947 Town and Country Planning Act. The Highways Act of 1959 was perhaps the most obviously anti-Gypsy post-war legislation. It stated: 'if a hawker or other itinerant or other itinerant trader or Gypsy pitches a booth, stall or stand on the highway, without lawful excuse, he shall be guilty of an offence'.[13]

The same act by a non-itinerant, someone who was not a hawker or Gypsy, was not considered to be an offence. Other legislation existed that acted as deterrents to an existence based on travelling and temporary work. The various post-war Social Security Acts had a collective impact and isolated Travellers from the system of social insurance through the relationship between the national insurance number, work and benefits. This effectively disqualified casual/ itinerant workers from State welfare, creating a pressure to abandon the 'no fixed abode' status.[14]

The legislation of the 1950s worked alongside the 1960 Caravan Sites and Control of Development Act and served to make its impact all the more profound. At the same time the 1960 Act promoted violations of previous legislation. However, in themselves, they undermined the viability of a travelling way of life. Although there are no figures to substantiate the claim that the legislation had an effect on the numbers of individuals and families giving up permanent caravan-dwelling, it could be realistically asserted that many did.

The 1960 Caravan Sites and Control of Development Act

The 1960 Caravan Sites and Control of Development Act was, at one level, the product of confused governmental thinking. At the time of the Act official government rhetoric did not portray people living in caravans as an ethnic group, although Gypsy and other organizations at the time of the Act were emphasizing such ideas. The whole force of the Act was to minimize caravan-dwelling under anything but the most strictly regulated conditions. Hence the inclusion of the, 'Control of Development' aspect.

The 1960 Caravan Sites and Control of Development Act can be seen as a piece of legislation mainly concerned with stricter control on caravanning in general, in that it was not specifically addressed to Gypsies; Gypsies were not mentioned in the Act.[15] The simplicity with which a caravan site could be opened, without adequate facilities and in locations that were unsuitable, was seen to have encouraged site owners to take advantage of the situation. The Act required site owners to obtain planning permission and a licence for their facilities. Under the Act local authorities could make discontinuance orders or require that sites be run down. Travellers who were settled or using sites in long-term transit were severely hit by this legislation. Private owners not wanting to provide expensive new provisions, failed to gain or in some cases even apply for planning permission. Many owners and renters[16] could simply not afford the improvements demanded under the Act, although many had improved facilities and paid rates.[17] Thus the 1960 Act was extremely detrimental to Travellers, who were constantly prosecuted and fined under the legislation. Following the legislation of 1960, Travellers could be seen to be subjected to discrimination in social practice and law, being without civil rights.[18] Official antagonism existed towards those categorized as Gypsies who were not familiar with legal and semi-legal practices and found it impossible to benefit from the theoretical existence of rights. It was claimed in 1971 by the Gypsy Council that more pitches were lost under the 1960 Act than were gained through the legislation of 1968.[19] Up to the mid-1990s sites were still being closed under the 1960 Act.

The evolution of the 1968 Caravan Sites Act

The legislation of 1960 had given local authorities the power (not the duty) to set up sites and a small minority did. Throughout the 1960s, governments became increasingly aware of the numbers of individuals and families that were not amenable to the conventional housing market of rent or mortgages. But they were caught between recognizing the need for sites and wanting to keep the numbers who might have resorted to such areas to a minimum. A Ministry of Housing circular of 1962 demonstrated this and recognized the need for sites; however, it significantly asked that such sites be limited to 'true Gypsies or Romanies'. It stated that such people would need 'help and encouragement to find a settled way of life . . . .'.[20] The circular pointed out that the movement of people from place to place, from one unauthorized site to another was ineffective, but at no point did the government do anything to prevent the continued harassment of Travellers, which was consistent throughout the 1960s. Local authorities allocated relatively huge resources to dozens of strategies to remove Travellers or to make life on unauthorized sites intolerable.[21]

In the same 1962 circular the then Conservative Government's Minister of Housing, Keith Joseph, called for a survey of 'Gypsies and itinerants' living on unauthorized sites. At approximately the same time he gave permission for a site to be opened at Cobham in Kent, against the wishes of local authorities. Thus, even before the 1968 Act, government policy amounted to the use of pressure (via the enforcement of the law) and the marginal treatment of those who could not be squeezed out of living in caravans (by the way of site provision). The use of harassment and site provision, alongside categorization and numeration created a policy of rationalization and isolation of those unable to reach or conform to the norms of the housing market. In many cases this was effected by the use of direct, physical force.

During the 1960s local authorities used the legislation with increasing vigour. Local politicians, driven on by the fear of the electoral retribution of their constituents, were prime movers in this process. Another ministerial circular of 1966, which incorporated the 1965 census of Gypsies, kept up the pressure for site provision. At that point it must have been clear that, despite all of the State's efforts, the problem was becoming more critical. The 1966 circular called for the improvement of Gypsy living conditions and advised that they should be 'encouraged to settle down and send their children to school'.[22]

The circular also recommended that as many Gypsies as possible be housed. The effect of policy becomes all the more obvious as 1968 drew closer. The lack of condemnation for the actions of local authorities towards Gypsies cannot be put down to ignorance. Every section of the media gave regular attention to the situation. Members of Parliament were constantly lobbied on the subject. The process in operation followed a line of controlling the travelling population, keeping numbers to a minimum.

It can be seen that the 1968 Caravan Sites Act came after a decade of conflict largely created by the 1960 Act. The 1968 Act was largely ignored by local authorities.[23] This can be understood as a reflection of the different attitude taken by the majority of local authorities to that of central government in terms of their approach towards Travellers, but this position neglects the underlying nature of the Act taken together with the actions of the local authorities. The potential result was a huge fall in the numbers resorting to caravans as permanent homes and a rise in the proportion of those that remained who would be confined to permanent sites. Local government action towards, and central government legislation regarding, Travellers worked in parallel in that both had the built-in effect of keeping down the numbers of people resorting to caravans as permanent mobile homes whilst isolating and controlling the minority of people who would not or could not resort to any other form of dwelling. The 1960 Act had obliged those caravan-dwellers who were able to find alternative housing options. In effect this caused a residuum to be identified: those who, for whatever reason, had no choice but the caravan. The effects of the 1968 Act, that took site provision out of the hands of the entrepreneurial/commercial sector[24] and placed it in the hands of local authorities, showed that at least some people could not be pressurized into conventional or sedentary housing.

Where do they all come from?

Certain theorists[25] have seen the constant movement involved in the enforcement of the 1960 Act and the lack of sites up to 1970 as increasing the visibility of Gypsies and as such giving rise to the notion of Gypsy invasions in the non-Gypsy consciousness, creating a false impression of a dramatic rise in the numbers of Travellers. This visibility has, by the same writers, been seen as the main cause of Gypsy persecution in the 1960s. Travellers who were evicted were likely to move to another site within much the same locality, maybe further down the road.[26] Terry, now a settled Traveller recalled:

> When you were moved on the cops just wanted you out of their jurisdiction. So they would make sure you were over the border and then they were satisfied. You might spend as little as a night in say Suffolk before you were moved back into Essex.

This meant that in many cases the same trailers were visible to the same community after eviction, as was the case before movement.

For all this, the new visibility of the Traveller population may have been due to more than the kind of trick of the light suggested in the literature. It is likely that the general public would know something of what was going on in the next county or borough. People would have been capable of making connections between events in other locations and their own area. Questioning local people about the movement of a contemporary group of Travellers around East London and north-west Essex reveals such awareness. Comments included:

> I saw that a large number of caravans were parked in the 'Homebase' car park in Canning Town. They suddenly disappeared – overnight. Within a

day a number of caravans turned up in the car park of 'Safeway's' in Stratford. They were the same people. I recognized the kids and the cars. I don't think it's right, but I suppose they didn't have anywhere else to go.

And

They just pulled into the supermarket car park. They were there when I came into work. I knew they were the same group that had been over at Canning Town, I remembered the vans, mostly new ones with the names of building and plumbing firms on the sides. A week or so after they were moved on I noticed that part of the same group of trailers were parked on a verge along the A406 in Barking. They came into the shop. I chatted up a couple of the girls and they had been born in houses. Their people had to move about for work.

These comments support the contention, given access to a range of public and private transport together with the commentary of local and national media, that it would be likely that most people would understand that the so-called increased visibility of Travellers during the 1960s was a direct consequence of them being moved on and that this was necessitated by of a lack of provision. With this in mind, together with an awareness of:

1   poor housing provision throughout the 1960s;
2   the constant use of compulsory purchase orders by local authorities from the late 1950s onwards (a response to the demand for land);
3   the widespread use of motorized transport amongst Travellers, that had become common in the 1950s;[27]
4   the movement of Traveller work locations from rural to urban areas;

the concept of a Gypsy invasion can be understood to reflect a general understanding that the Traveller population was growing. This apparent rise in numbers may have been going on for some time unnoticed. The 1960 Act could well have had the effect of making the rise perceptible to the public for the first time. To this extent it could be said to have facilitated visibility.

Although harassment has been a feature of the contemporary response to Travellers it would be too simplistic to argue that this has taken place as an end in itself, as has been claimed in the literature.[28] Persecution of Travellers has been part of a process aimed at obliging this group to conform to the norms of the housing market and social norms in general. The general response by local and national government was demonstrated by the activity of the Gypsy Council at the time. Just prior to the development of the 1968 Act, in 1966, the Gypsy Council demanded that local authorities should set up more sites under and up to the standards laid down in the 1960 Act.[29] Work areas on sites, transit pitches and the right to reserve pitches were also demanded. This illustrates that more space was needed to house the growing number of Travellers. The Gypsy Council began to actively support and organize resistance to evictions, which indicates that such activity was growing.

Resistance to evictions only became an offence in 1977, about ten years after the height of resistance. It is not clear why such legislation was not generated earlier. Perhaps the government and local authorities did not want arrests for this reason in the 1960s; resistance can mean more damage to homes and risk to families, in effect laws against resistance could mean less harassment. Here again policy appears to have been engineered to enable the forced removal of people out of caravan-dwelling and destruction of the home achieves this. That Traveller children could be placed in care and adults in hostels or other low-quality housing must also have been a continuing and harassing anxiety for travelling families.

Pressure for sites

Also in 1966 Members of Parliament for Kent were active in exerting political pressure on the government regarding site provision, goaded by Kent County Council.[30] As a result of a census of travelling people conducted in Kent in 1951, the county had planned to provide ten sites, each with 12 pitches. The Kent MPs concluded that the sites that had been set up were acting (by 1966) as a magnet to the displaced Travellers from other areas, creating a huge influx into the county, described in some areas as an invasion. It is possible the council also feared any future legislation which might have threatened to make adequate site provision the responsibility of local authorities. Therefore they would be obliged in the areas they represented to take on not only the Gypsies that were indigenous to Kent, but others who had sought refuge in the county.

Implicit political and legislative thinking in Kent at this time was based on the assumption that a set population of Gypsies existed. There is no evidence that there was any conception that the numbers of people taking to caravans in the area might be swollen by local people with no other alternative. In the same period the National Council for Civil Liberties[31] began to exert pressure on the Minister of Housing and Local Government to draw up a national plan for the local authority provision of sites. The publication of *The Ministry of Housing Census and Other Studies* in October 1967[32] backed up this demand, pointing out a need for a network of sites providing a variety of provision, both permanent and transitory. This study also argued that housing should be made available to Travellers[33] and that Gypsies should be encouraged to stop travelling and send their children to school. This demonstrates that by 1967 people, at a range of levels, were recognizing that there was both a section of the travelling population whose only option, in terms of a roof over their head, was the caravan and that many categorized as Gypsies had no wish to travel constantly or spend their lives in a trailer.

The 1967 study was the last critical policy action concerning Travellers before the 1968 Caravan Sites Act. In April 1967 Councillor Barry Smith of Hitchin Council called for 'concentration camps' for Travellers. Previously to this the leader of Birmingham Council had advised 'the extermination' of Gypsies.[34] As such, the time and political mood seemed ripe for draconian measures and this gives some clue to the actual nature and direction of the 1968 legislation.

Given the above it is possible to argue that the era of the site had been ushered in with the covert realization that the number of Travellers was growing, that this group included many who had come from a sedentary background and an appreciable number who did not desire a caravan-dwelling way of life. At the same time it was clear that constant harassment of this group was having little effect in terms of driving them into conventional forms of housing. Therefore a more rigorous strategy was needed to transform caravan-dwelling into a form of housing consistent with the norms of this sector.

The 1968 Act

The 1968 Caravan Sites Act set local authorities[35] the task of providing sites for Travellers. It is perhaps the most important piece of Traveller legislation in that it only applied to Gypsies. The Act came into force in 1970, a quarter of a century before its demise under the 1994 Criminal Justice and Public Order Act. Many authorities either failed to meet the conditions laid down in the legislation or achieved exemption from the Act. Where provision was available it often lacked adequate resources and was located in dangerous and remote areas. Although the Act never had the force to adequately provide for those who followed a travelling life-style, it was, alongside other legislation,[36] to have some negative effects beyond this.

The 1968 Caravan Sites Act required county councils and boroughs, 'so far as may be necessary', to provide accommodation for Gypsies residing in or resorting to their area. The Act was seen by some as marking a change in the approach of government legislation used to deal with the travelling population.[37] Before the 1968 Act legislation had been generally directed towards the dispersal of Travellers and added to levels of persecution suffered by people who found themselves following a nomadic way of life. In that the 1968 Act obliged local authorities to provide official sites for Gypsies it was seen by many as a humane piece of legislation. For all this the 1968 Act had built-in characteristics similar to previous legislation in that it would result in the dispersal of those on whom it was focused and act to extend control over these people.

After providing a stipulated number of pitches local authorities could make application for 'designation' or 'control' powers, under the Act.[38] Translated, this meant that all remaining Travellers in a designated district, residing on unauthorized sites, or the number above the amount of authorized pitches on authorized sites, could be removed from the area of the designated authority's responsibility. In some instances the 1968 Act enabled authorities to be designated where insufficient sites had been provided, 'where in all the circumstances it is not necessary or expedient to make any such provision'.[39]

The Act also made provision for local authorities to seek exemption from making any provision whatsoever. If exemption was granted to an authority it was able to use the same powers as provided under designation. To become an exempted area an authority needed to convince the Minister that the area concerned did not have 'sufficient' numbers of Travellers, 'residing in or resorting to' its area of jurisdiction in a period of five years before 1 May 1968. Exemption was also granted if no available land could be found for site development.

The main immediate effects of the 1968 Act were:

1   It further pressurized those living an itinerant, caravan-based way of life, to take to the conventional housing market.
2   Following on from the 1960 Act, it identified a 'hard core' of Travellers.
3   It provided the regulation by which this group could be dealt with – legal harassment/the site.
4   The site was thus encompassed by the norms of the housing market in a symbolic way (relative to the ad hoc nature of site provision under the 1960 Act). One paid a rent and was 'located'.

The nature of sites may have further cut-down the hard-core group of Travellers, conditions being such that housing alternatives, less attractive than the caravan off the site, might have been taken up. This being the case the 1968 Act maintained the potential to pressurize people to leave caravan-dwelling, but at the same time brought the site fully into the conventional housing market as a type of low-level local authority provision in the tradition identified by Orwell.[40]

Post-1968

The 1968 Act did little to help people living in caravans, although the awful conditions of the time caused many families to take eagerly to sites provided under the Act. In the main, the legislation was used by local authorities to obtain powers to control through the implementation of minimal provision of pitches. It might be construed that the ultimate aim of the government was to provide sites to attend to the need and that many local authorities did what they could to avoid their responsibilities or to carry them out in a manner that made resort to their jurisdiction unattractive to Travellers. Adams *et al.*[41] argue that the local authorities insisted on coercive powers in return for their acquiescence to site provision and they quote Eric Lubbock[42] who introduced the bill, which was to become the 1968 Act, informing the House of Commons that 'the stick' was the Minister's directive and 'the carrot' was the much stronger control powers to be made available once sites had been provided – to enable local authorities to move Gypsies from land they might be occupying without permission.[43] This had not been the first hint as to the underlying meaning of the legislation. An earlier paper[44] had set the scene for government strategy in calling for legislative action, with an emphasis on control with regard to Gypsies.[45]

Through the 1968 Act the government recruited local authorities and used them to force Travellers off the road on to sites or else into alternative ways of life. Smith[46] argues that the legislation itself could be taken as offensive in the race relations context, but the 1968 Act created the situation wherein isolated and controlled pockets of Gypsies existed on sites, the location of which was not decided by Travellers or their representatives. The legislation categorized people and defined their 'lawful place'. The designation powers made it a criminal offence, in a designated area, for a Gypsy to 'station a caravan for the purpose of residing for any period'[47] and enabled magistrates to make expedited eviction orders in respect of such Gypsies.[48] It assumed a racial or ethnic category existed (Gypsies), the members of which belonged on sites. In the same way Smith[49] also assumes a racial category.

This analysis can be taken to demonstrate that the 1968 Act was not merely used by local government to control Travellers. The controlling elements were built into the legislation for the use of local authorities. Local government made use of the legislation that was framed to be used to control Travellers. Central government, by way of the legislation, obliged local authorities to operate in a coercive manner towards Gypsies.[50] The essential element of control is fundamental to understanding the nature of the legislation affecting Travellers. Hawes and Perez[51] argue that local prejudice has corrupted the relatively humane nature of the legislation, but it is the Act's defining quality that discriminates against Travellers and reveals the social and political context of legislation.

The 1968 Act was never applied with any rigour,[52] so relatively few authorities made appropriate facilities available to Travellers. Those authorities that did respond were often those that had traditionally been host to and provided facilities for Traveller groups. However, authorities infrequently went beyond the Act's minimum level of accommodation of 15 spaces. No time limit was set for the provision of sites despite the known reluctance of local authorities to provide facilities. As such, by the summer of 1972, only 50 sites had been made available. Over one quarter of these had been established before the 1968 Act had made such provision mandatory.[53] By January 1977 there were 1,759 permanent pitches, each pitch being a space for one caravan. There were 495 temporary pitches.[54] At this time 15 London boroughs and ten of what had been county boroughs had obtained designation. None of the areas had provided more than the minimum provision of 15 pitches. Two London boroughs had obtained exemption.[55] Designation had also been granted to 26 county boroughs, which after exemption meant that they were not obliged to provide sites. Thus by the end of the 1970s, site provision was practically at an end in many parts of the country and in nearly all the most densely Gypsy-populated areas.

Population figures used in the preparation of the 1968 Act, that were widely acknowledged as inaccurate[56], were also used to decide on areas of designation and exemption. These statistics came from a census carried out on 22 March 1965 by the police and public health inspectors. They were analysed in *Gypsies and Other Travellers*.[57] The census returns grossly underestimated the numbers of Travellers.[58] This was partly due to the lack of co-operation on the part of Travellers and partly because of the actions of local authorities towards Travellers in the weeks leading up to the census, that involved hounding as many as possible out of their areas of responsibility in an attempt to minimize future obligations under any legislation. The census showed the travelling population to be around 15,000 individuals from 3,356 families. Even on the strength of these figures, provision of sites was over 30 per cent short of need by the late 1970s. However, just ten council sites existed at that time, accommodating a mere 4 per cent of the known population of Travellers and there were only 29 licensed private Gypsy sites recorded. This being the case, it is likely that the unauthorized figure accounted for almost 80 per cent of the total count.[59]

Even without the latter consideration, by the 1980s there may have been provision for less than 30 per cent of the travelling population in terms of sites. The constant lack of sites has meant that for the best part of 40 years many Travellers have been subjected to a consistent process of eviction from unofficial sites that has left little or no alternative other than the resort to other unauthorized sites.

By 1981, although 42 local authorities achieved designation, the numbers of people resorting to unofficial sites had been fairly constant since the mid–late 1960s.[60] However, the biannual counts of the Caravans in England and Wales indicate that around one in three Travellers in England and Wales were obliged to resort to sites that contravened the law. The January 1994 count for example illustrates that of the 13,794 Traveller trailers in England and Wales, 4,118 could not resort to a legal encampment.[61] These figures do not include many so-called New Age Travellers as the count focused on caravans, not mobile homes (buses, lorries etc.). The final count before the abolition of Part II of the Caravan Sites Act 1968 recorded that of the 13,329 caravans in England and Wales 6,063 were on a total of 324 council sites and 3,204 on private licensed sites. Around 300 public Gypsy sites were provided under the 1968 Act; in the final analysis 4,062 caravans, around 30 per cent, were on unauthorized sites. Despite the seeming 400 per cent rise in caravan-dwelling from 1968, the Act had succeeded in reducing the numbers of caravans resorting to unauthorized sites from 80 to 30 per cent.

The legislation was also used to restrict the number of unnecessary evictions.[62] However, although over 180 local authorities were granted designation powers, most of them failed to provide sufficient sites. The overall poor provision, together with the criminalization of a life-style, was seen as a form of inhumane treatment by the European Commission of Human Rights, upholding a complaint made by a Gypsy living in a designated area.[63]

The four main long-term effects of the 1968 legislation were:

1   The creation of competition for places on sites (sites became desirable for those who had to live in caravans).
2   Those who gained places on sites stayed there (site living became habituated).
3   Individuals who took up an itinerant, trailer-based way of life were assured of nothing more than the threat of legal harassment – mobile caravan-dwelling was made unattractive.
4   Individuals who could get out of the cycle of harassment did.

Poor implementation of the 1968 Act made the option of trailer living unattractive. Sites were rarely anything more than poorly serviced, often vandalized, and the focus of local prejudice, discrimination and police surveillance. In effect many sites could be likened to small Bantustans, sometimes surrounded with deep ditches, corrugated iron and/or barbed wire.[64] Occasionally, on first sight they were reminiscent of the rough concentration camps of latter-day Eastern Europe. In many instances these conditions have changed little over the last 30 or so years.

The 1968 Act in context

The 1968 Act cannot be viewed adequately in isolation from legislation affecting Travellers that preceded and succeeded it. The closure of sites via the 1960 Act was just the tip of the proverbial iceberg. When viewed alongside previous legislation of the post-Second World War period, the 1960 Act can be seen to be the start of a cycle of coercion.[65] Unlike the 1959 Highways Act, the 1960 Act did not legislate against activity or behaviour. It did not focus on identity but it forced those identified as Gypsies onto the roadside to be immediately threatened by the 1959 Act because of their activity. The 1960 and 1959 Acts taken together forced people to move onto land where prosecution was less effective and harder to carry out: commons, wasteland, areas that had been polluted by chemical or industrial activity, or land where the government were the owners. Thus, lack of sites provided under the 1968 Act meant that this situation continued for decades to come. However, the 1968 Act was more specifically focused on Gypsies than other post-Second World War legislation. It set the scene for what followed, and as such has become something of a milestone in the nearly 50 years of policy (and non-policy) that has negatively impacted on Travellers. The 1968 Act reveals much about the nature of previous and subsequent legislation affecting Gypsies and the underlying character of such legislation.

Other legislation

After 1968 other legislation complements the nature of the Caravan Acts of the 1960s and begins to demonstrate a growing web of policy control surrounding Travellers and their way of life.[66] The State has a range of powers too numerous to detail in this work. There are a huge number of by-laws and statutes.[67] Together, this array of legislation has a huge impact on potential and actual Traveller activity. I have included the following examples to demonstrate two effects: identification/categorization through legislation and, at the same time, the extension of control over those identified and categorized.

Criminal Justice and Public Order Act 1994

The 1994 Criminal Justice and Public Order Act did not affect Part 1 of the 1968 Act.[68] It is Part 2 of the 1968 Act, which put a duty on local authorities to

provide sites and deals with designation that was affected by this piece of legislation. The 1994 Act repealed designation provisions and in their stead put in
place more expansive and coercive powers.[69] Therefore, the Criminal Justice
and Public Order Act 1994 can be understood as being consistent with previous
governmental/legislative activity that has made a travelling way of life less and
less viable following the Second World War. However, it continued the effort to
force people into the conventional housing market in a much more overt manner
than its legislative ancestors and as such made anyone considering taking up a
transient existence think twice. It left those who, by choice or circumstance, lived
a travelling way of life, the rather limited option of acquiring land and seeking
planning permission for residential purposes. In other words, it obliged conformity to the prevailing housing market norms of the 1990s that encompassed
the diminishment of the public rented sector[70] and the promotion of private
ownership. This made the 1994 Act relatively honest when set alongside other
post-war legislation affecting Travellers – it openly required compliance with
conventional housing options, premised on State ambitions relating to private
ownership of property.

The expansive nature of the 1994 Act is exemplified in sections 72 to 76, that
provide new and amended powers in respect of displaced residential or intending occupiers.[71] This effects a revision of squatting rights, and the force and
conditions of the Act could be applied to those resorting to squatting, which
meant speeding up their potential removal from property. This enlarged the
potential number of people who might have been obliged to resort to caravan-
dwelling. Earle *et al.*[72], in noting how the effects of the Act reached beyond
Travellers, also noted that those at the receiving end of the pressurized housing
market suffered parallel experiences to those of Travellers:

> In 1991, more than 1,000,000 private houses were deemed unfit for human
> habitation; an increasing number of homes are repossessed as the recession
> continues; squatting has been made almost impossible; young people cannot
> claim housing benefit. So where are these Travellers supposed to go? With
> laws impounding their homes; authorities dividing their families, and im-
> prisonment for resisting arrest; the future seems bleak . . .
>
>   They don't just inhibit us, they inhibit everybody. The general public has
> lost the use of common land, not just the Travellers. And if they hadn't
> restricted us from common land, there wouldn't be a problem.[73]

Earle *et al.* point out this relationship of Travellers to those on the fringes of
the housing market, whilst noting that overall the Act was not an instrument
of ethnic oppression or persecution: 'Travellers cannot be classified as an ethnic
minority, having no common cultural or religious bond . . .'[74]

Legislation, of any ilk, constitutes a means of social control. However the post-
war legislation affecting Travellers is collectively an extension of State control
in the interests of capital that addresses certain contradictions arising out of
the housing market and those that the market produces who are obliged to seek

alternatives outside that market. That the 1994 Act legislated against minorities was perhaps a symptom rather than something that was central to the processes of law embedded in the legislation.

The Act also had a system of time control. Section 70 placed a new section (14A) in the Public Order Act 1986. This applied when the Chief Constable reasonably believed that a seriously disrupting and/or damaging unlawful assembly was intended. This being the case, s/he could apply to the local district authority for an order that would prohibit the conducting of a trespassory assembly for a period of not more than four days. A number of offences were brought into being by this section for persons contravening such orders. Section 71 even had a prophetic nature, giving police the power to stop persons 'thought' to be making their way to seriously disrupting and/or damaging unlawful assembly. Such people would be deemed to be in contravention of an order under section 70.

Given the above, it is clear that the 1994 Act was not just motivated by the actions of Travellers, Gypsies or even the much publicized New Age or Hippie convoys. The moral panic surrounding the so-called Hippie bands and the accompanying litter problem camouflaged other larger governmental concerns. However, it seems unlikely, given the disadvantages suffered by many of the travelling community in terms of access to educational provision and economic circumstances, alongside the prevailing housing, economic and employment environment, that entry to the housing market or the acquisition of land and the obtaining of planning permission, presented viable alternatives to informal caravan-dwelling. Considering the level of repossessions and homelessness amongst the sedentary population during the 1990s, most of whom started out with at least a rudimentary financial base and a range of access to social, educational and housing services, the picture of the typical Traveller as a likely candidate for a mortgage or as a land-owning bureaucrat seems fanciful. It seemed more likely that the 1994 Act would at best lead to the construction of a network of privately owned, commercially oriented, Traveller sites, based on minimal provision, act-ing as the market basement of the reviving private rent sector reminiscent of that described by Orwell.[75]

Post-1994

Looking at the 1994 Criminal Justice and Public Order Act is useful in that it can be seen as idiomatic of the social response to Travellers throughout recent history. It is congruent with the effects of the Acts of the 1960s. It reveals something of the nature of this population group when viewed in the context of post-war legislation affecting Gypsies and Travellers that tends to be framed at times of acute housing shortage. It could be argued that the visibility of Travel-lers, to the extent that provokes legislative action, seems to correlate with a heightened awareness and growth in numbers of homeless people.[76]

The 1994 Act had a consistency with the 1960 and 1968 Acts and other legislation in that it provided mechanisms for the exertion of discipline, through law, promoting conformity to housing norms and punishing those who would not or could not accomplish the same by way of poor quality provision and categorization as 'the other'.[77]

Despite the ravages of legislation since the early 1960s, when one begins to analyse site provision, alongside the pressure put on those with nomadic propensities to give up their wandering ways, it would be fair to expect that fewer people would need to resort to unauthorized sites. This would certainly be true if one was talking about a closed population that was not being added to by incoming personnel. However there were still 3,469 caravans on unauthorized encampments in England in July 1996, which was only 93 less than in 1968. The total count was almost 13,000 caravans. This represents a growth of around 4,500 families (caravans), more than 50 per cent, in a 13-year period. Some of the 10,000 or so caravans on authorized sites, one might assume, would have formally been included in the counts for unauthorized sites and many formally unauthorized sites did become official.[78] As such, it seems that the numbers of people resorting to unauthorized sites may not have decreased,[79] but this may have appeared to be the case as unauthorized sites became stepping stones to placement on an authorized site.

On closer inspection of the numbers of caravans, considering the problems with the accuracy of the caravan counts[80] and the non-inclusion of some groups of so-called New Age Travellers and non-Gypsy caravan-dwellers in the caravan counts[81] a possible pattern of caravan-dwelling emerges:

1   A seeming overall decline in the number of caravans parking illegally, established via counts of caravans on unauthorized sites, masks the likelihood that this number has remained constant, or has even grown.
2   Continued harassment, through law, may have obliged some people to give up a nomadic existence, either by finding places on official sites or moving out of caravan-dwelling altogether; however, their place has been taken by others, for example homeless families.
3   The current caravan-dwelling population, living on unauthorized sites, although it may include some long-term members, in the main represents a steady stream of people resorting to an illegal nomadic way of life over the last couple of decades.
4   Within this situation individuals and families move from illegal to legal status and perhaps back again, being literally in transit between travelling and non-travelling ways of life.
5   This suggests that a significant number of caravans included in any given count of unauthorized sites are part of a population flow, rather than a static group.
6   This means that the total number of individual households resorting to illegal caravan-dwelling, on count evidence alone since 1979, is potentially something in the region of 75,000.

Population growth of what might be recognized as traditional, long-term Travellers, via birth-rate might create a higher demand in the long run[82] if the majority of families could sustain site living, but this alone cannot explain the potential numbers of people resorting to unlawful sites over recent years. Unless significant recruitment from the sedentary population has taken place it means that the growth in population via birth-rate was approximately 50 per cent over the ten years between 1986 and 1996. At the same time it would also indicate that the Traveller population has remained relatively unscathed by the effects of legislation.[83] This general proposal does not seem feasible, particularly given that the infant mortality rate amongst the Traveller population is some 50 per cent higher than the national average and that parental mortality is around 80 per cent above the national norm.[84] As such, together with the effects over time of consistent harassment of traditionally itinerant groups, it would seem that the travelling/caravan-dwelling population must have absorbed considerable numbers of formally settled people into its ranks. This being the case, it is clear that there is a resilient development of the caravan-dwelling population, a large proportion of which, at any given time, resist or are unable to conform to housing market conventions. This development has not been overcome by the whole battery of post-war legislation, which has only served to demonstrate that this group is perhaps necessarily symptomatic of the nature and functioning of our society.

The Traveller Law Reform Bill 2002

In this section I am going to analyse the Traveller Law Reform Bill 2002[85] as it appears to be a significant change in direction in terms of policy impacting on the Traveller population of England and Wales, but, as I will argue, its logic and potential effects have much in common with previous legislation.

Introduction

The Traveller Law Reform Bill[86] is the product of over four years of discussion and collaboration by Gypsies and Travellers and their representative organizations and service providers in the United Kingdom (although individuals and organizations throughout Britain contributed to the process, the Traveller Law Reform Bill applies only to England and Wales due to the different constitutional arrangements in Northern Ireland and Scotland). This being the case the Bill can be understood to reflect the ambitions and purposes of these organizations,[87] the social pressures on Travellers and the political manipulation this group are subject and react to.

The process that concluded with the Bill formally commenced in 1997 when a proposal was made to create a common 'platform' to take forward the reform debate. The concept behind this collaborative grouping was explained at a meeting in August of that year:

> [A] 'platform' is not owned by any organization: it is not an organization in itself: it is, rather, the space between organizations. A platform does not restrict participating organizations, or remove their differences. A platform

exists whilst there is a common purpose in a particular area. It has limited objectives and ceases to exist when those objectives have been realized. In the present instance, the common platform is one for the promotion of law and policy reform: based upon equality, valuing diversity . . .

However, perhaps the most telling phrase in terms of the platform's purposes was the wish to promote 'integration not assimilation and build upon Traveller representation'.[88]

The reform process produced a law reform document[89] and was accompanied by a number of significant governmental policy changes, including such matters as:

- planning development advice;[90]
- DETR advice concerning toleration of unauthorized encampments;[91]
- NHS guidance specifically drawing attention to the health care of Travellers;[92]
- amendments to the housing repair grants regime to include caravans on publicly owned Gypsy sites;[93]
- ministerial endorsement concerning the 'best value' implications for local authority site provision and toleration policies;[94] and
- voting rights for Travellers.[95]

As such, this document might be seen as prompting first legislative acceptance that sites are a social fact of life for a growing group of people; that there exists a population who, for traditional, social and/or economic reasons cannot or will not access conventional housing options. This spirit was evident in the 1968 Act but tinged with efforts to minimize the numbers resorting to a caravan-dwelling option.

The impetus of reform was aided by a report by the Organization on Security and Co-operation in Europe (OSCE) produced in 2000, which (amongst other things) reviewed Britain's legal treatment of Gypsies and Travellers.[96] This underlined the need for lawful places wherein Travellers might be ensconced, the legitimate home of the Traveller being taken to be a caravan on a designated site. To this extent it echoes part of the motive for the Caravan Sites Act 1968. It also identified that the then current practice relating to the treatment of Travellers was unlikely to be socially or financially effective.[97]

The purpose and structure of the Bill

Many of the clauses in the Bill make important amendments to remove seemingly discriminatory statutory provisions. The Bill's most significant impact however, is the extent to which it apparently seeks to remove from the political stage, decisions concerning site provision and site toleration. In effect it creates self-enforcing provisions; measures which do not depend upon political will for their subsequent enforcement, but the force of law. It proposes a kind of mechanical liturgics to given demand. This again demonstrates official acceptance of the need for sites given the contemporary state of housing supply/access.

A major weakness of the Caravan Sites Act 1968 lay in the fact that it relied upon local politicians to approve sites in their areas and Ministers to use their powers of enforcement (under section 9) against recalcitrant authorities. Given the extent of prejudice against Gypsies and Travellers, the failure of this aspect of the 1968 Act is hardly surprising. Local authorities initially failed to approve sites, surrendering to local opposition, and Ministers failed to use their available powers. The 1968 Act only began to be effective when the High Court found against individual authorities, and in particular quashed eviction proceedings taken by authorities that had failed to provide sites.[98] The Bill proposes that the Gypsy and Traveller Accommodation Commission (GTAC) will be responsible for collecting data on the accommodation requirements of Gypsies and Travellers and for issuing guidance to authorities as to what provision they should make. If an authority fails to facilitate the provision of sufficient sites, or does not co-operate with other authorities in this endeavour or fails to provide adequate planning policies in its Development Plan, then these failures will become material considerations for courts and planning inspectors. This means that authorities that fail to take appropriate action may be penalized, effectively a reversal of the present situation. However, the Bill provides, relative to past legislation, a range of attractive financial incentives for local authorities to co-operate with the GTAC.

It is envisaged that the GTAC will have specifically targeted responsibilities directed at ensuring that there is adequate provision of suitable accommodation for Gypsies and Travellers in each locality. In the planning arena it will fulfil a function analogous to that of the House Builders Federation in relation to land allocations for housing. It will, in addition to vetting Development Plans, have other important and associated functions, including:

- The power to issue formal statements as to what constitutes adequate provision for the purposes of clause 1 of the Bill.
- The duty to oversee and collate biannual counts of Gypsy caravans.
- The power to issue general and specific guidance concerning the adequacy of local authority accommodation programmes.

As such, the GTAC can be understood as a tool for observing, recording and thus controlling Traveller housing issues, but as housing is such a central aspect of Traveller culture (and most other cultures) the level of intervention will be potentially huge, particularly in forming the future of the lawful locating of the Gypsy and Traveller population.

This represents the continuation of a control focus in terms of the official response to Gypsies in England. However, instead of identifying a rump population of belligerent caravan-dwellers to be effectively penalized, it makes provision for the widespread use of the site as a form of lawful accommodation to which caravan-dwellers might be assigned. At the same time, through the evocation of Traveller involvement in consultation about and implementation of proposals

and the repression of some of the more overt forms of harassment and undermining of Traveller civil liberties, the Bill placates European and other concerns
relating to the persecution of Gypsies.[99]

It should be noted that the Bill was drafted in a compartmentalized manner
(it was divided into separate 'Parts'). This was done to enable a piecemeal implementation should the Bill not be supported in its entirety at the end of the
legislative process.[100] This gives a great deal of flexibility and allows for strategic
manoeuvring if required.

The Bill was presented to the House of Commons as a Private Members
Bill (10 Minute Rule) on the 10 July 2002 by the Conservative MP Mr David
Atkinson. It was unopposed at its first reading and received cross-party support
from 11 other MPs. The Bill was scheduled to receive a second reading on
Friday 19 July. However, as there were a large number of other Bills due to
receive second readings on the same day it did not have a second reading. The
result of this was that the Bill could not received a second reading in that
Parliamentary year, and therefore, the whole process of introducing the Bill had
to begin again at the start of the new Parliamentary year in October 2002. Up to
the time of writing, the bill has not progressed. However, a pressure group, the
'Traveller Law Reform Coalition' that has the support of the 'All Party Parliamentary Group for Traveller Law Reform' continues to campaign for the progress
of the Bill.

It is the case that the Bill was generated from the basis of a consultationary
process[101] and was based upon a Bill produced by the Traveller Law Reform
Unit at Cardiff University Law School, an ally of the Gypsy cause in Britain,
with a small number of additional amendments/schedules. However, David
Atkinson's Bill has much about it that reminds the analyst of Keith Joseph's
circular of 1962.[102] Atkinson's Conservative forefather and, in 1962, the Minister
of Housing, openly aimed, by 'rationalization and isolation' of 'Gypsies and
itinerants', to categorize these people and 'define their lawful place'.

This being the case, and given the welcome and co-operation the Bill has
received from those who have hooked on to and largely defined the Traveller
cause (mostly non-Gypsies – interested academics and well-meaning professionals) it might be argued that the State has recruited this disparate group to
support the means of control of Travellers by use of the bait of adequate site
provision (the long awaited nirvana for the 'Traveller patrons'). As such, the Bill
could be understood as a sublime piece of State chicanery that offers a path to
fulfil an agenda that has stood for more than half a century. Its potential outcomes are the contemporary equivalent to those realized on *The Road to Wigan
Pier*.[103] Whilst the progress of the Bill has somewhat blunted its potential impact,
its original content is important in terms of judging the future direction of legislation. This is of particular import given the expansion of the European Union
and the possible effects of an influx of Eastern European migrant labour on
housing provision in Britain. The Traveller Law Reform Bill provides intriguing
strategic options in terms of a new base level of housing provision and social
control.

The social generation of legislation: beware of cultural care

This section shows that the Traveller Law Reform Bill is a logical progression of former legislation. It has, like former strategic proposals focusing on Travellers, come into being at a time when governmental attention is being paid to the state of the housing market. However, under the guise of cultural care, the provision of Traveller sites and the apparent facilitation of a nomadic life-style,[104] it proposes a more covert and administrative form of control than its precursor, which was based on overt force and clearly ineffective. The Bill can be understood as an effort to address issues and concerns relating to the Civil Rights of Travellers but also as a means to bring the former alternative of caravan-dwelling into the mainstream of housing provision; it seeks to reform what has been a deviant housing resource, echoing part of the ambition of the Caravan Sites Act 1968. However, it also has the potential to expand the Gypsy site as a form of general accommodation. This expansion is likely to result in an increase in the numbers of people subject to the ethnic categorization that may accompany their resort or assignment, as caravan-dwellers, to the only lawful place of residence open to them – the site. This group, or members of it, can, potentially, be socially allocated and legally designated to the Gypsy population.

Throughout this chapter the aim has been to review the crucial post-war legislation affecting Gypsies and Travellers in order to illustrate that the law has had an underlying focus on the control and categorization of this population. It has also been argued that the momentum of this legislation has been to make a travelling way of life unattractive or untenable. In this respect legislation has worked to limit alternative informal options to conventional forms of housing and as such is set within the context of the economics or the housing market (rent/mortgage). It is this that is the fulcrum of the legislation affecting Travellers and not a kind of first cause, pariah status of Gypsies. This legislation has affected those unable or unwilling to take up house-dwelling and who have resorted to informal forms of caravan-dwelling, be they Gypsies or non-Gypsies. Such people have been, by their behaviour or life-style, described as an ethnic type – Travellers. Travellers have become a focal point of legislative action as they represent a counter cultural alternative to the capitalist enterprise of housing, but the legislative deterrent has been set against contravention of market norms and not a particular ethnicity. Travellers have been defined, within the legislation, as a category to be 'reformed' by reconnection to the market. In the 1960s this was achieved via harassment and the official site. Post-1994 a more direct, *laissez-faire* legal conduit of control bypassed the site. It seems, at the start of the twenty-first century that the ambitions of the 1960s have been reincarnated. However, the effort to minimize the potential 'client population' seems to have been replaced with the embracing (in policy) of caravan-dwelling as a viable addition to housing provision and the market. Given the lack of provision of cheap housing in the areas most traditionally associated with caravan-dwelling (the south east) the widespread development of site living seems to make at least some kind of economic sense.

The Traveller Law Reform Bill 2002 embodies the potential for the provision of a mass of prefabricated, and in terms of living space and amenities, relatively low quality housing. No matter how well maintained, the modern caravan was designed as a leisure vehicle, for transient and temporary inhabitancy. What might be understood as a traditional Traveller would change caravans regularly and of course use them to travel. Many would resort for varying periods to more conventional housing according to disposition, necessity, taste and/or season. The permanent/semi-permanent 'sited' caravan has little to do with a Gypsy or Nomadic propensity. However, contradictorily, the Traveller Law Reform Bill 2002 carries a categorizing power that, given the dominant response to place Travellers as caravan-dwellers (or the other way round) in an ethnic slot, can potentially be creative of a Gypsy ethnicity.

Conclusion

In this chapter I have placed the post-war legislation affecting Gypsies in its political context. I have shown how the 1960 Caravan Sites Act was consistent with other post-war policy that impinged on the lives of Travellers in that it acted as a deterrent to a travelling way of life and legitimated harassment of Travellers. I went on to illustrate how the legislation of 1968 continued to make an itinerant life-style problematic, in effect serving to pressurize travelling people into resorting to conventional forms of housing. The fact that many local authorities sought to keep provision of sites to a minimum meant that supply of sites fell short of need. This enabled local authorities, which had provided a minimal provision or achieved designation, to use powers of legal harassment against Travellers illegally parked in their area of jurisdiction. I have argued that this process would have produced a hard core of Travellers, those unable or unprepared to comply with housing-market norms. I went on to suggest that what was seen as the increased visibility of Travellers in the 1970s was due in part to the effects of the 1968 Act and also the continued problem of access to housing in England.

In this chapter I have also suggested that the 1994 Criminal Justice and Public Order Act continued to reinforce the logic of previous post-war legislation affecting Gypsies, having in practice made a nomadic way of life illegal. I have argued that although the 1994 Act was framed with a much wider constituency than Travellers in mind, it represented for Travellers an extension of State control and its ability to categorize them as a homogeneous ethnic group whilst further promoting conformity to housing-market norms. I went on to analyse how the Traveller Law Reform Bill 2002 continues this legislative path by facilitating movement towards the integration of caravan-dwelling into the conventional housing-market. I have argued that as such the Traveller Law Reform Bill 2002 represents not only acceptance of the necessary presence of the site as an alternative form of accommodation, but facilitates its growth as a means of categorization and control.

5 Power, knowledge, truth and the prison

Introduction

In the literature concerned with Gypsies and Travellers human agency is (preponderantly) described in terms of the psychology of discrimination and prejudice. These phenomena are seen as key factors in the framing of legislation. For example: 'We set modern responses against an historic backdrop, in the hope of illustrating somewhat deeper arguments about the process by which prejudice, fear and antagonism to minority peoples becomes fixed in the formal structures of society.'[1]

This exemplifies the neglect of a broad sociological perspective in the literature. In this chapter I want to address this by providing an analysis of social mechanisms that drive the social responses framed in legislation impacting on travelling people. The following will suggest that the social formation will move to eliminate structures outside of its logic, the logic of the current social formation being that of capitalism. It will control, via law that is framed in the interests of capital, structures or movements that contravene market norms. Travellers are thus the focus of legislation and harassment because they reject or fail to access the norms of the housing market. This being the case, it is not psychological dispositions that give rise to social responses to Travellers; legislation is not just a matter of will or the general attitude of a particular group.

In this chapter I will expand on this perspective via the thought of Michel Foucault. It will argue that the legislation affecting Travellers, being essentially a part of the general social process of control and discipline, elaborates, exemplifies, complements and confirms the nature of the social form in which it is wrought. I will suggest that the character of the legislation and governmental activity demonstrates the operation of Foucault's notion of the 'carceral'.[2] I will argue that ethnicity, its narrative and sentimental attachments, is used as a means of social control and regulation of specific groups including Travellers.

Mother Courage

For Marx:

> In the social production of their life, men enter into definite relations that are indispensable and independent of their will, relations of production which correspond to a definite stage of development of their material productive forces. The sum total of these relations of production constitutes the economic structure of society, the real foundation, on which rises a legal and political superstructure and to which correspond definite forms of social consciousness. The mode of production of material life conditions the social, political, and intellectual life process in general. It is not the consciousness of men that determines their being, but, on the contrary, their social being that determines their consciousness.[3]

According to Marx, social being determines consciousness. Marx was drawing on the Hegelian dialectic, an important factor in shaping thinking about the modern notion of the individual. The notion is that as soon as one begins to define oneself as an individual, isolated and separate, one needs to exclude something else.[4] In the end this process of exclusion becomes so crucial, because identity is dependent on it, that the individual becomes understood as the product of the 'other'. We are moved by great social events, wars, revolutions and social conditions that affect masses of people in profound and lasting ways, these have an impact on housing, employment and economic institutions. The extent of this is well elaborated by Bertolt Breht's 'Mother Courage', the great figure in his play *Mother Courage and Her Children*.[5] She thinks she is choosing, she thinks she is making her life, but in fact what is happening is that she is being absolutely destroyed and pulled apart by great historical contradictions. Maybe this is the human consequence of Marx's insight.

According to Marx, it is the 'economic structure of society' which is 'the real foundation on which rises the legal and political superstructure', for example the 1994 Criminal Justice and Public Order Act and the Traveller Law Reform Bill 2002. However, the idea that the character of society is fundamental to what happens in society is of course not just a Marxist concept, indeed it is a basic tenet of most sociology, be it Marxist, Weberian or Durkheimian. The notion that society, and its legal and political superstructure[6], are built by or on psychological, attitudinal forces of individuals has a distinctly right-wing ancestry:

> The State as conceived and realized by fascism is a spiritual and ethical entity for securing the political, juridical and economic organization of the nation, an organization which in its origin and growth is a manifestation of the Spirit. . . . Far from crushing the individual, the Fascist State multiplies his energies, just as in a regiment a soldier is not diminished but multiplied by the number of his fellow soldiers.[7]

If one sees legislation affecting Travellers as being possibly derived from the spiritual or ethical premises, as put forward by the likes of Hawes and Perez,[8] then this means seeing society ordered in much the same way as Mussolini describes. But if one understands society as:

not resting upon law. This is a juridical function. Just the reverse is the truth. Law rests on society, it must be the expression of the general interest that springs from the material production of a given society against the arbitrariness of any single individual.

Here, the code of laws which I hold in my hands has not created modern civil society. It happened just the other way. The civil society . . . found its legal expression in the code. As soon as it ceases to correspond with the social conditions, the code will be as effete as waste paper.[9]

Taking this into consideration it can be understood that the law affecting Travellers is the legal expression of society and corresponds to social conditions – that are capitalist in character: 'men do not make their own history . . . not just as they please; they do not make it under circumstances chosen by themselves, but under circumstances directly found, given, and transmitted from the past'.[10]

Foucault and genealogy

According to McNay[11] Michel Foucault sees traditional historiography as representing the passage of time as a logical stream of causally linked events, each event having a discrete significance helping to form part of the greater pattern of meaning that is history. This is what Foucault describes as a 'formless unity of a great becoming'.[12] For Foucault, these events are slotted into an all-embracing explanation of things, producing an artificial unity. What might be called the conventional view of Traveller history and the identity arising out of this exemplifies this process. According to Foucault, this teleological interpretation deprives events of their uniqueness and immediacy. For him:

> The world we know is not this ultimately simple configuration where events are reduced to accentuate their essential traits, their final meaning, or their initial and final value. On the contrary, it is a profusion of entangled events.[13]

This being the case, for Foucault, Traveller identity and history would need to be understood as the product of a vast complexity of events, situations and incidents and not the type of linear formation suggested by, for example, Fraser.[14] Foucault perceives history in its traditional translation as a lie, highlighting seminal moments and at the same time placing the self-reflexive subject in the middle of the flow of history. What is generated is a kind of mythology wherein the human character becomes central to the movement of history, which becomes an interpretation and playing out of human nature within the changing context of society; many Travellers have taken to housing and merged into the sedentary life, while non-Gypsies take up ambulant life-styles; individuals exchange communities and cultures. This occurs as a result of the impact of economic and/or social considerations on individuals, families or groups. It is the collective effect of this intermingling and interchange that for Foucault drives the historical process. At any time or place the particular circumstances give rise to the emergence of a travelling population. Thus, there would be, for Foucault, any number of Traveller aetiologies, histories and identities. However, the recording of history is carried out in what McNay[15] calls 'a logic of identity'. For him, 'history is read narcissistically to reconfirm one's present sense of identity and any potentially disruptive awareness of alterity is suppressed'.[16]

The analysis of the travelling population offered by Hawes and Perez is typical of the type of response that McNay (and Foucault) critiques. It is what Foucault would see as traditional historiography. Hawes and Perez place human characteristics at the centre of historical process.[17] They cite psychological intention, discrimination and sentiment for example, as the forces that define Gypsies, their activity and what happens to them. It takes the situation of Travellers at face value and builds an analysis on the basis of prescribed identities, Gypsy/non-Gypsy. Accusation, by theorists, that provoke resentment on the part of Travellers and guilt in non-Travellers (psychological states) bind together in a blinkered perspective that clinically isolates the travelling population as a discrete category (ethnicity or race). At the same time this group are cut off from wider social issues, roots, interaction and causation.

In an attempt to address this problem of cultural discrimination I employ Foucault's use of the Nietzschean idea of 'effective' history or 'genealogy' linked to a notion of 'analysis of descent' or 'emergence'. This enables a view of history wherein events emerge by chance within the process of history in a discontinuous and divergent manner. Genealogy, 'the philosophy of the event',[18] is the analytical method that follows the disruptive and erratic dispersion of processes, which overlap and accrue, that give rise to the event. A genealogical analysis of the Traveller population would understand this phenomenon as arising out of a complexity of social interactions and conditions, which themselves are subject to chaotic ebb and flow. This population would also need to be comprehended as a complicated mixture of groups, prone to change and flux, like everything else, in a constant state of emergence or 'becoming'.[19] Thus we can never say definitively what the travelling population is, or who they are. However, at any given time their presence has a meaning.

For Foucault, conditions, events and situations and our response to the same provoke and stimulate our propensity to adapt behaviourally, culturally and socially. It is precisely because we are socially mobile in this way that we move between identities; this is something that arises out of being human. Anything that impedes this development, that categorizes by force of law or even academic practice for example, is inhumane. The genealogical perspective is the antithesis to the contention that a secure connecting line of Traveller identity or ethnicity exists and that this joins current Travellers living in Britain to travelling groups emanating from Asia hundreds or even thousands of years ago.

The concepts of power and the body derive from the notion of genealogical analysis. Foucault utilizes Nietzsche's idea that force has primacy over meaning, seeing that history is a result of an ongoing battle between power interests which seek to dominate. For him human history does not slowly move between conflicts to reach a moment at which consensus under the law takes the place of war. Rather violence becomes systematized and applied through regulations facilitating a movement in time from one form of control to another;[20] history is the playing out of a sequence of violence. From this standpoint the contemporary position of and perspective on Travellers can be understood to emerge from a stream of legislation and the means of housing supply/production. The power interests that are expressed in this relationship seek to dominate through the establishment and enforcement of housing norms.

Although Foucault sees the orthodox Marxist analysis of power relations as being set in the economy and class conflict as a functionalist oversimplification,[21] a slightly more complex application of the same enables the Traveller population to be understood, at least in part, as a phenomenon arising out of a conflict/contradiction within capital. This contradiction gives rise to groups that are unable to respond to the market; at the same time it creates legitimate forms of violence[22] with the purpose of bringing about conformity to the existing social norms of the housing market.

Power and the 'Gypsy'

For Foucault, at the heart of the continuing conflict lies the human body. The forces of history act through and on the body in a way that cannot be understood from what McNay calls 'a totalizing historical perspective',[23] the type of focus adopted by many theorists interested in Traveller affairs.[24] The body, for Foucault, is a most revealing tableau in terms of the exercise of power; it illustrates the nature of disciplinary power. The body is moulded and remoulded by the power blocs that are involved in the constant conflict that constitutes history. According to Foucault the body constitutes a record of events, how they happened and what effects they have. Genealogy is, as such, exposed through the means of the body and history. It can function to 'expose a body totally imprinted by history' and how the process of history destroys the body.[25] As such, power relations, the continuing conflict of the historical process, infuse every facet and level of social existence.

The history of Gypsies presented in the literature is essentially teleological, tracing the origins of Travellers along an ethnic/racial/cultural path.[26] What this book has tried to present is a more genealogical analysis; seeing the travelling population as a product of definite power relations that operate on a defined body (labelled as the Gypsy). The reader has been asked to consider the Traveller as 'a body imprinted by history'. In the process of history the human body of the Gypsy has been destroyed, leaving naught but the Gypsy. Thus, the power that isolates and oppresses the Gypsy derives from that label placed on the body. This person can be treated in a particular way because s/he is a Gypsy. This application of power on the body is used by Gypsiologists.[27] Such an analysis cannot regard legislation as the result of diverse and divergent events emerging out of the continuous struggle between various power blocs. Unlike Foucault, the literature concerning itself with Travellers consistently suggests that power is exercised with intention, as a negative force of oppression, which is the property of an elite. Foucault on the other hand does not see power necessarily being applied from above, in Hawes and Perez's[28] terms, the State. According to Foucault one needs to be involved with an 'ascending analysis of power from below'.[29]

This being the case, legislation such as the Acts of the 1960s, the 1994 Criminal Justice and Public Order Act and the momentum behind the Traveller Law Reform Bill 2002, can be understood as exemplifying the ongoing struggle of power within the social realm. Such legislation is partly energized by the accepted notion of what a Gypsy is, as applied to individual bodies. Whilst the legislation has no necessary consistency, it does chart a line of interest or power obliging conformity to conventional forms of housing, consistent with the logic of capital.

The site of control

It would appear that the caravan site is the only future for a growing number of individuals and groups, yet even this resort has been in short supply. Site provision under the 1968 Caravan Sites Act was slow.[30] By the summer of 1974 just over 100 sites had been built, with an average of 15 pitches each, this to meet a demand of around 8,000 families.[31]

Although it is clear that the option of the site cannot, at the moment, be available according to need, the Traveller Law Reform Bill 2002 shows the potential for the site to be made to conform to the housing market[32] as a cheap form of housing, in the hands of social landlords. It provides guidance for the development of a new base level of housing provision. The 1994 Criminal Justice and Public Order Act did not disallow this.[33] There was the potential for a large number of sites to fit such a purpose, if unwanted, dangerous or isolated ground were utilized on a temporary or semi-permanent basis, with low minimum standards. This would have provided areas for those excluded from conventional housing. However, with the probable growth of this group the Traveller Law Reform Bill 2002 sets an agenda for a large outcast housing-underclass to be penned into sections of the urban, industrial wastelands. This final section will use Foucault's[34] ideas on the nature of prison to explore how this relates to the site as a form of discipline on the body of the Traveller.

Foucault argues that the prison is the most overt testimony of the 'disciplinary society'. For him the development of modern society has produced a situation wherein each individual has been objectified and from this point subjected to the manipulation of forces driven by a 'power-knowledge' dynamic. The individual objectified as a Gypsy emerges from this dynamic and thereafter is open to manipulation appropriate to this label.

For Foucault, there is no historical moment at which the prison erupts into existence. The prison, as we recognize it, is at once generated by and is instrumental in the creation and sustaining of contemporary society; given the nature of society, the prison is a necessary and complimentary artefact. We cannot escape from the prison; it at once accompanies and is of the prevailing social form. As we stare into the 'stern', as we analyse what it means to be 'put away', according to Foucault, we translate the society we live in; we uncover its evolution and make manifest its inner rationale. The Traveller site, that is a product of social forces, is another manifestation of this inner rationale.

This model is founded on a conception that knowledge is formed within a power system. Knowledge has to be accrued, communicated and ordered. These mediating factors are invested with the prevailing dominant forms of power that in turn affect and create knowledge. As such, the person, understood to be a Gypsy, has, in the process, been exposed to forms of power that infect the final object (for the person has been objectified) presented (the Gypsy). At the same time any power is reliant on knowledge. What can be said about Gypsies is reliant on the knowledge of this category. Knowledge is a constituent factor of power, as applied in our society. Power is power because it applies knowledge in a characteristic manner, to sustain the power structures. Sets of knowledge have to be gained, applied and retained in order to deploy power. So, Gypsies are presented in the way that they are in order to complement existing formations of power. This relationship of 'power-knowledge' forms the basic building blocks of the institutions that make up and dictate the character of modern society. What we call the Gypsy is a product of knowledge; they live in this or that way, they do 'A' and not 'B'. The category thus established is treated within the existing power system (which is a disciplinary system). The product of this is the site.

According to Foucault, an 'economy of truth' dictates the nature of a society. This is arrived at via power-knowledge, that is, according to how knowledge of certain types is extracted, presented and distributed, how an order is established between these knowledge types and how they operate socially. 'Truth' is knowledge laundered by the prevailing articles of power; knowledge is saturated and coloured by power. This is the fundamental flaw in much of the literature pertaining to Travellers. It starts out as taking the Traveller as a fact, an ethnic given. This however is knowledge mediated by existing power interests. At the same time this 'truth' produces forms of power. For example, Hawes and Perez confirm the 'fact' of Gypsiness and the requirement of sites is an accompaniment to that 'fact'.[35] Any given form of power gives rise to a nexus of truth that is necessary and adequate to it,[36] whilst certain articulations of truth produce forms of power that are requisite to them, the way Travellers are treated.

This is Foucault's 'economy of power', a self-reinforcing mechanism that exists to perpetuate itself, a corollary to the mechanistic metaphor of capitalism. Thus the analyst of power must refer to the knowledge(s) that is embedded in the mechanisms of power, whilst understanding that any knowledge is formed via these mechanisms. As such, in a system that promotes conventional forms of housing as the norm,[37] forms of housing that undermine this system cannot be sustained or tolerated. A certain species of 'truth' is needed to accommodate this, for example, the 'truth' that Travellers naturally require/desire sites; sites are linked[38] to the ethnic/cultural drives of Travellers; they are taken to need and want them because they are Travellers.

For Foucault the prison produces and applies knowledge and in turn implicates it to generate power. Prison is a power station, fuelled by a hot core of knowledge. The human sciences emerge from the disciplinary social institutions (of which prison is one) as the apex of the techniques of power therein employed. Foucault[39] deploys a description of the generation of the prison as a power mechanism. A product of this was 'the criminal'; the individual, isolated and so able to be observed and described on the basis of this observation and on the basis of this process defined in terms of like-individuals; the criminal population.[40] The criminal is thus understood according to a particular power context. This understanding will complement the power formation that created it. The criminal is thus a product of knowledge imbrued with power. The Gypsy can be understood to be generated in a similar manner through the site. So the existence of the Gypsy produces sites, and sites confirm the existence of Gypsies.[41]

Foucault portrays the prison in a whole landscape of power-knowledge. The site can be understood as part of this. The rationale of this panorama is to take the individual identified as deviant or abnormal through, 'coercion by means of observation'[42] and, in the case of Gypsies, assign them to the site – via categorization. At this point a campaign is waged on the interior of the defined Gypsy, with the object of normalization. This is the current function of the site and it is enshrined in the Traveller Law Reform Bill 2002. The site imposes a discipline on its inhabitants and this is put on show for others as the consequence of moving outside the housing norm.

Foucault's analysis[43] describes the disciplinary ethos of the workshop facilitating capitalist production. The disciplinarization of a workforce was the means of transforming labourers into labour power, thus economic considerations merged with the aims of subjection and control. Production became dependent on control that was founded on knowledge of the worker and their work; the breaking down of tasks necessary to production into absolutely controllable units of work. This allowed the closest scrutiny. In effect this production of labour power leads Foucault to conclude that, 'power produces reality' in that 'it produces domains and objects of truth'.[44] The prison and the site are areas that fulfil the same ends; a production of reality, through a defined 'truth'. They are both a means to an end; promoting a regime of normality within society – conformity to the needs of capitalism. In a similar way to the factory, in the jail each action of the prisoner is reduced to its most precise elements, so observation may be total and thus control maximized. Research into life on the site can be understood to function towards the same ends. The prison complemented the factory by acclimatizing those who deviated from the social norm (the deviants) to the regime of production, whilst the workplace informed the prison in the disciplinary strategies. The site can be seen in the same way; it is, in effect, an area of punishment, either through poor conditions (relative to conventional housing) and/or through the control systems focused on the illegal site.

For Foucault no individuated person is free from the process he describes; all are normalized to a greater or lesser extent. No one operates outside of the institutions of the disciplinary society. This landscape is Foucault's 'carceral', the social apparatus of control based on an integratory and reintegratory force directed and informed by the knowledge it extracts. The prison is the most obvious aspect of this landscape; as such it can be perceived as a crystallization of this whole environment that grows by implosion of power-knowledge, but the site can be understood as one of its progeny.

Power relations

Foucault can be seen to be illuminating power relations with two distinct hues, one at the level of the body, the individual, the other referring to a whole politico-philosophical, socio-historic spectrum. This book has undertaken something of the same exercise with regard to the Traveller.

Placing the site in a cavalcade of power relations, as one application of power within the great 'economy of power', we can argue that it is part of the expansive logic of the prison that spreads throughout the social field. The site, with no relation to nomadic existence, as a place of intransigence, or semi-permanence, like the prison, has a social meaning beyond the position of Travellers. The site tells us something about the nature of our society. The Gypsies are the focus of law because they breach the means of establishing market norms in housing. The whole history of Travellers can thus be seen to be enveloped in Foucault's carceral; the site is another application in the 'economy of power'.

For Foucault, from the seventeenth century onwards a new economy of power was necessary to the social form in which crime against property had become the principal transgression in the capitalist 'economy of illegalities'. Contemporaneously, the 1994 Criminal Justice and Public Order Act has addressed part of a particular economy of illegalities, being in essence framed around principles of property (rather than ethnicity). Out of this bourgeois economy of power emerges the power tactic of penal reform. For Foucault, the whole end of this movement, which arose alongside the prison, was the carrying through of the bourgeois economy, albeit by ostensibly humanitarian means. It was an attempt to make punishment more efficient whilst removing what would have become a mode of punishment dangerous to the new social form (emerging capitalism). The Traveller Law Reform Bill 2002 might be understood as a product of the same kind of motivations within the realm of Traveller concerns. Within it the site is set up as a humanitarian response but it is the place where the 'unamenable' in terms of the housing market, are to be placed. When the Gypsy has been located on the official site a type of reform has been enacted. Council tax and rent can be extracted from named individuals who fall into a category (Traveller).

The individual = punishment = abstraction

Foucault illustrates the percolation of the 'carceral' environment, creating an atmosphere of reciprocal institutions that at first informed prison and then became informed by it. The range might include the school, the 'madhouse', the hospital, the site and so on. This matrix of power-knowledge is the basis of Foucault's 'genealogy'. As the criminal is created, so the lunatic, the student, the youth, the Gypsy are produced, all controllable according to their individuation, all objectified within this. Disciplinary society creates individuals and attaches these to definite populations. Hence the system reproduces itself. For Foucault, the individual is thus a constructed entity, through the techniques of power.[45]

Foucault focuses on the body to show how subjects are formed, how they are made objects of knowledge and regulated through this knowledge that is unique knowledge. Thus the travelling population are publicly defined as abnormal and are abstracted, placed on the periphery, their destiny to reintegrate or be increasingly alienated. Some might see the self-confidence or assertiveness that has arisen amongst many groups of Travellers because of this situation as a benefit, and maybe there are positive side-effects. This is an area of weakness in Foucault's analysis in which he shows the tendency to deny individuals the chance to reassess human agency and intentions through self-confidence and resistance. However, as outlined in Chapter One, solidarity can act to identify and solidify type or category in a negative way.[46]

Foucault describes the prison as having a contemporary function in the pro- duction of a 'delinquent milieu' useful to the ruling class for the management of delinquency.[47] Here the site can again be seen as an extension of the prison, which operates to manage housing delinquency. According to Foucault, prison manages illegality, it does not repress or overcome it. The site has similar limita- tions. In contemporary society prison is, to a great extent, the depository of the prostitute, the shoplifter and the traffic and drug offender. The site is the as- signed dwelling place of 'the Gypsy', s/he who is unwilling or unable to conform to the norms of housing discipline. The school, the workplace, the necessity to fit an acceptable mode of behaviour for success or even the least personal or famil- ial security are the appliances used to control the potential for political activity that threatens the norm. But the prison today is not reform, it is not cure and it is not management. It is possible that prison is not even essentially punishment, although it may have been at given periods in the past. The prison is now something other, where the 'other' is assigned – it is a dumping ground for those who are not amenable to social norms. Yet again, in terms of housing, for the groups that have rejected or been ejected from conventional resorts, the site has a similar function to the prison.

For Foucault power is not to be found in the amorphous State; hence the analysis offered by Hawes and Perez[48] who see Travellers as the victims of the State, would be, for Foucault, fundamentally flawed. The technology of power, for Foucault, is dispersed throughout the social body. The State actually exists on the foundation of this diffusely exercised discipline – places such as the site, the designated locations for the categorized group, named Travellers.

Conclusion

I have, deploying Marxist and Foucauldian theory, suggested that post-war leg- islation impacting on Travellers is congruent with a social formation that will in its workings eliminate or reform structures and activity that fail to conform to the market norms on which it is premised. Within this argument I have employed a

Foucauldian genealogical analysis that defines the Gypsy as a product of power relations. I argue that the category Gypsy has been created as a deviant and consigned to a place of control. As such, the legislation surrounding itinerant life-styles and the site can be understood as mechanisms of discipline, complementary to and confirming of capitalist society.

Conclusion

A central concern of this book has been to highlight the role of social and economic forces in the generation of ethnicity in general and Gypsy ethnicity in particular. As O'Connell argues, 'ethnicity is something which is produced in historically specific contexts and it emerges, changes and adapts in meaning over time'.[1] In keeping with this the conceptual framework of the book proposes that forces other than biology and tradition have shaped what we perceive to be the Traveller population. Throughout the book the position that in effect argues for Gypsy ethnicity based on biological reductionism has been exposed. The literature concerned with Traveller identity, whilst conceding that the travelling population of England has consistently recruited numbers of people from the settled community[2] has, with a few recent exceptions[3] claimed that Travellers have preserved a blood-line[4] and/or maintained themselves as a 'distinctive cultural group'.[5] From this background the analysis of the Traveller population in the book considers a range of issues including the efficacy of notions of ethnic difference and the social purpose/meaning of the existence of the taxonomy of ethnic types.

In the opening chapter I argued that theories and descriptions of Gypsy ethnicity have been articulated on a range of abstract assumptions, coloured by romanticism, ideas about Gypsy language,[6] travelling, self-identification,[7] ritual and rite.[8] These suppositions are set in a background of a supposed underlying group unity that is seen to emerge out of the diversity of the travelling population.[9] I went on to suggest that organizations claiming to support and/or represent Traveller interests and concerns reinforce this perspective of Traveller identity.

Consideration of relevant theory[10] referring to the nature of ethnicity led to the conclusion that race, culture and ethnicity have become interchangeable terms[11] and that each are, at least in part, social constructs.[12] This motivated a critical analysis of the notion of Traveller ethnicity, which highlighted the limitations of the literature that fails to adequately consider the broader social context in which the Traveller population exists.

My critique of the current paradigm of Traveller identity argued that the proposed markers of Traveller ethnicity identified in the literature are fragile indicators in terms of identity categorisation and that 'ethnic homogeneity' has arisen out of a range of heterogeneous travelling groups is suspect. On this basis

I suggested that in order to establish a clearer aetiology of travelling population a broader theoretical perspective needs to be developed that includes consideration of social and economic factors, moving beyond ethnic and cultural determinants.

The development of a perspective of Gypsy and Traveller existence that exposes the role of social generation in the creation of such categories may have broader connotations. The whole notion of ethnicity and some of the basic tenets of this realm of anthropology might come into question and this would have exceeded the aims of the book. Instead it was more practical to consider Travellers in a broader framework when looking at Traveller identity, taking into account the insight of A. Rehfisch and F. Rehfisch when studying Scottish Travellers:

> Literally gallons of ink have been utilized developing theories as to the origin of these people. It would seem to me to be an exercise in futility to review all of these and even more to attempt to justify any of them. Their origin is lost in the far past and can hardly be reconstructed. For many centuries references exist mentioning the presence of nomadic bands wandering through the length and breadth of Scotland and occupying the economic niche, to a greater or lesser degree, that Travellers do today.[13]

This stance seems to counter a disturbing undercurrent within the literature, the effort made to propose a definite, pure group, being sustained over hundreds of years.[14] This striving to present a unified whole, an identifiable grouping that may be categorized as a type, harks back to authoritarian Fascist regimes. Although this analysis is couched in terms of anti-racism and political correctness, it seeks to differentiate people in terms of a typology based on custom, tradition, ethnicity or race; it also proposes (mostly by inference) that this group belong in certain situations (on sites, in trailers). This seems an inherently racist analysis. The promotion of a non-social, non-contextual perspective only serves to heighten the ethical, moral and analytical flaws in the literature. However, this perspective has other implications. Setting the position of Travellers within a discourse of ethnicity and race with a focus on discrimination, racism and oppression, that turns non-Travellers into the pariah group[15] does not adequately explain a possible relationship between the Traveller population and homelessness. This book proposes that the ethnic/racial focus is unable to account for the maintenance and growth of the travelling population, despite continued pressure from legislation. Neither does it have the capacity to explain why so much governmental, academic and legislative effort has been expended on what is a relatively small group of people. This is because the writing on Travellers tends to be highly emotive, set in romanticism, promoting a subjective analysis based on notions of individual and group psychology. It does not allow for the possible effects of phenomena like social action,[16] social closure,[17] or the dynamics of disciplinary society that move inextricably towards social norms that complement and confirm the character of the social formation, in areas like housing, by means of social control and punishment.[18] Therefore, the analysis of the situation and nature of the Traveller population, as contained in the literature, is partial.

The critique presented in Chapter One does not support a universalistic/non-ethnic outlook; the aim has been not to destroy the Gypsy. I have tried to demonstrate the fragile character of ethnic and racial distinctions as a critique of the explanatory power given to the same in the literature focusing on Traveller issues with regard to the generation and development of the Traveller population.

In Chapter Two I argued that ethnicity is primarily a social construct. From this standpoint I suggested that ethnicity can be understood as a product of social closure,[19] illustrating the potential role that access to social resources has on the creation of solidarity within excluded groups and how this might evolve into an ethnic definition. I then explored how the notion of a Gypsy diaspora may be seen as being part of an ethnic narrative. At this point the analysis suggests that ethnic identity or feelings of affiliation to an ethnicity can emerge out of a shared social anxiety fostered by the inequalities in the distribution of social resources. At the same time this association with an ethnic whole meets sentimental and emotional needs connected to notions of belonging. However, calling on the thinking of Fanon,[20] it was suggested that interlocking and interactive narratives can produce colonial narratives wherein the Gypsy can tap into an ethnic affiliation that is seemingly political,[21] but is, in practice, based on taking on the identity as one of the oppressed. I argue that the resultant ethnic identity is forged not so much out of a fundamental feeling of ethnic unity, but as a response to the oppressor's definition and treatment of the Traveller.

Overall, Chapter Two confirms that the academic response to Gypsy identity departs from the contemporary discourse on ethnicity. It has much more in common with older reductionist notions of race.[22] A central theme of the chapter is to challenge those seeking to establish or confirm the idea of a Gypsy ethnicity to consider this.

Chapter Three critiqued the notion, which runs through the literature and theory pertaining to Travellers, that the groups that make up this category have an assumed rightful or natural place in society. The resultant position questions the emphasis on cultural homogeneity and ethnicity that dominates the theory focusing on Travellers and that reinforces assumptions about the racial, cultural and traditional origins of the Traveller population. As such, the chapter also critiques the position that places biological determination to the fore. From this standpoint Chapter Three argues that cultural responses, in terms of education, housing and social provision, often demanded by theorists and those claiming to represent Travellers, may not be applicable to the whole of the caravan-dwelling population, providing an analysis that includes the inaccessibility of employment and in particular housing as contributing factors to the development of the caravan-dwelling population. This position is established in the first part of the chapter via interviews with Travellers, material drawn from media sources, family history, biography and literature focusing on post-Second World War housing. An analysis of Orwell[23] that illustrated a consistent historical relationship between homelessness and caravan-dwelling was also presented.

I went on to analyse the research carried out in Holland into the origins of the Dutch caravan-dwelling population.[24] Pre-empting Chapter Four this includes an examination of legislative activity in Holland and its marginalizing and so defining function in terms of caravan-dwellers. The resultant distinctions are, according to Cottaar, adopted by Travellers as part of a defensive strategy in response to continued State pressure via legislation.

The hypothesis that the caravan-dwelling population might, in part, be made up of 'migrants' from the settled population and not wholly a product of ethnic/biological inheritance is explored further in the final part of the chapter through the presentation of empirical data. This material illustrates that similar patterns exist in the national figures relating to those defining themselves as homeless and the biannual caravan counts carried out in England and Wales. It is suggested that the level of like demographic traits shared by these groups over an extended period of time illustrates a statistically analogous relationship between homelessness and caravan-dwelling. This implies a connection between economic and social considerations and the development of the Traveller population. Given the partial character of the respective data and the limited comparison of just two populations, this comparative exercise could not claim to demonstrate a definitive connection between homelessness and caravan-dwelling. However, the characteristic shape of these respective populations repeated in the graphical representation of both groups over nearly two decades suggests the possibility that they may be generated out of a single population pool, by similar socio-economic factors. This, together with the qualitative data of an illustrative character presented in the chapter, whilst not providing definitive evidence, does strengthen the contention that the Traveller population would be better understood in relation to social and economic environment.

In Chapter Four I undertook a detailed analysis of the legislation affecting Travellers and this was linked to the ideas of Foucault[25] in Chapter Five. After demonstrating that the contemporary interpretations of Traveller identity fail to stand-up to Foucauldian genealogical analysis, the chapter goes on to suggest that ethnic categorization can serve the control structures inherent in the workings of capitalism. I suggest that legislative marginalization is consistent with and part of the whole panoply of discipline[26] that is premised, in terms of Gypsies, on the need to comply with housing market norms. This analysis highlights the partial treatment of legislative activity within the literature concerned with Gypsy affairs that portrays the policy which impacts of Travellers as arising out of a psychological disposition rather than being the product of social environment.[27] However, this legislation has a discernible linkage that is founded in the nature of the social formation of our society and has both a limiting and disciplinary function.

I have argued that the analysis presented in Chapters Four and Five departs from conventional standpoints found in the literature, that are generated on the basis of assumptions about psychological dispositions rather than social imperatives. Out of this analysis arises a general conception of the meaning of Traveller identity and the response to Travellers. Travellers are the 'other' because they represent an alternative to market norms, departing as they do from housing conventions and, importantly, from the accompanying norms of housing that act as means of observation and control; through known location and patterns of consumption and communication. Given this position the argument that the irrational/psychological response of discrimination is the *fundamental* factor motivating the harassment and oppression of Travellers can be seen to be flawed. It lacks an appropriate analysis of the societal context within which Travellers are defined as a category. Existing accounts of Gypsy culture do not have a full grasp on what the role of Travellers is within the social environment. Neither do they appear to wholly understand how legislation affecting Travellers relates to their social location and how this relates to why Travellers emerged (and persist) as a social category.

Towards a new paradigm of Traveller identity

It is clear from the material presented in this book that a different standpoint on Traveller identity is required and that the whole emphasis on ethnicity relating to Travellers needs to be reassessed. Whilst the development of the kind of universalism suggested by Gilroy[28] might be too idealistic at the present time, given the impact of social and economic inequalities inherent in the current social formation (capitalism) as Gilroy[29] suggests, contemporary society may have reached a moment wherein there is the opportunity to rid itself of the human taxonomies of race and ethnicity that have been shown as partial, flawed and destructive. It seems, given our current knowledge and awareness of the biological, psychological and social make-up of humanity, we need to develop a new paradigm with regard to our relatedness. In the building of this new perception of our interaction, we may do well to ask if our need to categorize ourselves and others as specific 'types' of human being is in some way intrinsic to our being, or just the product of a particular social mileu.

The analysis presented in this book allows Travellers to begin to be situated within the general social context; it seeks to show that the treatment they receive is appropriate and logical to that context. It is an attempt, through the development of social understanding of Travellers, to go beyond the vague notions, premised on mystery, subjectivity, romanticism and near superstition that surround the study of this population. The book as a whole is arguing for a change in perspective in terms of establishing the character and nature of Traveller identity. This does not merely demand a different emphasis. What is required is a movement away from an essentialist analysis premised on biological assumptions and romantic folklore traditions, towards a commitment to a broader conceptual framework that is able to encompass wide social and economic considerations as crucial factors in the generation and categorization of populations. Given the inherent contradictions in the notion of Traveller ethnicity exposed in this book it is clear that a new paradigm of identity formation with regard to this group is needed.

In the book I have consistently argued that Travellers should be understood as being a heterogeneous population,[30] developing out of and reflecting the social and economic situation in which it exists. This proposal does not disqualify hereditary or biological links between individuals and families within this group, but it questions these as necessary qualifications or the absence of blood ties as a limiting factor in terms of identity. In short, this perspective questions the 'Traveller phenomenon' as necessarily a 'type', set in a permanent, unchanging ethnicity, race or history and presents a more balanced paradigm of Travellers as a group of people responding to definite social, including family and institutional, conditions and/or economic exigencies, choices, obligations or pressures.

The idea of Gypsy ethnicity as essentially a social construction represents a serious challenge to the idea of a homogeneous Gypsy identity, founded on hereditary or biological factors. As such it is a threat to the dominant academic discourse relating to Travellers as it is founded on notions of ethnic attachment. These include sentiment, vague political standpoints, the consequences of ambitions of State power, as exemplified in legislation[31] and obscure folk mythologies.[32] As Hetherington has pointed out, we now choose groups rather than identify with 'primary groups' like the family, and more and more people are becoming part of what Hetherington has described as 'neo-tribes' and 'elective communities'.[33] Social change is now the motivator of identity formation; the family, kinship and community pressures, what might be called traditional generators of identity, are shrinking in significance in terms of their effect on identity formation.

This undermines the notion of Traveller ethnicity as portrayed in the literature that places 'primary groups' at the centre of ethnic construction. However, as this book has shown, in terms of Traveller identity, the traditional mechanisms of identity are at work alongside social and economic influences and it might be argued that it is this combination of effects that give rise to Traveller ethnicity. The book has argued that this amalgamation of social and economic phenomena arises out the social formation (the political environment) and as such would be seen by Weber as having the capacity to motivate the development of ethnic identity:

> ethnic membership does not constitute a group; it only facilitates group formation of any kind, particularly in the political sphere. On the other hand, it is primarily the political community, no matter how artificially organized, that inspires the belief in common ethnicity.[34]

Perhaps the greatest obstacle to the development of a new paradigm of Traveller identity is the apparent inability of theorists and those involved in Traveller issues to make this connection.

Montagu[35] quotes J. S. Mill's *Autobiography*. Writing in 1873 Mill makes a strikingly original and, relatively, contemporary point:

> I have long felt that the prevailing tendency to regard all the marked distinctions of human character as innate, and in the main indelible, and ignore the irresistible proofs that by far the greater part of those differences, whether between individuals, races, or sexes, are such as not only might but naturally

> would be produced by differences in circumstances, is one of the chief
> hindrances to the rational treatment of great social questions, and one of the
> greatest stumbling blocks to the human improvement.

This seems to be the fundamental problem about conflating differences, be they
'innate' as in the concept of race, or 'indelible', in terms of tradition, rite, ritual
and culture, with situations/events/issues that are profoundly intertwined with
social forces and the character of the social formation. The myth, as Montagu
would have it,[36] can prevent appropriate action. For example, if homelessness is
a large contributory factor to the numbers of people being obliged to take to
caravan-dwelling, it would seem the creation of adequate, conventional provision is an obvious need. However, if the ethnic paradigm is favoured, this would
mean that most people living in caravans represent a population that have
traditions/cultural drives/social propensities for an itinerant way of life. In this
case the need is converted to the provision of a network of temporary and
permanent sites; this is the facility which most Gypsiologists favour and which
seems to be imminent by way of the Traveller Law Reform Bill 2002. The latter
requires a socio-cultural response; the former demands a socio-political initiative,
probably involving a commitment to social housing provision and an accompanying massive reform of the housing market.

   Given this, and the possible dire consequences of sticking stoically to ethnic
distinctions one wonders if the whole project of ethnic categorization has out-
lived its usefulness as a successor to the damaging categorization of race. Ethnicity does seem to be spiralling into the same problems of contradiction in use
and confusion of definition that marked the demise of its theoretical predecessor.
If indeed ethnicity has its roots and force in social change, why do we need to
align with it anymore? If the travelling population is a product of social conditions and interactions, would it not be more accurate and productive to admit
that the phenomena involved are the generators of the crucial factors in human
distinction and the resulting inequalities, rather than to seek to make marginal and
fragile hereditary and biological boundaries the pivot of perceived difference?

Appendix 1 Methodology

Introduction

In the book I have linked biographical material with ethnographic data and theoretical interpretation in order to try to generate rigorous research whilst at the same time ensuring, as much as possible, the material presented stays in touch with the reality of lives lived. I have said something about how this was body of the text; however, what follows is a more detailed summary of how I went about bringing the research, in particular the biographical and ethnographic elements, together.

Researching Travellers

The response Travellers make to researchers may not only be tainted by what they see as the wants and needs of the researcher. Feelings about their own position might not facilitate a clear reflection of their situation:

> any English Gypsies who presented themselves as victims of members of their own nation or as drop-outs from the dominant 'superior race' would appear to question the values of those in power and those with whom they had a supposed 'natural' affinity. Much better if the English Gypsies could be said to be descendents of exotic outsiders who had migrated.[1]

The response given by Travellers is also as fragile as the reaction of any respondent to the gaze of research: 'the way Travellers choose to describe themselves to outsiders depends on who is asking the questions, what the context is and what the Travellers stand to gain or lose by the labels'.[2]

With this in mind I chose to use a range of research tools. I will now look at each of the research methods deployed with the object of elaboration and justification.

Ethnographic and biographical material

Personalized and biographical data

Personalized and biographical material has been called upon to demonstrate how movement and employment impacts on families.[3] The data has been included because of its illustrative qualities. It exemplifies how individuals can, through social processes, move across communal boundaries, demonstrating the possible cultural interchanges between Traveller and sedentary groups, showing the contribution of social influences to the generation of the Traveller population. However, it has also been given a place with the understanding that the biographical tradition seeks to give voice to those who have previously been mute. Relative to the academic writers these 'voices' often speak with more accuracy and perceptive clarity about their life situations, given their proximity and relatedness to the events and conditions that impact on their existence. This perspective can avoid the distortions made by theorists and polemicists who frequently commentate from a social and geographical distance, through vested and/or professional interests.[4]

The Minster research: the Community Club

In order to maintain research confidentiality the names of research locations have been changed. As such, 'Criton', 'Arfom' and 'Rangly' are all pseudonyms given to areas of 'Minster', which is a *nom de plume* given for a city in the north of England. Likewise the 'Community Club' is a fictitious title given to the agency that was at the focus of the research in Minster.

The main site of qualitative research was a long-term study centred in the Community Club (CC) club. This took place between 1993 and 1998. The CC is a voluntary community project in the Criton area of Minster that had been in existence for approximately ten years at the start of the research. The management of the project is supported by a religious organization. The CC, for the latter part of its history, has been almost exclusively used by young Travellers and their families who come to the club from a number of authorized and unauthorized stopping places within the Minster area.

The CC facility offered flexible, negotiable boundaries of language, space and time. This provided an environment wherein there was room for users to rebel, or organize, rant or participate. No particular regime was imposed, but forms of inclusionary community practice and democracy were nurtured. Acceptance of behaviour, points of view, dress and language opened up the possibilities of expression. This environment eased access.

The history of the Traveller population in Minster

The travelling population of Minster has a history that is set in the background of the area's general agricultural and industrial past. This become evident throughout the course of the research as individual and family situations have been described. Dave, a Traveller and local youth worker stated:

> Travellers in the Minster area seem to move between Minster, Doncaster and Hull. Not all, but most, consistently move around this triangle. Most of the younger Travellers I work with have not been outside of Yorkshire (this, for them, includes Hull).
>
> Family ties between towns are very strong. The young Travellers often talk about cousins in the area and occasionally these relatives visit the club when they are in Minster. If a family leave Minster they usually stay within this 'traditional territory'.
>
> Most Travellers in the 16 to 24 year old age group report parental origins as being within the Minster, Doncaster, Hull triangle. However, grandparent origins have been located in Leeds, Durham, Middlesborough, Newcastle and Manchester.

The Minster interviews

Approximately 200 recordings of interviews with around 30 Traveller respondents were generated. About 30 interviews were initially retained from around a dozen respondents. The decision to retain this particular material was based on the clarity, usefulness and representative nature of the interviews. The material picked for inclusion in the chapter was chosen on the basis of its illuminative power in terms of the whole 'sub-sample' and its relevance to the subject area.

Access to respondents was gained through undertaking the research within an existing community project. Because community workers known to the respondent group undertook the interviews within the process of their practice a level of trust existed between respondents and interviewers. The content of each interview was discussed during and after the write-up of the same, first within the project and then in terms of its place in the research structure.

This part of the research has relied on verbal contacts made within everyday practice with Travellers. This methodology enabled a range of responses to be considered. Whilst carrying out interviews with Travellers it was important to grasp that the research focused on quite different cultural, educational or class experiences from some of those carrying out the interviews. Thus it was important to allow the research subjects to express their opinions, feelings, perceptions, understandings, insights and ideas etc. on their own terms. Introductions, when necessary, were made in non-threatening ways through project workers who had established a level of trust with Travellers. Throughout the research every effort was made to allow respondents to do the talking. This meant that interviewers, including myself, made interventions mainly in the form of questions and statements that might motivate individuals to develop their input.

In that respondents were defining themselves as Travellers the reliance on the rather suspect visual clues – colour of skin, dress, language/accent – could be dispensed with. This was just as well because most Travellers in the Minster area cannot be picked out by these visual criteria. Visual clues based on dress or demeanour are necessarily partial and ambiguous. It may be true that standards of dress within the Traveller community in Minster might not always be sartorial, but this of course is true of a number of groups in the area, obliged by class, income, fashion or personal/family decisions about material or even ecological considerations.

A number of specialist youth and community workers also contributed to the research. Five were called upon in the construction of the final research.

Age and gender make-up of the Minster sample

Whilst, in the first instance, no conscious effort was made to achieve a gender balance, the sample included approximately an equal number of males and females. This appears to be a consequence of the following situation:

- More males than females attended the project.
- More females were present when interviewers visited sites.

The youngest respondent was seven years of age, the oldest were in the mid- to late fifties bracket. However in terms of the gender/age range the following situation prevailed:

- Most Travellers who attended the project were under working age.
- Of those Travellers attending the project who were of working age more were female.
- When sites were visited by interviewers there were more female Travellers of working age present.

Overall this meant that the female age range of the sample was more balanced than the male age range.

The specialist youth and community workers who contributed to the work included more men than women. This situation reflected the gender balance of those working within the CC. Of those called upon in the construction of the research four were male.

Other interviews/conversations

I have drawn on material collected from family members, neighbours, colleagues and those I have worked with and supervised in an informal education/youth work context. Through my involvement I have also used contacts with activists within Gypsy politics. As part of my role in professional education I have organized and attended many training and educational events focused on issues surrounding the Traveller population, including specialized training specifically for young Travellers involved in youth work and have called on contacts made in these contexts. Other data has come from chance meetings with Travellers and informal conversations undertaken on unauthorized, short-term encampments.

Names

During the period of qualitative research it became obvious that many respondents were using false or adopted names. Sometimes former respondents were referred to by others by names other than the title given by the respondent. At other points respondents would use names that differed partly or wholly from the names previously given. All this could indicate fluctuations in trust/confidence or anxiety about the conversations and information passed on, but equally it might have been related to 'having fun' or 'a laugh'. It was not unusual to come across an encampment where everyone would claim the surname of 'Smith'. This would often be met with amusement by respondents when referred to at a later date. This was not a surprise to me on reflection. As a child I had often been instructed by my Gypsy grandmother to refer to myself on enquiry as 'Morris' (my mother's maiden name), or Stone (my grandmother's maiden name).

In all cases where I have given names I have used the initial titles given. Some respondents refused outright to tell me their names. Often children would only give first or nick-names. I have also been asked not to record names and sites of some respondents. In all such cases I have respected the wishes of respondents to be known by the names they have chosen or to remain anonymous.

Radio interviews

Reflection on radio material has enabled me to include a wider perspective of 'the travelling experience' and has provided comparative material with regard to the opinions and attitudes of Travellers. This has also helped expose some of the problems and contradictions involved in the adoption of and/or the social designation/ascription to the category of 'Traveller'.

Analysis of post-war housing and exploration of the literature pertaining to the links between caravan-dwelling and homelessness

An exploration of literature and statistics pertaining to the housing situation of the period of interest has been included to demonstrate the critical level of homelessness in the contemporary period. This, alongside a critical review of literature/theory pertaining to Travellers, provides an illustrative analysis of social and economic motivations to take up caravan-dwelling.

Summary of the research aim

Collectively, the data aims to illustrate the social origins as opposed to ethnic and cultural roots of many Travellers.

Overall, the book provides a heterogeneous body of research that offers a broader view of the nature and generation of Traveller identity that gives much more consideration to social imperatives than found in most other writing focusing on the Traveller population, as exemplified in Chapters One and Two.

Appendix 2 Formal Gypsy organizations

Introduction

What follows continues the analysis[1] of some organizations whose focus of concern is Gypsies and Travellers. It is not an exhaustive catalogue but an illustrative selection of agencies that exhibit something of the range, direction and purpose of such organizations.

Travellers school charity

This was established in 1988 and distributes 'culture friendly' resources to home-educated Traveller children and seeks to provide schools on sites for Traveller children.

National Association of Teachers of Travellers (NATT)

Founded in 1980 in order to decrease the isolation of teachers of Travellers and to support and encourage their work the NATT sees its role as facilitating the sharing of ideas and developing good practice, providing and creating a system of continuity of schooling for children as they travel.

The NATT describes itself as 'Working to promote and improve the education of Travellers.' The principles of the NATT are:

- A commitment to justice for all and equality of opportunity as a fundamental purpose and value.
- A demonstration of the belief that society is strengthened and enriched by pluralism of background, culture, religion and perspective.
- A recognition of the inequality of opportunity which exists within society for individuals and groups and a determination to take positive action to enable everyone to participate equally, to raise expectations and to enhance performance.
- A commitment to question and counteract all forms of prejudice and discrimination.
- An entitlement to quality, self-respect, respect for others, a broad and balanced education and a supportive environment as a basis for successful learning participation.[2]

The NATT claims to support its members by being proactive in liaising at local, regional, national and European levels, looking to improve the education of Gypsies and Travellers including fairground, circus and barge children. It provides a forum for the exchange of knowledge, information and materials including culturally specific materials for the education of all children.

According to the NATT a great many Gypsy and Traveller children experience difficulties in terms of access to schooling, the curriculum and continuity of education. It aims to:

- promote access to educational opportunities for Gypsies and Travellers;
- seek recognition of Gypsies and Travellers as minority/cultural/ethnic groups and for education to be provided within the framework of equality;
- draw attention to the educational rights of Gypsies and Travellers where they are not being met and seek justice.

For its members the NATT organizes conferences, provides advice and support, information packs, mailing support, regional representation, reports, surveys and questionnaires and professional development, and has revealed instances of subtle and not-so-subtle discrimination.[3] The three NATT working groups focus on policy and strategy, professional development and European developments.

Publications include the *NATT Information Pack, Parent Education Contact Booklet, Schools Report* in *World's Fair, Euroline – up-to-date Information on Involvement in European Projects.*

The NATT is a founder member of the European Federation for the Education of Children of Occupational Travellers (EFECOT). Members are involved with EFECOT projects and also with projects focused on improving the education of Gypsy and Traveller children through the Commission of the European Union's educational programmes. It sees itself as proactive in record and transfer systems, distance learning and new technology, secondary education, early years education for mobile children, circus children's education and structuring national and international networks. It undertakes to disseminate its activities to colleagues and partners in mainland Europe.

The Patrin website (http:www.geocities.com)

Partrin is a web journal that promotes a perception of Travellers that conforms to the general portrayal of this group in the literature.

The National Association of Gypsy and Traveller Officers (NAGTO)

NAGTO was formed to enable local authority Traveller officers engaged in similar work practices the opportunity of meeting and corresponding with colleagues.

The Association's objectives include the spreading of good practice concerning site management, treatment of encampments and relationships between local authorities, Gypsies and Travellers. Full membership is limited to local authority officers engaged in work with Travellers and/or Gypsies, although associate membership may be offered to other persons working with Gypsies and/or Travellers employed by non-local authority organizations acting as agents or sub-contractors for a local authority.

The Romany Guild

The Romany Guild emerged in 1972 with help and finance from the NGEC. It was linked with ACERT[4] and published several reports. After it ended its association with ACERT the Romany Guild was mainly concerned with planning issues. It looks to provide an authentic ethnic leadership for Romany people in Britain.

The Traveller Law Research Unit, Cardiff Law School (TLRU)

Arising out of the Telephone Legal Advice Service for Travellers that existed between 1995 and 1998, the TLRU is involved in research into the impact of the Criminal Justice and Public Order Act 1994 on Travellers. It also organizes conferences and facilitates networking and research on issues related to Travellers and the law. It publishes a Newsletter, *Travellers' Times*.

Romani Studies at the University of Greenwich

This is a group of courses run within the School of Social Science at the University of Greenwich. It portrays Gypsies as a group 'that left India 800–1,000 years ago who are currently in the news partly' because of 'the controversy over caravan sites in the UK'.

The studies are premised on Gypsies 'being an ethnic group – or range of ethnic groups – with their own history . . .'

Romanestan Publications (E Patteran)

This is a publisher specializing in texts relating to Traveller issues. Its mission statement is written in Romany. Whilst this might be a statement about use of Romany, it, in effect, limits access to 'host communities'.

The National Gypsy Council

This was first formed as the Gypsy Council in 1966 in part to emphasize 'the essential unity of travelling people, irrespective of group and origin' and their right to 'self-determination . . . their traditional mode of life . . . and a legitimate need for camp sites'. At first it was mainly concerned with site provision, but developed its role to support 'Gypsies as defined in legislation'[5] in the obtaining of permanent residential and transit sites and emergency stopping places through the planning process. It sought to promote an 'integrated, State school education for Gypsy children',[6] assist Gypsies in obtaining access to health care and address social welfare problems experienced by Travellers.

The National Gypsy Council is essentially a pressure group made up of Gypsies and Gypsy sympathizers, who claim to represent Gypsies. At its beginnings it was questionable if the Gypsy Council represented a large body of feeling amongst travelling people. This is illustrated by a subscription scheme giving affiliation to the Council that was inaugurated in 1969. At first it was aimed at heads of families, but the distinction was never strictly applied.[7] It was estimated that five or six thousand people would apply. In fact barely one thousand did.[8] It was thought that this number might represent up to 25 per cent of Gypsies on the road. However, it is likely that many of these subscriptions came from settled Travellers and people who were not in any way Gypsy, but who had sympathy with the Council's aims. As such, the Gypsy Council could only claim to represent a few hundred Travellers. Even if one accepts that the membership represents families one still has no evidence of a broad representation of Gypsy feeling.

The Council went on to be able to call on a range of expertise and after becoming affiliated to the Campaign for Civil Liberties could command some respect for its knowledge of Gypsy affairs.

The Gypsy Lore Society

This society was founded in 1888 by a number of non-Travellers.[9]

Contemporary political issues at first received scant attention in the pages of its journal. The society lasted until 1892, and was then revived in 1907, surviving with a few intermissions up to present times. Having managed to attract to its ranks most of the authorities in Europe and North America on Gypsy lore and language, its primary objective was to gather together scholarly material. Not until 1908, by which time a run of attempts to pass a Movable Dwellings Bill was again starting, did the GLS set out to influence opinion as to the way in which Gypsies ought to be treated.[10]

The Gypsy Collections at the University of Liverpool

These collections are comprised of the Gypsy Lore Society Archive, and the Scott Macfie Gypsy Collection of books, manuscripts, prints, photographs, sound recordings and press cuttings. The holding encompasses over 50,000 items in various media.

The Collections represent one of the prime sources of Romani studies in Europe, and are particularly strong in material relating to the culture and language of British Roma/Gypsies. They also include information on the social history of European Roma/Gypsies and travelling people in general. The Collections are mainly historical and include many rare items including genealogies, vocabularies, photographs and recordings of Romani music and newspaper and magazine cuttings. In general the collection does much to complement the contemporary perspective on Traveller culture whilst at the same time being informed by the same.

The Department of the Environment, Transport and Regions

This department is responsible for the biannual caravan counts and has a role in the collection, summation and dissemination of information connected with the provision of sites.

The Gypsy Council for Education, Culture, Welfare and Civil Rights (GCECWCR)

The National Gypsy Educational Council (NGET) was formed in 1970 with the main aim to make education available for the vast number of Gypsy children identified in the Plowden Report as receiving no schooling whatsoever, estimated to have been 90 per cent of the total.[11] The NGET became the Gypsy Council for Education, Culture, Welfare and Civil Rights in 1991. This marked the recognition of the Council's involvement in issues affecting the education of Gypsys including the lack of stopping places, inadequate and unhealthy official sites, racism, inefficient health-care, government and institutional harassment. The GCE, which is affiliated to the International Romani Union, claims to be a 'Gypsy based organization' but it states that it 'welcomes members from all Traveller groups'.[12] It is involved with support and liaison work assisting Gypsies in planning applications and legal matters, promoting work with outside bodies and organizations, 'Gypsy and non-Gypsy'.[13] It emphasizes that, 'The Gypsy people are a recognized ethnic group . . .'.[14] It also mediates in issues relating to Gypsy rights, lobbying politicians and political parties, dealing with government bodies, local authorities, health and social services, police and legal advisors, education departments and schools. It offers advice to Travellers and acts as a point of contact for the national media.

The GCECWCR has a large resource library and sends representatives to conferences, seminars and public meetings throughout the UK and Europe. It has its own representatives to the European Union and the United Nations. It publishes a newsletter and other periodical reports and journals.

Appendix 3 Caravan-dwelling and homelessness

A statistical comparison

Introduction

The data presented below elaborates on the material presented in Chapter Three of the main text.[1] This, together with the preamble on this data[2] and reflection[3] in the body of the main text outlines what the figures that follow might indicate and the limitations of this aspect of the research. However, each regional set of data is introduced by a short amplification.

South East

Homelessness climbs steadily in the area up to 1995/6. The overall trend in the caravan counts is similar up to the early 1990s. There is then a decline in numbers until 1996 when the numbers of caravans increase again. The figures present a similar profile to that generated by the combined numbers in the figures for England. As such a similar empathy, in terms of reaction to social conditions, is suggested.

West Midlands

The extraordinary rise in those identifying themselves as homeless in 1991/2 makes the overall trend appear quite distinctive. However, this does coincide with the all-time high of the July caravan count.

Yorkshire and Humberside

Although the peak periods do not coincide, the homelessness high occurs in the early 1990s whilst the caravan counts show a later high; the general pattern of a rise in numbers from the late 1970s/early 1980s is discernible in both populations.

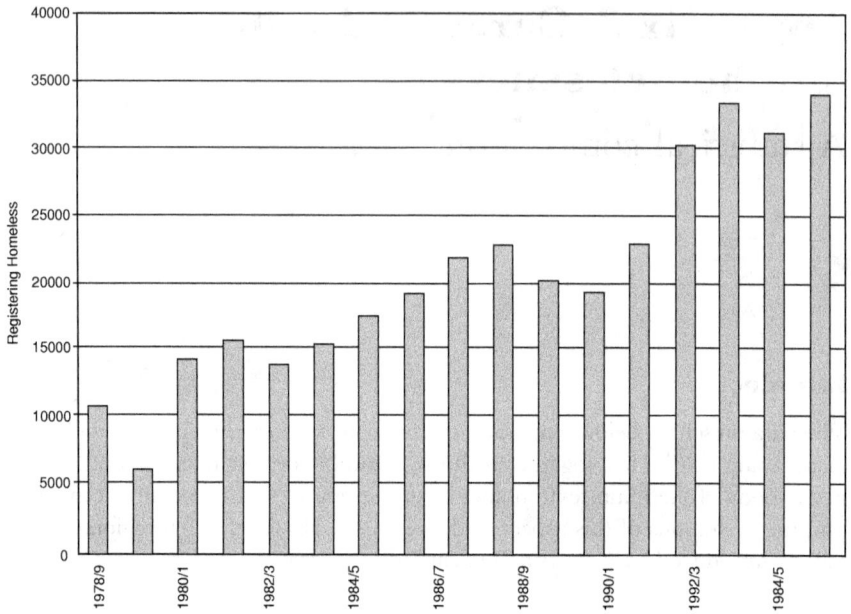

Figure 5 Homelessness – South East, 1978/9–95/6.

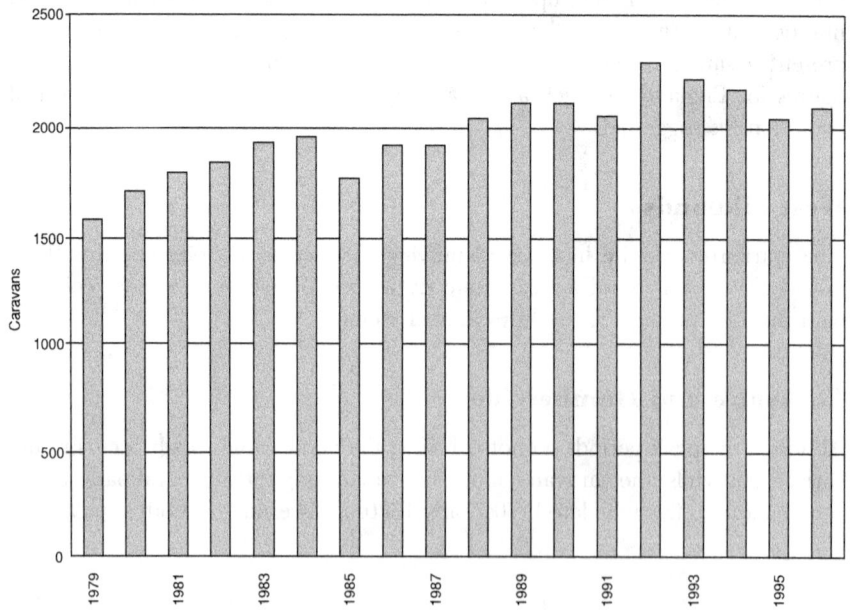

Figure 6 January caravan counts – South East, 1979–96

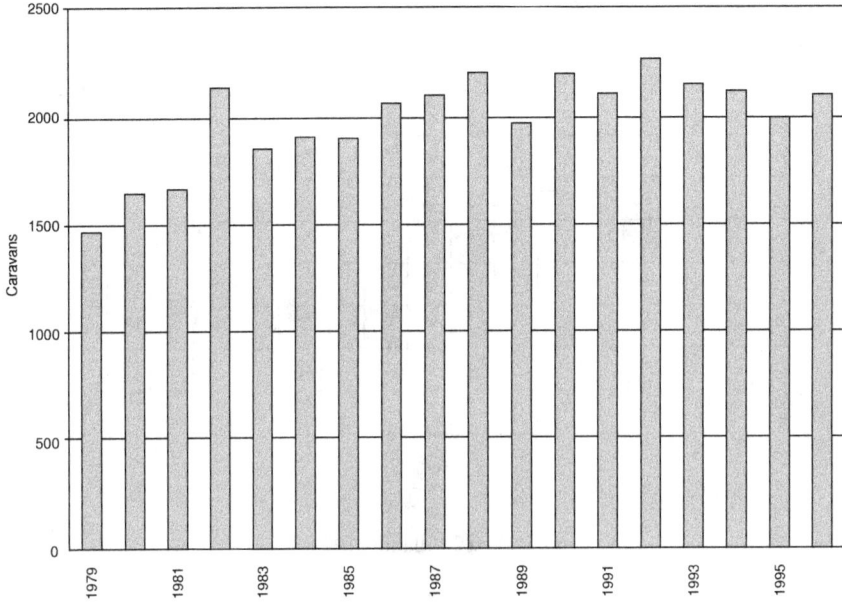

Figure 7 July caravan counts – South East, 1979–96.

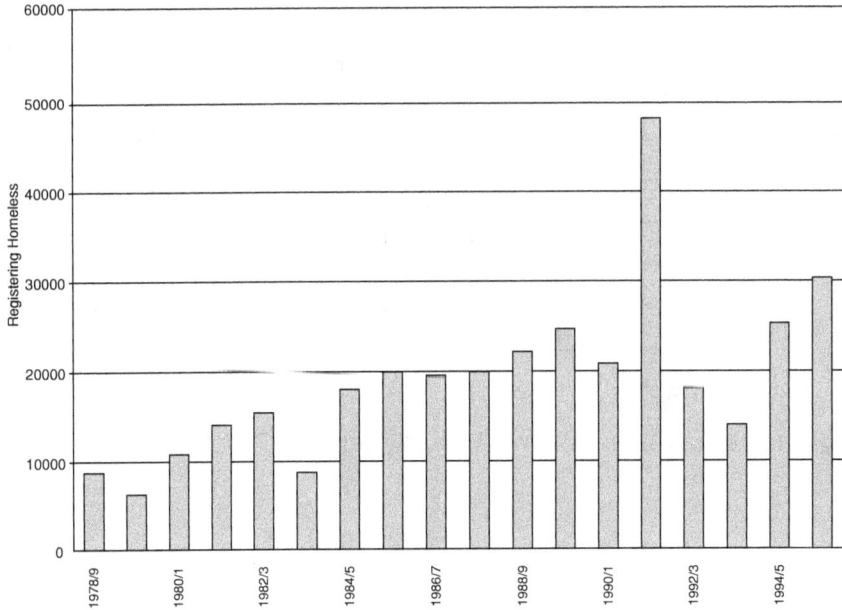

Figure 8 Homelessness – West Midlands, 1978/9–95/6.

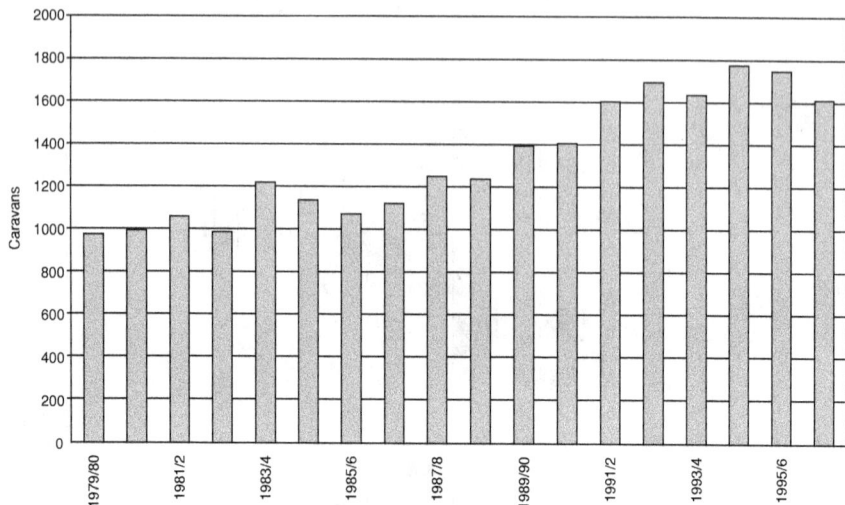

Figure 9 January caravan counts – West Midlands, 1979–96.

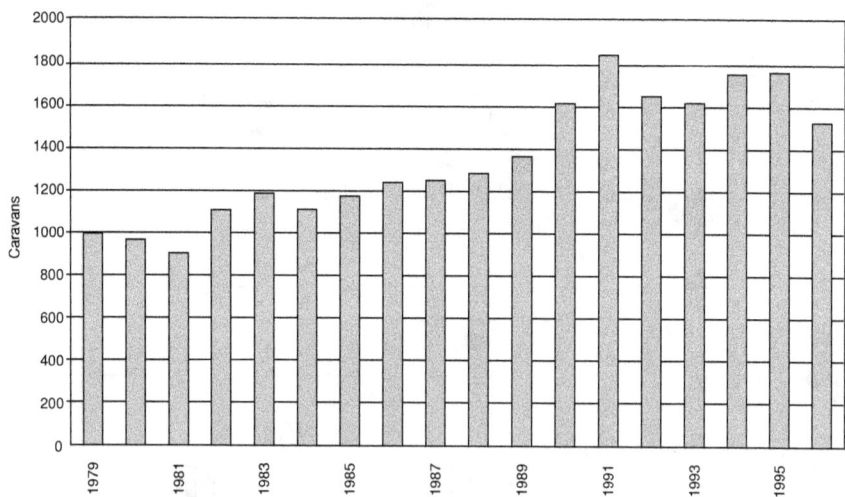

Figure 10 July caravan counts – West Midlands, 1979–96.

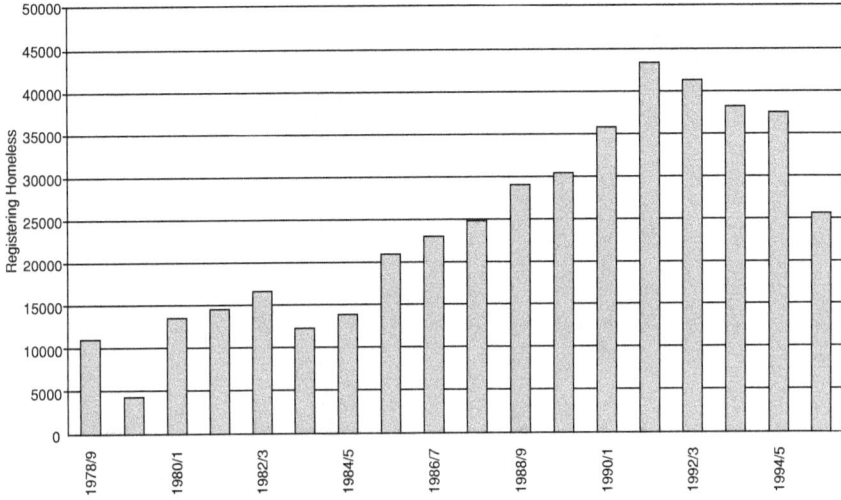

Figure 11 Homelessness – Yorkshire and Humberside, 1978/9–95/6.

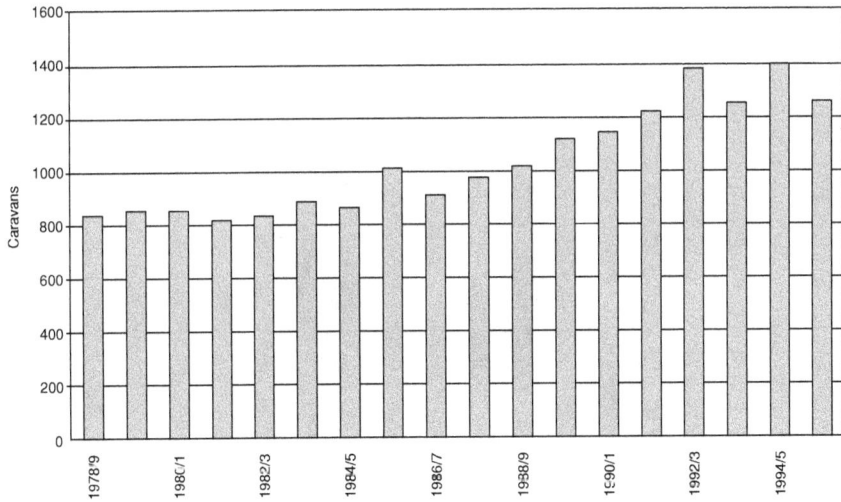

Figure 12 January caravan counts – Yorkshire and Humberside, 1979–96.

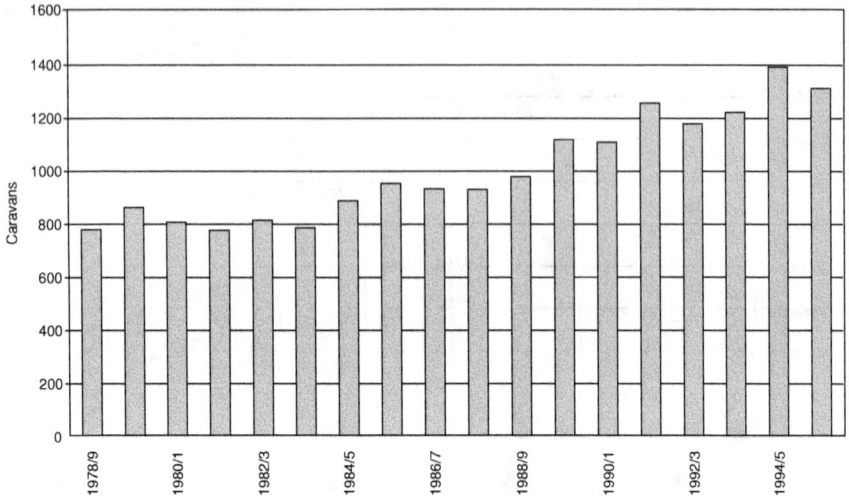

Figure 13 July caravan counts – Yorkshire and Humberside, 1979–96.

Appendix 4 Legislation and Travellers

Introduction

The following details post-Second World War legislation that has a significant impact on Gypsies and Travellers. It supplements and elaborates on the analysis contained in Chapter Four of the main text. It is not meant to be an exhaustive list, but it does aim to illustrate, alongside Chapter Four, how legislation can act, in unison with other conditions and phenomena, to facilitate the social generation of ethnicity.

After the Second World War a range of new legislation began to impinge on the nature of Traveller life-styles. For example, the 1954 Scrap Metal Dealers Act had a specific effect on Travellers that had taken to trading in scrap metal. This employment-related legislation was detrimental to many Travellers, curtailing part of or, in some cases, their entire means of earning a living, this group often being practically and socially debarred from employment of a permanent, non-mobile, non-trade-related nature. This situation was sometimes exacerbated by being constantly moved on. The 1967 Civic Amenities Act is a later example of legislation that curtailed an itinerant way of life by way of employment-related legislation.

Alongside other legislation,[1] a great deal of pressure and effort was exerted by the force of law on making a travelling way of life impossible for many and unattractive to many who had traditionally lived an ambulant way of life. From the mid-1980s other legislation continued this process.

The Children Act 1989 and the Housing Act 1985

The Children Act 1989 and the Housing Act 1985 can be understood as providing some help to Travellers. Social services departments have a duty to safeguard and promote the welfare of children in need in their area under section 17 of the Children Act. Under section 20 this duty includes accommodation when a child's carers are prevented from providing the child 'with suitable accommodation or care'. This could include provision of a site. However, this section can in effect play a part in the categorization of a child and its family. Once suitable accommodation is linked to the site other options may be passed over. The individual or group is labelled as a type, the type for whom a site is suitable;

other 'types' are not suited to sites. The result of this is that other types, slum types for instance, are suitable for slums; semi-detached types are suitable for that kind of provision.

The duty to accommodate homeless people under Part III of the Housing Act 1985 encompasses those who have no place to station their trailer. Paragraph 12.16 of the Code of Guidance allows for provision of accommodation under the Act, in respect of Travellers. This may mean the provision of a pitch for a trailer.[2] The danger of this is that those who have no wish to be placed anywhere permanently will experience permanent placement. It also opens the door for homeless people, maybe with no background in caravan-dwelling, to be placed on sites.

The Town and Country Planning Act 1990

To station a trailer generally requires planning permission.[3] If planning controls are flouted the planning authority can issue a notice of enforcement.[4] Since the introduction of an amendment to section 9, Planning and Compensation Act 1991, a stop notice may also be served. This must be complied with.[5] If one fails to comply with a stop notice one is guilty of a criminal offence under section 187 Town and Country Planning Act 1990.

The government has tried, without a great deal of success,[6] to limit the use of these powers. Department of Environment Circular 28/77 para.36 counsels toleration, 'until enough sites have been provided Gypsies should not be moved from place to place', whilst 1/94 paragraph 26 advises that in deciding whether or not to start enforcement procedures, 'the existence or absence of polices for Gypsy sites in development plans could constitute a material consideration'.[7] This legislation has made life very difficult for those who cannot find, leave or choose not to live on sites. In this respect it reinforced the effects of the 1968 Act.

Hawes and Perez call the period between 1960 and 1993 an 'era of consensus'.[8] From the above analysis this epoch can be seen as a time of increasing control and discipline of Travellers. What followed can thus be understood as a logical extension of policy rather than, as Hawes and Perez argue,[9] a 'radical departure' from what had gone before.

The Criminal Justice and Public Order Act 1994

The definition of a Gypsy made in section 16 of the Caravan Sites Act 1968 remained unchanged in the 1994 legislation. The definition was approved by the Court of Appeal[10] and effectively excluded so called New Age Travellers by use of the word 'nomadic', a notion of travel with a purpose, economic independence (to some extent) together with a travelling tradition. But perhaps of more concern is that it defined a category of people that could be criminalized because they are defined as falling into this grouping. It created a situation wherein an individual could in effect be guilty of a crime not primarily for something they have done, but because of 'what' they seem or are taken to 'be'.[11]

However, the criminal designation provision, which was established by section 10 of the Caravan Sites Act 1968, was amended by section 77 of the 1994 Act. This made the failure to leave land as soon as was practicable following the receipt of a direction to move from the local authority an offence. This applied to any person residing in a vehicle:

1   on any land forming part of a highway;
2   on any other occupied land; or
3   on any occupied land without the consent of the occupier.

This section applied to 'any person' whereas section 10 of the 1968 Act was restricted to Gypsies; the new offence would therefore also affect so called New Age Travellers. As the offence was limited to persons who are 'residing' in a vehicle, it in effect remained focused on Travellers. This new section criminalized all Travellers without a secure pitch in England and Wales. Section 10 of the 1968 Act applied only to districts where there had been sufficient site provision or where the Secretary of State saw it as expedient for other reasons.

The heading of the section deployed the expression 'unauthorized campers'. This was not the case in reality as the offence could be committed where a Traveller was on unoccupied land with the owner's consent, whilst causing no nuisance or other interference to neighbours.

Sections 78 and 79 in effect replaced the powers of section 11 of the 1968 Act. They were subject to the same observations made in relation to section 77. A local authority could apply to a magistrate's court to obtain an order requiring the removal of a vehicle from land that contravened a direction to leave given under section 77. The authority had the power, on providing 24 hours' notice to individuals, to remove the vehicle(s).

During the debate on section 77 in the House of Lords, Lord Ferrers gave assurances concerning its implementation saying:

> We fully understand the problems which are experienced by genuine nomads without proper site accommodation; and we intend to reinforce our advice to local authorities that they should not evict Gypsy families needlessly where they are camped on council or unoccupied land and are causing no nuisance. We will also advise authorities to continue to make emergency stopping places available to Gypsies where they may stay for short periods . . . We intend to reinforce our advice to local authorities that they should not evict without good cause.[12]

Draft guidance was issued by the Department of the Environment for consultation on 20 September 1994: the draft guidance consisted of eight paragraphs; it counselled only temporary toleration of Gypsy encampments, although in relation to all Travellers (Gypsy or New Age Traveller) it reminded local authorities of their duties under the Education, Housing and Children Acts.[13] This can be seen to have invited poor provision in order to comply with legislation, duty and swift action against those resorting to caravan-dwelling. Despite the assurances of well meaning and good intentioned individuals in the policy making process, the mechanisms that accompanied the Act addressed not humane exigencies but the interests of housing capital by removing alternatives to the housing market that in effect contradicted the norms and conventions of this market.

An authority's power to move Travellers without the duty to provide accommodation seemed destined to reproduce conditions which gave rise to the 1968 Act. This power has been called 'thoroughly reactionary, taking us back to the bad old days prior to the 1968 Act when Gypsies were harried from pillar to post'.[14]

Section 80, Abolition of Duty to provide sites and power to pay grants, was perhaps the most damaging section of Part V of the 1994 Act. It was the focus of heated exchanges in Parliament, and embodied the market protection explicit throughout the Act. It repealed Part II of the 1968 Act and removed the Treasury's power to pay grants to local authorities to cover the capital costs of creating and maintaining Gypsy sites. Part II of the 1968 Act included crucial sections which gave local authorities the duty to provide sites,[15] the power of the Secretary of State to direct local authorities to comply with this duty,[16] together with designation provisions.[17] The repeal of this part of the 1968 Act put Travellers in a difficult situation: those living on sites were less able to take part in seasonal travel, as the new powers under sections 77 to 79 disallowed this. Those not able to resort to site-living risked prosecution under the same new powers.

The Department of the Environment capital programme was used to renovate vandalized and run-down sites and new construction.[18] The abolition of the power to make 100 per cent capital grants towards the capital costs of Gypsy sites took the risk of limiting the construction of sites for Gypsies. It also meant that existing sites were less likely to be maintained and eventually be closed. Section 80 was criticized by such unlikely organizations as the National Trust, the Country Landowners Association, the Town and Country Planning Association, National Farmers Union and the association of County Councils.[19] The Association of Chief Police Officers also came out against the repeal of the duty to provide sites and the general effect of the legislation 'to criminalize the act of living in a caravan'.[20] The Journal of the Police Federation described the proposals as,

> At best a knee-jerk reaction to the Government's wish to be seen to be doing something about this year's particular problem. At worst they can be construed as direct discrimination against a minority – a discrimination that would not be tolerated if Gypsies were black, came from another country, or were homosexual.[21]

The House of Lords did amend the proposed repeal of the duty to provide sites, however this was reversed by the House of Commons and the legislation was given Royal Assent. The power to make new grants disappeared with the duty to provide sites. It began to look increasingly likely the situation would eventually come before the European Court of Human Rights. Lord Avebury in the House of Lords debate gave warning of this likelihood;

> The criminalization of the Gypsy way of life under this clause would violate the recommendations made by the Committee of Ministers against Gypsies. The Committee declared that in their law and practice regarding the movement and residence of persons, States should refrain from any measure, which would lead to discrimination against nomads for reasons of their lifestyle. Will the Government say whether they have considered the possibility of a flood of applications under Articles 8 and 14 being declared admissible by the Commission, and how they answer the charge that I now make, that what they are doing in this clause is a deliberate violation of our obligations under the convention?[22]

The 1994 Act motivated the creation of private sites by law. It inevitably meant eviction from land where permission for parking had not been given, and perhaps the confiscation of the offending homes. In short, the 1994 Act made a nomadic way of life a criminal way of life and at the same time enforced conventional housing market norms.

The 1994 Act repealed section 39 of the Public Order Act 1986 and put in its place broader police powers in section 61. This section exemplified how the 1994 Act made it almost impossible for Travellers to make use of land. It applied to two or more trespassers[23] when reasonable steps had been made by or on behalf of the occupier to ask them to move. In such a case the most senior police officer present could direct them to leave if:

1   Any of those persons had caused damage to property on the land or the land itself, or used abusive, threatening or insulting behaviour or language towards the occupier, and member of his/her family, agent or employee or those persons have six or more vehicles between them on the land.

It was a criminal offence if such a direction was not complied with.

The definition of 'land' did not include buildings unless used for agricultural purposes or scheduled monuments. What is new here is that the powers were initiated by:

2   The trespassers causing 'damage to the land'. It was stated in section 61(7) that this took in 'the deposit of any substance capable of polluting the land'.

On this area Mr Maclean, the Minister of State in 1994, identified that urinating on land used for pasture would be 'polluting the land', however it 'would be a matter for the court to decide' should a sweet wrapper be deposited on the same land.[24]

3   Six or more vehicles on the land.[25] A vehicle was defined as, 'any chassis or
     body, with or without wheels, appearing to have formed part of such a
     vehicle, and any load carried by, and anything attached to, such a vehicle'.

This greatly extended former definitions. A pram could fit the description.

Existing Chief Constable Guidance in respect of proper use of these powers
continued.[26] The government indicated that further detailed guidance would be
issued on this and other police powers introduced by the Act.[27] The same applied to court decisions on section 39,[28] which stated that what was a reasonably
practicable period for a trespasser to leave the land could not be established by
the police but was ultimately a question for the court to decide.[29] In effect this
meant that any action against Travellers could be undertaken swiftly with minimal public and judicial scrutiny.

Section 62 of the Act enabled the police to seize and remove vehicles from
land after the powers under section 61 (see above) had been utilized. Seized
vehicles could be held under section 67. This outlined the regulations for the
recovery of charges relating to the vehicles seized, including disposal of the same.
This meant that homes could be confiscated and held until bail was paid, or
Travellers might even be dispossessed. The 1994 Act could make the decision to
seize a home the responsibility of any police officer. This reneged on the Department of the Environment's undertaking that the seizure of caravans would not
be permitted.[30]

A superintendent was given the power to direct 10 or more people to leave
land under section 63 of the 1994 Act, if s/he reasonably believed that they were
waiting for 100 or more people to come together with music that was likely to
cause serious distress to neighbours.[31] It was a criminal offence not to comply
with such a direction. Section 63 applied even if the gathering and music was
taking place with the consent of the owner of the land, unless the owner had an
entertainment licence for the gathering.[32] This exemplified how the lineage of
legislation of which the 1994 Act was a part is more than just a means of control.
It carried out the very logic of capital, translating the informal, through law, to
the commercial. Within this, what McKay sees as 'the spark of transgression',[33] is
not, as he implies, 'resistance' to Thatcherism, it is a cultural response to a brand
of New Right economic policy. New Age Travellers can be understood as a
contemporary incarnation of a continuing social trend that is part and parcel
of capitalist enterprise. Being alienated from the housing market people adopt
alternative/informal-housing options. At this point the tentacles of the State
exert the discipline of capital. New Age Travellers, and other 'counter culturalists'
are not, as McKay might have it, 'outside' State/capital control, the treatment
New Age Travellers receive exemplifies the ubiquitous nature of control in our
society and how the logic of capital exerts this control. This analysis is further
elaborated in Chapter Five of the main text, but it is clear, via this legislation,
mere control is not the issue, control can be exerted to a point of confiscation
and destruction of property of any description. Police had the power under
section 64 of the Act to:

1   Enter land with no warrant, if direction under section 63 is considered.
2   Seize and remove sound equipment and vehicles where a section 63 direction has been obtained.

Following the enactment of Section 63, Section 65 of the Act gave police the authority to stop persons reasonably believed to be going to a gathering within a five-mile radius of land currently under the jurisdiction of section 63. The court had the power under section 66 to confiscate sound equipment seized under section 64 when the owner had been convicted of an offence under section 63. Section 67 gave the power for property to be seized as a result of police powers under sections 62 and 64. This could be retained, disposed of or destroyed. Charges could be made on the persons from whom the property was seized for the recovery of the removal, storage or destruction of that property.

At the same time the legislation allowed the removal of persons from any place that was not their personal property. An offence was created by sections 68 and 69 of the Act. These sections also enabled the police to remove people from land where they trespassed on land in the open air intending to:

1   intimidate persons engaged in lawful activity on or adjoining that land, so as to deter them or any of them from engaging in that activity,
2   obstructing that activity, or
3   disrupting that activity.

These sections were not restricted to Travellers; they could also have had an impact on hunt saboteurs for example, but they may have had an important effect on Travellers involved with protests against road construction for instance, it being stated that these sections were 'kept as broad as possible to embrace anti-roads protests'.[34]

The Traveller Law Reform Bill (2002)

The following elaborates on the analysis of the Traveller Law Reform Bill 2002 undertaken in the main text.[35] It is a clause by clause consideration of the Bill that is placed here to further illustrate the logic of post-war legislation and its effect in terms of the generation of ethnicity.

Clauses 1–2: The Gypsy and Traveller Accommodation Commission

The Gypsy and Traveller Accommodation Commission (GTAC) will be a non-political body charged with ensuring that there is adequate (and suitable) accommodation for Gypsies and Travellers in England and Wales. In the planning arena it will act like the House Builders Federation in ensuring that Development plans incorporate adequate policies and land for site construction. The GTAC will assume responsibility for ensuring that biannual counts of Gypsies are accurate and that each authority complies with its duty to prepare detailed 'accommodation programmes' (clause 5). The Commission has the power to issue guidance (clause 7) and a failure by an authority to comply with this guidance will be a material consideration for courts and planning inspectors when determining any planning appeal or any other enforcement proceedings (clause 6).

The composition of the authority is detailed in Schedule 1 of the Bill: at least half of its members must be Gypsies and Travellers.

Analysis

Given these powers and this control the GTAC will become the wielder of huge authority in terms of those resorting to caravan-dwelling, charting the development and providing for the growth of this population. It will also exist to make the site an accepted form of accommodation, locating it within the mainstream of housing provision. It will do this by the cooption of Travellers into its own functioning systems, replicating the practice familiar in the colonial context, recruiting 'natives' to carry out the functioning of colonial control.

Clauses 3–4: Duty to facilitate site provision

These clauses recast the previous obligation to provide sites by enabling local authorities to discharge this duty by adopting other measures that facilitate this goal. 'Facilitating' could include tolerating (or 're-securing') traditional stopping places, obtaining grants for self-build sites, ensuring sufficient planning applications are approved, as well as supporting the construction by Housing Associations of sites[36] under clause 15.

Local authorities are provided with powers to seek the co-operation of adjoining authorities in promoting sufficient sites.[37] A failure by an authority to co-operate in such a programme would be a material consideration for any court or planning inspector when determining any planning application or enforcement application connected with that authority.[38] The use of this provision could help negate the so-called 'honey pot' effect; namely that an enlightened authority that provides sites experiences a disproportionate responsibility, because its humane action encourages Travellers to move into its area away from less tolerant authorities.

Local authorities powers in relation to site construction are widened to enable safe play spaces to be created, and any other facilities which promote safe and healthy environmental conditions on sites.

Analysis

These clauses provide the means for the insertion of the site into the realm of legitimate housing provision.[39] They literally restructure the role of local authorities from being providers of sites to becoming part of the facilitation of site development. Potentially it adds to the proliferation of sites across authorities, providing the means to avoid the concentration of site provision to discreet districts.[40] This reinforces the integration of the site into the overall landscape of housing provision. Health and safety powers give authorities potential influence and a means of intervention.

Clauses 5–6: Accommodation Programmes

Local authorities are required to prepare Gypsy and Traveller Accommodation Programmes which spell out precisely how they are going to comply with their 'site facilitation' duty.[41] The programmes must incorporate all the available information, not only about the accommodation needs of Gypsies and Travellers, but also issues such as management policies and practice for existing sites. The preparation of such plans will be subject to specific guidance by the Secretary of State and the Gypsy and Traveller Accommodation Commission, which will include procedures for consultation with local Gypsies and Travellers[42] and (it is anticipated) the requirements of 'Best Value'.

The adequacy of a local authority's Accommodation Programme will be (amongst other factors) a material consideration when a court or planning inspector is making a decision in proceedings concerning that authority which relate to Gypsies and Travellers.

Analysis

These clauses fortify clauses 3 and 4 but also provide the means and the force for the generation of accurate population profiles, whilst seeking to ensure a standardization of treatment and provision, using the yardstick of 'Best Value'. This exposes an underlying economic motivation of the Bill that undermines its overtly stated aims and purposes that are presented as social and humanitarian in character.

Clause 7: Guidance issued by the GTAC or Secretary of State

This clause makes explicit the requirement that courts must have regard to guidance issued by the Secretary of State or the Gypsy and Traveller Accommodation Commission.[43]

Analysis

This is an assertion of the power of GTAC, giving it influence and authority at law, beyond mere overseeing of legislative requirements and recommendations. Its weight is, in theory, equivalent to that of the Secretary of State, thus integrating it into State mechanisms, near to a sort of 'Ministry of Travellers'.

Clause 8: The right to live a nomadic way of life

This clause establishes the right of Gypsies and Travellers to pursue a nomadic habit of life, by asserting the responsibilities that come with this right. These responsibilities are most clearly articulated in the European Convention on Human Rights,[44] the wording of which is adopted by this clause.

Analysis

The 'right' this clause apparently provides is rendered almost meaningless by the 'responsibilities' that come with it. In short Gypsies are free to be nomadic as long as they travel from recognized site to recognized site and make the appropriate prior arrangements for this. They may be nomadic, but only to a standard that would apply to most of humanity, within certain prescribed parameters.

Clause 9: Non-discrimination

This clause amends the Race Relations Act 1976 to make explicit that the Act protects, in addition to Romany Gypsies, traditional Gypsies and Travellers of Irish, Scottish and Welsh descent.

Analysis

This clause widens the categorization of 'Gypsy' in law and thus the constituency for 'lawful' placement.

Clauses 10–12: Education provisions

The proposed amendments to the School Standards and Framework Act 1998 will require local education authorities to prepare effective strategic programmes[45] which will ensure that the educational needs of Gypsies and Travellers,[46] are satisfied. In order to support such authorities in this endeavour the Bill amends the grant support provisions of the 1996 Act to ensure:

1   continuity of funding (for 5 year periods); and
2   that Gypsies and Travellers are able to receive funding from the ethnic minorities grant, notwithstanding that some Traveller groups might not otherwise be deemed to constitute an 'ethnic minority'.

Analysis

These clauses, by asserting 'the educational needs of Gypsies and Travellers' and opening up grant funding by way of 'ethnic' identification, promote the notion that those living on sites are, unproblematically, an ethnic grouping.

Clause 13: Criminal trespass provisions

The Bill amends section 61 of the Criminal Justice and Public Order Act 1994 by restoring the 'purposive' approach of the Public Order Act 1986. However the 1986 wording is strengthened by emphasizing that the powers can only be used in cases of mass trespass[47] and subject to stringent obligations on the police in terms of the service of notices, the recording of reasons for the use of the powers and by clarifying the statutory defences for failing to comply with such an order.

Analysis

Clause 13 means that smaller groups of Travellers cannot be summarily removed from informal/illegitimate sites. Whilst this is, in practical terms, a humane effect, it gives time for a more effective bureaucratic processing of such groups and increases the potential for their allocation to their 'lawful' place.[48] However the clause preserves potential powers for the use of overt force in the face of 'mass' trespass.

Clauses 14–15: Public funding for site construction

Clauses 14 and 15 remove the present anomaly whereby public funds are available to subsidize the construction of housing accommodation but not for caravan site accommodation. This amendment is achieved by widening the potential powers of housing associations[49] and then amending the powers of the Housing Corporation to use its resources to fund the construction or maintenance of caravan sites.

Analysis

This clearly is another aspect of the Bill that brings the site into the wider 'legitimate' housing realm. It helps integrate caravan-dwelling into the housing market, subjecting it to 'social landlords'. At the same time it widens the opportunities for and means of site construction, so making it a potentially broad housing option.

Clauses 16–17: Security of tenure provisions

At present Gypsies and Travellers residing on local authority Gypsy caravan sites have appreciably less security of tenure than residents on other caravan sites which are protected by the Mobile Homes Act 1983. These provisions remove this anomaly and increase protection from eviction for such residents.

Analysis

Here again the effort to underpin the 'Gypsy' caravan sites as a secure housing option is clear. Local authority action in terms of eviction is curtailed, thus allowing for the 'rooting' and so permanency of sites; a contradiction with regard to a nomadic way of life.

Clause 18: The Court's discretion in relation to public land

This clause ensures that courts have the power, in appropriate cases, to refuse relief to a local authority that has failed to comply with its obligations under Part II of the Act.[50]

Analysis

This is another clause that seeks to ensure the broad geographic development of site provision.

Clause 19: Repeals

This section repeals:

1   the power of the police to seize and impound caravans which are the living accommodation of Gypsies and Travellers; and
2   the enhanced powers of eviction available to local authorities which apply to encampments on highways and land of uncertain ownership.

The current legislation enables eviction to occur even where the encampment is causing neither nuisance, annoyance nor indeed any interference with the rights of the landowner. It is legislation which clearly offends the European Convention on Human Rights.[51]

Analysis

Clause 19 will pacify those with concerns relating to the civil/human rights of Travellers and help mollify European apprehensions with regard to the response of English law to Gypsies. See also clause 13 above. However, it also clearly shows that the treatment of Travellers will move from an emphasis on harassment to the development of a systematic, bureaucratic placement of caravan-dwellers.

Clause 20: Wales

This provision extends the powers under the Bill to Wales.

Analysis

This is probably self-explanatory given the above.

Clause 21: Financial provision

Since the Bill may result in an increase in the expenditure of local authorities this 'money clause' enables Parliament to pay funds to cover any such additional expenses they may incur. Provision is already made for the costs attributable to the Gypsy and Traveller Accommodation Commission expenses in clause 1(2).

Analysis

This clause provides further impetus and motivation for local authorities with regard to site expansion and development.

Clause 22: Commencement provisions

This is a routine provision, which provides (amongst other things) that once the Act has received Royal Assent it is up to the Secretary of State (in England) and the National Assembly of Wales to determine when it will actually come into effect.

Analysis

As with all legislation the provision of some tactical 'time placement' facility is desirable.

Notes

Introduction

1 Housing supply has been chosen as it provides a definite social barometer by which the pressure placed on individuals and groups to resort to alternative forms of shelter can be measured. The book argues that shortages of flexible housing provision may add to the numbers of people categorized as Gypsy and/or Traveller.

2 L. Clements, 'The Traveller Law Reform Bill' in *Travellers' Times* magazine (TLRU, Cardiff Law School, Issue 9, August 2000).

3 See D. Hawes and B. Perez (1995) *The Gypsy and the State* (Bristol: SAUS Publications), A. Fraser (1992) *The Gypsies* (Oxford and Massachusetts: Blackwell Publishers Ltd); and J.-P. Clebert (1963) *The Gypsies* (London: Readers Union Ltd) for example.

4 W. Willems (1997) *In Search of the True Gypsy: From Enlightenment to Final Solution* (London: Frank Cass Publishers), p. 36.

5 W. Guy (1975) 'Ways of Looking at Roms: The Case of Czechoslovakia', in F. Rehfisch (ed.), *Gypsies, Tinkers and Other Travellers* (London: Academic Press), p. 203.

6 K. Hetherington (2000) *New Age Travellers: Vanloads of Uproarious Humanity* (London and New York: Cassell) pp. 92–3.

7 Ibid., p. 93.

8 D. C. Harvey, R. Jones, N. McInroy and C. Milligan (eds) (2002) *Celtic Geographies: Old Culures, New Times* (London: Routledge).

1 Who are the Travellers?

1 A. Sampson (1997) *The Scholar Gypsy* (London: John Murray); I. Fonseca (1995) *Bury Me Standing* (London: Chatto and Windus); M. Stewart (1997) *The Time of the Gypsies* (Oxford: Westview Press).

2 J. Okely (1983) *The Traveller Gypsies* (Cambridge: Cambridge University Press).

3 W. Willems (1997) *In Search of the True Gypsy: From Enlightenment to Final Solution* (London: Frank Cass Publishers); J. Lucassen, W. Willems and A. Cottaar (1998) *Gypsies and Other Itinerant Groups: A Socio-Historical Approach* (Basingstoke: Macmillan).

4 See D. Hawes and B. Perez (1995) *The Gypsy and the State* (Bristol: SAUS Publications).

5 W. Willems, 'Ethnicity as a Death-Trap: the History of Gypsy Studies', in L. Lucassen, W. Willems and A. Cottaar (1998) *Gypsies and Other Itinerant Groups* (Basingstoke: Macmillan), pp. 17–34.

6 The period of concern to this book.

7 This literature includes the most influential of the texts relating to Gypsies and Travellers. It is understood that certain authors have added to the statements made in these seminal works; for example, T. Acton (1974) *Gypsy Politics and Social Change* (London: Routledge and Kegan Paul), was prolific throughout the last part of

the twentieth century. It is also understood that the likes of J.-P. Clebert (1963) *The Gypsies* (London: Readers Union Ltd) has been discredited by a number of writers concerned with Gypsy studies. However, I have chosen to include his work as it exemplifies many of the problems and flaws found in the literature relating to the field. Even his most ardent critics can be seen to follow his attitudinal trail, for example Acton, *Gypsy Politics*, p. 87, calls Clebert 'offensive and inaccurate'.

8 Lucassen, Willems and Cottaar, *Gypsies and Other Itinerant Groups*.
9 A. Fraser (1992) *The Gypsies* (Oxford and Malden, MA: Blackwell).
10 Lucassen, Willems and Cottaar, *Gypsies and Other Itinerant Groups*, p. 5.
11 Ibid., p. 5.
12 Fraser, *The Gypsies*.
13 Encarta Online (1998) *Social Science: Anthropology Roma* in *Encarta Concise Encyclopaedia* (Encarta Online), p. 1.
14 Willems, *In Search of the True Gypsy*, p. 17.
15 For example see Hawes and Perez, *The Gypsy and the State*, and Clebert, *The Gypsies*.
16 Lucassen, Willems and Cottaar, *Gypsies and Other Itinerant Groups*.
17 Fraser, *The Gypsies*.
18 Lucassen, Willems and Cottaar, *Gypsies and Other Itinerant Groups*, p. 6.
19 J. Okely (1994) 'An Anthropological Perspective on Irish Travellers', in M. McCann, S. O'Siochain and J. Ruane (eds), *Irish Travellers: Culture and Ethnicity* (Belfast: Institute of Irish Studies, The Queens University Belfast), p. 6.
20 Ibid., pp. 4–5.
21 Ibid., p. 8.
22 Lucassen, Willems and Cottaar, *Gypsies and Other Itinerant Groups*, p. 5.
23 M. Weber (1922) *Economy and Society (vol I)* (Berkeley, CA: University of California Press), p. 385.
24 Ibid., p. 389.
25 As Lucassen, Willems and Cottaar, *Gypsies and Other Itinerant Groups*, confirm.
26 See for example D. Kenrick and S. Bakewell (1990) *On the Verge: The Gypsies of England* (London: Runnymede Trust) and D. Kenrick, and C. Clark (1995) *The Gypsies and Travellers of Britain* (Hatfield: University of Hertfordshire Press).
27 See Lucassen, Willems and Cottaar, *Gypsies and Other Itinerant Groups* and Willems, *In Search of the True Gypsy*.
28 See for example I. Hancock, S. Dowd and R. Djuric (eds) (1998) *The Roads of the Roma* (Hatfield: University of Hertfordshire Press) and Dublin Travellers Education and Development Group (1992) *Traveller Ways Traveller Words* (Dublin: Pavee Point Publications).
29 See especially A. Cottaar in Lucassen, Willems and Cottaar, *Gypsies and Other Itinerant Groups*, pp. 114–52.
30 Ibid., pp. 1–16.
31 In as much as they have an overarching title – Travellers.
32 Acton, *Gypsy Politics*, pp. 76–9.
33 Ibid., p. 58.
34 Clebert, *The Gypsies*, p. xvii.
35 See for example Okely, *The Traveller Gypsies*, pp. 68–9.
36 F. Rehfisch (1975) 'Scottish Travellers or Tinkers', in F. Rehfisch (ed.), *Gypsies, Tinkers and Other Travellers* (London: Academic Press).
37 Weber, *Economy and Society (vol I)*.
38 Willems, *In Search of the True Gypsy* and Willems, 'Ethnicity as a Death-Trap', pp. 29–32.
39 See for example Okely, *The Traveller Gypsies*, pp. 72–3.
40 A. Samuels (1992) 'Gypsy Law', *Journal of Planning and Environment Law*, 719, p. 73.
41 For example Acton, *Gypsy Politics*, p. 54.

42 Ibid., p. 1.
43 Ibid., pp. 60–78.
44 This position is refined by later analysis, for example T. Acton (1985) 'The Social Construction of the Ethnic Identity of Commercial Nomadic Groups', in J. Grumet (ed.), *Papers from the 4th and 5th Annual Meetings of the GLSNAC.*
45 T. Acton, *Gypsy Politics and Social Change* (London: Routledge and Kegan Paul, 1974).
46 Clebert, *The Gypsies.*
47 But Acton denounces Clebert in Acton, *Gypsy Politics*, p. 87.
48 Clebert, *The Gypsies*, p. xvi.
49 Ibid., p. xvii.
50 Ibid., p. xix.
51 Acton, *Gypsy Politics*, p. 87.
52 D. Kenrick, and G. Puxon (1972) *The Destiny of Europe's Gypsies* (Hatfield: Hertfordshire Press), Chapter One.
53 Most writers agree that the word Gypsy is a derivative of Egyptian, a term give to people of eastern appearance, see Clebert, *The Gypsies*, p. 5, for example.
54 See K. Malik (1996) *The Meaning of Race* (Basingstoke: Macmillan), pp. 4–5 and Lucassen, Willems and Cottaar, *Gypsies and Other Itinerant Groups*, p. 6.
55 J.-P. Liegeois (1986) *Gypsies: An Illustrated History* (London: Al Saqi Books).
56 Ibid., p. 13.
57 Clebert, *The Gypsies* and Acton, *Gypsy Politics.*
58 Liegeois, *Gypsies*, p. 49.
59 Ibid.
60 Clebert, *The Gypsies*; Fraser, *The Gypsies*; and Hawes and Perez, *The Gypsy and the State.*
61 Willems, *In Search of the True Gypsy*; and Lucassen *et al.*, *Gypsies and Other Itinerant Groups.*
62 Liegeois, *Gypsies.*
63 Clebert, *The Gypsies.*
64 Acton, *Gypsy Politics.*
65 Okely, *The Traveller Gypsies*, p. 28.
66 Hawes and Perez, *The Gypsy and the State*, p. 7.
67 Ibid.
68 Ibid.
69 Ibid., p. 18.
70 Ibid., p. 20.
71 Public Order Act 1986 and The 1994 Criminal Justice and Public Order Act for example.
72 See Chapter Four.
73 Hawes and Perez, *The Gypsy and the State*, p. 12.
74 Ibid., p. 6.
75 Ibid.
76 Ibid.
77 Kenrick and Clark, *The Gypsies.*
78 A. Sutherland (1975) 'The American Rom', in F. Rehfisch (ed.), *Gypsies, Tinkers and Other Travellers* (London: Academic Press), p. 38.
79 Sutherland, 'The American Rom'.
80 Families spent between 6 and 66 per cent of their time travelling. Ibid., p. 15.
81 The exact character of travelling genealogy is not examined.
82 Sutherland, 'The American Rom', p. 22.
83 F. Barth (1975) 'The Social Organization of a Pariah Group in Norway', W. Kornblum, 'Boyash Gypsies: Shantytown Ethnicity', J. Okely (1975) 'Gypsies Travelling in Southern England' and W. Guy (1975) 'Ways of Looking at Roms: The Case of Czechoslovakia', all in F. Rehfisch (ed.), *Gypsies, Tinkers and Other Travellers* (London: Academic Press).

84 C. Miller (1975) 'American Rom and the Ideology of Defilement', in F. Rehfisch (ed.), *Gypsies, Tinkers and Other Travellers* (London: Academic Press), p. 41.
85 Guy, 'Ways of Looking at Roms', pp. 221–2.
86 F. Barth (1970) *Ethnic Groups and Boundaries* (London: George Allen and Unwin).
87 Quoted by Guy, 'Ways of Looking at Roms', p. 222.
88 For example see Okely, *The Traveller Gypsies*, pp. 49–65.
89 Kornblum, 'Boyash Gypsies', p. 131.
90 Kornblum, 'Boyash Gypsies'.
91 Willems, *In Search of the True Gypsies*, pp. 298–9.
92 Ibid., p. 299.
93 Ibid.
94 Guy, 'Ways of Looking at Roms', p. 202.
95 Willems, *In Search of the True Gypsy*, p. 301.
96 D. Mayall (1988) *Gypsy-Travellers in the Nineteenth-Century Society* (Cambridge: Cambridge University Press) and D. Mayall (1995) *English Gypsies and State Politics* (Hatfield: University of Hertfordshire Press).
97 H. O'Nions (1995) 'The Marginalization of Gypsies', *Web Journal of Current Legal Issues* (London: Blackstone Press), p. 1.
98 Ibid., p. 3, citing J.-P., Liegeois (1985) *Gypsies and Travellers* (Strasbourg: Council of Europe Press).
99 Ibid., p. 12.
100 Citing L. J. Nicholls, in *CRE* v. *Dutton*, 1989.
101 O'Nions, 'The Marginalization of Gypsies', p. 13.
102 Ibid., p. 3.
103 Acton, *Gypsy Politics*.
104 Willems, *In Search of the True Gypsy*.
105 For example see Willems, 'Ethnicity as a Death-Trap', p. 28.
106 Willems, *In Search of the True Gypsy*.
107 Lucassen, Willems and Cottaar, *Gypsies and Other Itinerant Groups*.
108 Willems, 'Ethnicity as a Death-Trap', pp. 22–4.
109 Weber, *Economy and Society*, p. 389.
110 See Clebert, *The Gypsies*, for example.
111 Such as the 1994 Criminal Justice Act.
112 J.-P. Liegeois, *Gypsies*.
113 Liegeois, *Gypsies*, p. 104.
114 Ibid., p. 139.
115 Ibid., p. 104.
116 Ibid.
117 Ibid., p. 136.
118 Ibid., Chapter Three.
119 Okely, *The Traveller Gypsies*.
120 S. Hall (1991) 'The Local and the Global', in A. D. King (ed.), *Culture, Globalization and the World System* (London: Macmillan), p. 34.
121 Okely, *The Traveller Gypsies*, p. 35.
122 Ibid., p. 77.
123 F. Fanon (1952) *The Wretched of the Earth* (Harmondsworth: Macgibbon and Kee/Penguin); F. Fanon (1961) *Black Skins, White Masks* (London: Pluto Press); and S. Biko (1987) *I Write What I Like* (London: Heinemann).
124 Okely, *The Traveller Gypsies*, p. 78.
125 N. N. Dodds (1966) *Didikois and Other Travellers* (London: Johnson Publications).
126 Ibid., p. 145.
127 One product and perhaps the zenith of this involvement is the Traveller Law Reform Bill 2002, see Chapter Four.
128 Dodds, *Didikois*, p. 146.

129 Ibid., p. 142.
130 Liegeois, *Gypsies*, p. 45.
131 Ibid., p. 84.
132 Ibid., p. 165.
133 Ibid.
134 Ibid., p. 180.
135 See A. Montagu (ed.) (1968) *Culture: Man's Adaptive Dimension* (Oxford and New York: Oxford University Press); A. Montagu (ed.) (1969) *The Concept of Race* (London: Collier Books, Collier-Macmillan); A. Montagu (ed.) (1975) *Race and IQ* (New York: Oxford University Press); A. Montagu (1997) *Man's Most Dangerous Myth: The Fallacy of Race* (Walnut Creek, CA: AltaMira Press); and N. Stepan (1982) *The Idea of Race in Science: Great Britain 1800–1960* (London and Basingstoke: Macmillan).
136 Acton, *Gypsy Politics*, p. 47.
137 See Chapter Three.
138 Acton, *Gypsy Politics*.
139 Ibid., Chapter 19.
140 Hawes and Perez, *The Gypsy and the State*.
141 Ibid., p. 1.
142 Department of the Environment 1992.
143 Hawes and Perez, *The Gypsy and the State*, p. 2.
144 Acton, *Gypsy Politics*.
145 Hawes and Perez, *The Gypsy and the State*, p. 17.
146 See Chapter Four.
147 Hawes and Perez, *The Gypsy and the State*, p. 4.
148 Ibid., p. 20.
149 Ibid., Chapter Seven, 'The Politics of Prejudice'.
150 Ibid., p. x.
151 'The Ethnic Cleansing of British Society'.
152 Acton, *Gypsy Politics*.
153 For example see Acton, *Gypsy Politics*, pp. 15–21, and more explicitly Kenrick and Bakewell, *On the Verge*, pp. 9–17.
154 F. Boas (1911) *The Mind of Primitive Man* (New York: Free Press).
155 E. Durkheim (1915) *Elementary Forms of Religious Life* (St Albans: Allen and Unwin).
156 Quoted in A. Kuper (1983) *Anthropology and Anthropologists: The Modern British School* (London: Routledge), p. 43.
157 W. Goldschmidt (1990) *The Human Career: The Self in the Symbolic World* (Malden, MA and Oxford: Blackwell Publishers), pp. 175–6.
158 T. Burns (1992) *Erving Goffman* (London: Routledge), p. 336.
159 Clebert, *The Gypsies*, Chapters Four and Five.
160 Okely, *The Traveller Gypsies*, p. 34.
161 Ibid., p. 77.
162 Ibid., p. 37.
163 Ibid., pp. 80–6.
164 R. Hoggart (1957) *The Uses of Literacy* (London: Chatto and Windus).
165 Okely, *The Traveller Gypsies*, p. 129.
166 Ibid., p. 35.
167 Okely, 'An Anthropological Perspective on Irish Travellers', p. 7.
168 Acton, *Gypsy Politics*, and more explicitly Kenrick and Bakewell, *On the Verge*, pp. 55–7.
169 Fraser, *The Gypsies*, p. 22.
170 D. P. O'Baoill (1994) 'Travellers' Cant – Language or Register', in M. McCann, S. O'Siochain and J. Ruane (eds) *Irish Travellers: Culture and Ethnicity* (Belfast: Institute of Irish Studies, The Queens University Belfast), pp. 155–69.
171 Clebert, *The Gypsies*, p. 191.

172 Ibid., Chapter Six.
173 Ibid., p. 191.
174 Ibid.
175 Fraser, *The Gypsies*, p. 25.
176 Willems, *In Search of the True Gypsy*, p. 80.
177 C. Renfrew (1987) *Archaeology and Language: The Puzzle of Indo-European Origins* (London: Cape); and J. P. Mallory (1989) *In Search of the Indo-Europeans: Language, Archaeology and Myth* (London: Thames and Hudson).
178 Willems, *In Search of the True Gypsy*, p. 83.
179 S. Jones (1993) *The Language of the Genes* (London: HarperCollins), pp. 186–7.
180 Guy, 'Ways of Looking at Roms', p. 202.
181 Nando.net (1996) 'Mrs. Clinton tells Gypsies not to give up', Associated Press, p. 2.
182 Kornblum, 'Boyash Gypsies', p. 131.
183 Guy, 'Ways of Looking at Roms'.
184 Clebert, *The Gypsies*, p. 246.
185 See Fonseca, *Bury Me Standing*.
186 Liegeois, *Gypsies*.
187 Ibid., p. 8.
188 Hawes and Perez, *The Gypsy and the State*, p. 7.
189 J. Sandford (1973) *Gypsies* (London: Martin Secker and Warburg), p. 181.
190 See for example Okely, *The Traveller Gypsies*, pp. 72–3.
191 M. McCann, S. O'Siochain and J. Ruane (eds) (1994) *Irish Travellers: Culture and Ethnicity* (Belfast: Institute of Irish Studies, The Queens University Belfast), p. xiii.
192 Okely, 'Gypsies Travelling in Southern England', p. 60.
193 Guy, 'Ways of Looking at Roms', p. 222.
194 Okely, 'Gypsies Travelling in Southern England', p. 61.
195 Miller, 'American Rom and the Ideology of Defilement'.
196 Sutherland, 'The American Rom'.
197 Okely, 'Gypsies Travelling in Southern England', p. 35.
198 Ibid., p. 67.
199 Ibid., p. 68.
200 R. Jenkins (1996) *Social Identity* (London: Routledge).
201 See Okely, 'Gypsies Travelling in Southern England', pp. 83, 94.
202 Ibid., p. 59.
203 Ibid., p. 15.
204 Ibid., pp. 173–4.
205 A. Rao (1975) 'Some Manus Conceptions and Attitudes', in Rehfisch, F. (ed.), *Gypsies, Tinkers and Other Travellers* (London: Academic Press), p. 139.
206 Ibid., p. 140.
207 Rehfisch and Rehfisch, 'Scottish Travellers and Tinkers'.
208 For example see P. J. Lee (2000) *We Borrow the Earth: An Intimate Portrait of the Gypsy Shamanic Tradition and Culture* (London: Thorsons); and W. Lee (1990) *Dark Blood: A Romany Story* (London: Minerva).
209 O'Nions, 'The Marginalization of Gypsies', p. 3.
210 I refer to Clebert, *The Gypsies*, extensively because it exemplifies the full range of excesses in the analysis of Traveller origins/background, which seems to be replicated to a greater or lesser extent across the literature.
211 Clebert, *The Gypsies*, p. 80.
212 Ibid., p. xix.
213 Ibid., pp. 8–25.
214 Ibid., p. 21.
215 Ibid., Chapter Two.
216 Ibid., p. 27.
217 Ibid., p. 23.

218 For example see A. Brah (1996) *Cartographies of Diaspora: Contesting Identities* (London. Routledge); J. Clifford (1997) *Routes, Travel and Translation in the Late Twentieth Century* (Cambridge, MA: Harvard University Press), pp. 283–9; S. Hall and P. du Gay (eds) (1996) *Questions of Cultural Identity* (London: Sage), pp. 92, 101; K. G. Azoulay (1997) *Black, Jewish and Interracial: It's Not the Color of Your Skin, but the Race of Your Kin, and Other Myths of Identity* (Durham, NC and London: Duke University Press), pp. 9, 51–2; S. Fenton (1999) *Ethnicity: Racism, Class and Culture* (Basingstoke: Macmillan), pp. 28, 30, 33; and J. Hutchinson and A. D. Smith (eds) (1996) *Ethnicity* (Oxford and New York: Oxford University Press), pp. 217–20.

219 S. Hall (1992) 'Our Mongrel Selves', *New Statesman and Society*, supplement, 19 (June), p. 8.

220 S. Cornell and D. Hartmann (1998) *Ethnicity and Race: Making Identities in a Changing World* (London and New Delhi: Pine Forge Press, Sage Publications), p. 250.

221 See E. V. Huseby-Darvas (1995) 'The Search for Hungarian National Identity', in L. Romanucci-Ross and G. DeVos (eds), *Ethnic Identity* (Walnut Creek, CA: AltaMira Press, Sage Publications), pp. 171–3.

222 The role of social closure is explored in Chapter Three.

223 Clebert, *The Gypsies*.

224 Ibid., p. 81.

225 Ibid., p. 213.

226 Willems, *In Search of the True Gypsy*.

227 Clebert, *The Gypsies*, p. 124.

228 Ibid., p. 72.

229 For example see Acton, *Gypsy Politics*, and Hawes and Perez, *The Gypsy and the State*.

230 Clebert, *The Gypsies*.

231 Fraser, *The Gypsies*.

232 Ibid., p. 22.

233 Ibid., p. 294.

234 Clebert, *The Gypsies*, and Dodds, *Didikois*.

235 Dodds, *Didikois*, p. 142.

236 Ibid., p. 17.

237 Ibid., p. 142.

238 Clebert, *The Gypsies*.

239 Acton, *Gypsy Politics*.

240 Fraser, The Gypsies.

241 Kenrick and Clark, *The Gypsies*.

242 Malik, *The Meaning of Race*, p. 225.

243 S. Hall (1978) 'Racism and Reaction', in Commission for Racial Equality (eds), *Five Views of Multi-cultural Britain* (London: Commission for Racial Equality), p. 26.

244 For example Clebert, *The Gypsies* and Acton, *Gypsy Politics*.

245 Kornblum, 'Boyash Gypsies', p. 131.

246 Barth, 'The Social Organization of a Pariah Group in Norway', p. 286.

247 Guy, 'Ways of Looking at Roms', p. 202.

248 Ibid., p. 221.

249 Ibid., p. 222.

250 Okely, 'Gypsies Travelling in Southern England', pp. 59–60.

251 Acton, *Gypsy Politics*.

252 This is mirrored in the layout of the book and chapter titles.

253 Acton, *Gypsy Politics*, p. 2.

254 Fraser, *The Gypsies*.

255 Whilst the author has elaborated, refined and adjusted his position since Acton, *Gypsy Politics*, it remains his most influential text and the foundation of his analysis of Gypsy culture and the politics surrounding this group.

256 Liegeois, *Gypsies*, p. 45.

257 Ibid., p. 18.
258 Ibid., p. 22.
259 Ibid., p. 23.
260 Ibid., p. 33.
261 Ibid., p. 102.
262 Ibid., p. 44.
263 Ibid., p. 45.
264 Ibid., p. 50.
265 Okely, *The Traveller Gypsies*.
266 Ibid., p. 77.
267 Ibid., p. 78.
268 Ibid., p. 47.
269 Ibid., Chapter Four, 'Economic Niche'.
270 Ibid., p. 49.
271 Ibid., p. 231.
272 A. Rehfisch and F. Rehfisch, 'Scottish Travellers or Tinkers', Preface.
273 Okely, 'Gypsies Travelling in Southern England', pp. 59–60.
274 Ibid., p. 60.
275 Guy, 'Ways of Looking at Roms', p. 223.
276 B. Barnes (1975) 'Irish Travelling People', in F. Rehfisch (ed.), *Gypsies, Tinkers and Other Travellers* (London: Academic Press), p. 258.
277 E. Hobsbawn and T. Ranger (eds) (1983) *The Invention of Tradition* (Cambridge: Cambridge University Press), p. 67.
278 Barnes, 'Irish Travelling People'.
279 Sandford, *Gypsies*, p. xv.
280 Ibid., p. 4.
281 Ibid., p. 3.
282 This is confirmed by Lucassen, Willems and Cottaar, *Gypsies and Other Itinerant Groups*, and Willems, *In Search of the True Gypsy*.
283 Sandford, *Gypsies*, p. 181.
284 Ibid., pp. 184–5.
285 Ibid., p. 184.
286 Not all organizations with a Gypsy/Traveller focus could be included and exclusions have been commented on and considered at the draft stage of this book. However, I present the contents of this section as illustrative of the purpose and direction of such organizations not as, in any way, an exhaustive catalogue of such organizations.
287 Hawes and Perez, *The Gypsy and the State*, pp. 63–4.
288 D. Kenrick (1993) *Gypsies: From India to the Mediterranean* (Paris: Gypsy Research Centre CRDP Midi Pyrenees), pp. 59–60.
289 Ibid.
290 Lucassen, Willems and Cottaar, *Gypsies and Other Itinerant Groups*, Willems, *In Search of the True Gypsy*.

2 What is ethnicity?

1 For example, J.-P. Clebert (1963) *The Gypsies* (London: Readers Union Ltd), pp. xvi–xix; T. Acton (1974) *Gypsy Politics and Social Change* (London: Routledge and Kegan Paul), p. 54; J.-P. Liegeois (1985) *Gypsies and Travellers* (Strasbourg: Council of Europe Press), p. 13; J. Okely (1994) 'An Anthropological Perspective on Irish Travellers', in M. McCann, S. O'Siochain and J. Ruane (eds), *Irish Travellers: Culture and Ethnicity* (Belfast: Institute of Irish Studies, The Queens University Belfast), pp. 34, 37, 67; and A. Fraser (1992) *The Gypsies* (Oxford and Malden, MA: Blackwell Publishers), p. 25.
2 J. Okely (1983) *The Traveller Gypsies* (Cambridge: Cambridge University Press), pp. 6–8.

3 S. Hall (1992) 'Our Mongrel Selves', *New Statesman and Society*, supplement, 19 (June), p. 8.

4 S. Hall (1990) 'Cultural Identity and Diaspora', in J. Rutherford (ed.), *Identity, Community, Culture and Difference* (London: Lawrence and Wishart), p. 227.

5 D. Kenrick and S. Bakewell (1990) *On the Verge: The Gypsies of England* (London: Runnymede Trust), pp. 16, 10, 56–7; and G. McKay (1996) *Senseless Acts of Beauty* (London and New York: Verso).

6 Okely, *The Traveller Gypsies*, p. 66.

7 S. Hall (1981b) 'Teaching Race', in A. James and R. Jeffcoate (eds), *The School in the Multicultural Society – A Reader* (London: Harper and Row), p. 69.

8 Ibid., p. 19.

9 M. Banton (2000) 'The Idiom of Race', in S. Back and J. Solomos (eds), *Theories of Race and Racism: A Reader* (London and New York: Routledge), pp. 51–63.

10 See also A. Montagu (ed.) (1969) *The Concept of Race* (London: Collier Books, Collier-Macmillan); and N. Stepan (1982) *The Idea of Race in Science: Great Britain 1800–1960* (London and Basingstoke: Macmillan).

11 L. Lieberman, A. Littlefield and L. T. Reynolds (1975) 'The Debate over Race: Thirty Years and Two Centuries Later', in A. Montagu (ed.), *Race and I.Q.* (New York: Oxford University Press), pp. 49–50.

12 K. Malik (1996) *The Meaning of Race* (Basingstoke: Macmillan).

13 Citing J. Rex (1986) *Race and Ethnicity* (Milton Keynes: Open University Press), p. 175.

14 W. Sollors (ed.) (1989) *The Invention of Ethnicity* (New York and Oxford: Oxford University Press), p. xiv.

15 See Clebert, *The Gypsies*, pp. xvi–xix; Okely, *The Traveller Gypsies*, pp. 34, 37, 67; and Fraser, *The Gypsies*, p. 25.

16 Sollors, *The Invention of Ethnicity*, p. xiv.

17 Ibid.

18 According to the *Oxford English Dictionary* (1999) (New York: Oxford University Press).

19 Malik, *The Meaning of Race*, p. 174.

20 D. McLoughlin (1994) 'Nomadism in Irish Travellers' Identity', in M. McCann, S. O'Siochain and J. Ruane (eds), *Irish Travellers: Culture and Ethnicity* (Belfast: Institute of Irish Studies, The Queens University Belfast), p. 80.

21 Malik, *The Meaning of Race*, p. 176.

22 Referring to M. Chapman (ed.) (1993), *Social and Biological Aspects of Ethnicity* (Oxford: Oxford University Press), p. 21.

23 Cultural norms.

24 Malik, *The Meaning of Race*, p. 186.

25 Citing R. Scruton (1990) 'In Defence of the Nation', in J. C. D. Clark (ed.), *Ideas in Politics in Modern Britain* (Basingstoke: Macmillian).

26 A. Montagu (1997) *Man's Most Dangerous Myth: The Fallacy of Race* (Walnut Creek, CA: AltaMira Press).

27 K. Lee (1997) 'Australia – Sanctuary or Cemetery for Romanies?', in T. Acton and G. Mundy (eds), *Romani Culture and Gypsy Identity* (Hatfield: University of Hertfordshire Press).

28 C. Geertz (1973) *The Interpretation of Cultures* (New York: Basic Books), p. 259.

29 W. Reid (1997) 'Scottish Gypsies/Travellers and Folklorists', in T. Acton and G. Mundy (eds), *Romani Culture and Gypsy Identity* (Hatfield: University of Hertfordshire Press), p. 29.

30 G. Laparge (1997) 'The English Folklore Corpus and Gypsy Oral Tradition', in T. Acton, and G. Mundy (eds), *Romani Culture and Gypsy Identity* (Hatfield: University of Hertfordshire Press).

31 Ibid., p. 19.

32 Reid, 'Scottish Gypsies/Travellers and Folklorists'.

33 Laparge, 'The English Folklore Corpus and Gypsy Oral Tradition'.

34 D. Mayall (1995) *Gypsy-Travellers in the Nineteenth-Century Society* (Cambridge: Cambridge University Press), p. 84.
35 Mayall provides evidence of intermarriage between Gypsies and non-Gypsies from eighteenth-century records.
36 Reid, 'Scottish Gypsies/Travellers and Folklorists', p. 30.
37 H. Henderson (1992) *Alias MacAlias* (Edinburgh: Polygon), p. 174.
38 Acton, *Gypsy Politics*, p. 44.
39 Sixteenth-century nomads.
40 Laparge, 'The English Folklore Corpus', p. 20.
41 F. Barth (1969) *Introduction to Ethnic Groups and Boundaries* (St Albans: Allen and Unwin), p. 16.
42 Quoted in Lee, 'Australia – Sanctuary or Cemetery for Romanies?', p. 68.
43 Ibid.
44 Barth, *Introduction to Ethnic Groups and Boundaries*, p. 38.
45 Lee, 'Australia – Sanctuary or Cemetery for Romanies?', p. 69.
46 E. H. Spicer (1971) 'Persistent Cultural Systems', *Science*, 174 (4011), pp. 795–800.
47 Quoted in Lee, 'Australia – Sanctuary or Cemetery for Romanies?', p. 69.
48 Spicer, 'Persistent Cultural Systems', p. 797.
49 R. Jenkins (1994) 'Rethinking Ethnicity: Identity, Categorization and Power', *Ethnic and Racial Studies*, 17(2), pp. 197–223.
50 M. Mann (1983) *The Macmillian Student Encyclopaedia of Sociology* (Basingstoke: Macmillian), p. 34.
51 Jenkins, 'Rethinking Ethnicity: identity', p. 203.
52 Lee, 'Australia – Sanctuary or Cemetery for Romanies?', p. 70.
53 M. Castells (1997) *The Power of Identity* (Malden, MA and Oxford: Blackwell Publishers), p. 8.
54 R. Sennett (1980) *Authority* (New York: Knopt).
55 For example, Fraser, *The Gypsies*; and D. Hawes and B. Perez (1995) *The Gypsy and the State* (Bristol: SAUS Publications).
56 A. D. Smith (1992) *Ethnic and Racial Studies* (London: Routledge), p. 513.
57 P. Gilroy (1993) *The Black Atlantic* (London and New York: Verso), pp. 201–2.
58 Jenkins, *Rethinking Ethnicity*, pp. 13–14.
59 M. Weber (1922) *Economy and Society (vol. I)* (Berkeley, CA: University of California Press), p. 385.
60 Ibid., p. 389.
61 This seems to include Barth, *Introduction to Ethnic Groups*, and E. C. Huges (1994) 'On Work', in L. A. Coser (ed.), *Race and the Sociological Imagination* (Chicago, IL: University of Chicago Press), pp. 91–6.
62 Weber, *Economy and Society*.
63 F. Parkin (1979) *Marxism and Class Theory* (London: Tavistock), Chapter Four.
64 See M. Hyman (1989) *Sites for Travellers* (London: London Race and Housing Research Unit).
65 Hawes and Perez, *The Gypsy and the State*, p. 89.
66 Ibid., pp. 109–12.
67 Hyman, *Sites for Travellers*, especially Chapter Ten.
68 See Chapter Four.
69 Barth, *Ethnic Groups and Boundaries*.
70 Quoted by W. Guy (1975) 'Ways of Looking at Roms: The Case of Czechoslovakia', in A. Rehfisch and F. Rehfisch (eds), *Gypsies, Tinkers and Other Travellers* (London: Academic Press), p. 222.
71 F. Fanon (1952) *The Wretched of the Earth* (Harmondsworth: Macgibbon and Kee/ Penguin), p. 217.
72 Ibid., pp. 83–108.
73 Ibid., p. 65.

74　A. L. Jinadu (1986) *Fanon: In Search of the African Revolution* (London: KPI), pp. 28–30.

75　See Chapter Four.

76　Ibid.

77　Fanon, *The Wretched of the Earth*, p. 97.

78　See Chapter Four.

79　Fanon, *The Wretched of the Earth*, p. 98.

80　See K. Hetherington (2000) *New Age Travellers: Vanloads of Uproarious Humanity* (London and New York: Cassell), p. 132.

81　For example see Sollors, *The Invention of Ethnicity*, pp. xiii–xiv.

82　Parkin, *Marxism and Class Theory*; Weber, *Economy and Society*.

83　Fanon, *The Wretched of the Earth*.

3　The social generation of the Traveller population

1　J. Okely (1983) *The Traveller Gypsies* (Cambridge: Cambridge University Press).

2　T. J. Cottle (1977) *Private Lives and Public Accounts* (Amherst, MA: University of Massachusetts Press), p. 2.

3　B. Adams, J. M. Okely, D. Morgan and D. Smith (1975) *Gypsies and Government Policy in England* (London: Heinemann), p. 9.

4　T. Acton (1974) *Gypsy Politics and Social Change* (London: Routledge and Kegan Paul), p. 191.

5　J. Greve (1991) *Homelessness in Britain* (York: Rowntree), p. 4.

6　J. Greve, D. Page and S. Greve (1971) *Homelessness in London* (Edinburgh: Scottish Academic Press), pp. 57, 66 – see Table 1.

7　Okely, *The Traveller Gypsies*, p. 31.

8　S. Hutson and D. Clapham (eds) (1999) *Homelessness: Public Policies and Private Troubles* (London: Cassell).

9　J. Manby (1956) *Pamphlet 188*, Fabian Research Series (London: Fabian Society).

10　In 1960, 56.5 per cent of permanent dwellings completed were for private use compared with 14.7 per cent in 1950 – Central Statistical Office.

11　S. Merrett (1979) *State Housing in Britain* (London: Routledge and Kegan Paul).

12　Ibid. – the lowest of any tenure.

13　96 per cent of the stock was built after this date.

14　J. Parker and C. Mirrlees (1972 and 1988) 'Housing' in A. H. Halsey (ed.), *Trends in British Society Since 1900* (Basingstoke: Macmillan), p. 303.

15　S. Lansley (1979) *Housing and Public Policy* (Beckenham: Croom Helm), p. 227.

16　Parker and Mirrlees, 'Housing', p. 368.

17　Greve, *Homelessness in Britain*, pp. 4–5.

18　Adams *et al.*, *Gypsies and Government Policy*, pp. 8–9.

19　No figures for this population were generated before this time.

20　Census Information, HMSO.

21　M. Smith (1975) *Gypsies: Where Now?* (London: Fabian Society), p. 4.

22　2,000 per annum – ibid.

23　Especially given infant and parent mortality rate amongst the Traveller population. In the 1990s infant mortality was approximately 50 per cent higher than the national average whilst parental mortality was around 80 per cent above the national norm (see D. Hawes and B. Perez (1995) *The Gypsy and the State* (Bristol: SAUS Publications), p. 107). It is likely that these disparities between the Traveller and non-Traveller population would have been even more marked in the 1950s.

　　Even if the population had grown to this size as a consequence of birth rate the extra 20,000 would have been between the ages of 0 and 10 and it is questionable how much impact this would have had in terms of 'visibility'. It is maybe more realistic, in terms of achieving general social discernment of a rise in the ambulant population, that the increase in numbers would be in post-school-age groups.

24 See Chapter Four.
25 Average caravan-dwelling household size had fallen from 2.44 to 2.33.
26 See Chapter Four.
27 Average caravan-dwelling household size was 2.21 persons.
28 See Chapter Four.
29 Perhaps as many as 9,000 people.
30 But the census returns did not include caravans on long-term residential sites.
31 Only about 30 per cent of the total housing stock had been available for rent in 1968.
32 Central Statistical Office.
33 Merrett, *State Housing in Britain*, pp. 196–31.
34 See Chapter Four.
35 Greve, *Homelessness in Britain*, p. 4.
36 Ibid., p. 18.
37 Ibid., p. 26.
38 Ibid., p. 18.
39 Shelter (1996) *Homelessness in England, the Facts* (London: Shelter).
40 R. Burrows, N. Pleace and D. Quilgers (1997) *Homelessness and Social Policy* (London: Routledge).
41 See figures in the last part of this chapter and Appendix Three.
42 Traditionally the most densely populated area in terms of Travellers.
43 See Chapter Four.
44 See J. Jusserand (1988) *English Wayfaring Life in the Middle Ages* (Corner House Williamstown MA and London: Methuen, repr. of 1974); and D. Mayall (1988) *Gypsy-Travellers in the Nineteenth-Century Society* (Cambridge: Cambridge University Press).
45 See Acton, *Gypsy Politics*, p. 66 for example.
46 *Oxford English Dictionary* (1999) (New York: Oxford University Press).
47 Mayall, *Gypsy-Travellers in the Nineteenth-Century*.
48 Statute of Labourers 1351.
49 See Jusserand, *English Wayfaring Life*.
50 See Chapter Four.
51 Okely, *The Traveller Gypsies*, p. 14.
52 E. Mandel (1979) *Introduction to Marxist Economic Theory* (London: Pathfinder), p. 34.
53 K. Marx (1818) *Capital Vol. 1* (Moscow: Foreign Language Publishing House, Lawrence and Wishart), p. 718.
54 See Mandel, *Introduction to Marxist Economic Theory*, p. 35.
55 J.-P. Clebert (1963) *The Gypsies* (London: Readers Union Ltd), p. 63.
56 F. Barth (1969) *Introduction to Ethnic Groups and Boundaries* (St Albans: Allen and Unwin).
57 Okely, *The Traveller Gypsies*, p. 15.
58 BBC Radio Four (FM), Monday, 28 September 1997, presenter, Rory Maclean.
59 D. McLoughlin (1994) 'Nomadism in Irish Travellers' Identity', in M. McCann, S. O'Siochain and J. Ruane (eds), *Irish Travellers: Culture and Ethnicity* (Belfast: Institute of Irish Studies, The Queen's University Belfast).
60 A fact that was not made clear during the programme.
61 That might be seen as representative of a wide range of rationalizations and justifications for travelling.
62 Bridget Gaffey in Southwark Traveller Women's Group (1992) *Moving Stories* (London: Traveller Education Team), p. 35.
63 Helen Gaffey, Ibid., p. 69.
64 Joannie McDonagh, Ibid., p. 69.
65 F. Earle, A. Dearling, H. Whittle, R. Glasse and Gubby (1994) *A Time to Travel* (Dorset: Enabler Publications).
66 J. Sandford (1973) *Gypsies* (London: Martin Secker and Warburg).
67 Clebert, *The Gypsies*, p. 212.

68 S. Toulson (1980) *The Drovers* (Aylesbury: Shire).
69 Dublin Travellers Education and Development Group (1992) *Traveller Ways Traveller Words* (Dublin: Pavee Point Publications).
70 P. Noonan (1994) 'Policy-making and Travellers in Northern Ireland', in M. McCann, S. O'Siochain and J. Ruane (ed.), *Irish Travellers: Culture and Ethnicity* (Belfast: Institute of Irish Studies, The Queens University Belfast).
71 David Ward – Stock Orchard Crescent 1991.
72 J. Okely (1975) 'Gypsies Travelling in Southern England', in F. Rehfisch (ed.), *Gypsies, Tinkers and Other Travellers* (London: Academic Press).
73 Male Traveller – Minster 1994.
74 Youth Worker – Minster 1994.
75 See in particular Earle *et al.*, *A Time to Travel.*
76 Noonan, 'Policy-making and Travellers in Northern Ireland'.
77 Earle *et al.*, (1994) *A Time to Travel*, p. 50.
78 Mary Theresa McDonagh, Dublin Travellers Education and Development Group, *Traveller Ways Traveller Words*, p. 55.
79 Margaret McDonagh, Ibid., p. 62.
80 Jim Belton snr., 1997.
81 Okely, 'Gypsies Travelling in Southern England'.
82 Violet, Canning Town, 1997.
83 Toni – unofficial site, Chigwell 1997.
84 Travellers/poorer non-Travellers moving into housing provision together.
85 Steve – unofficial site, Kent.
86 See Chapter Four.
87 Earle *et al.*, *A Time to Travel*, pp. 50–1.
88 Adams *et al.*, *Gypsies and Government Policy.*
89 Okely, *The Traveller Gypsies.*
90 G. Orwell (1937) *The Road to Wigan Pier* (London: Victor Gollancz), pp. 56–9.
91 The Traveller Law Reform Bill 2002 seems to demonstrate, to some extent, that this relationship has been acknowledged, at long last, by policy-makers.
92 See R. A. Leeson (1979) *Travelling Brothers* (St Albans: George Allen and Unwin); S. Toulson (1983) *Lost Trade Routes* (Aylesbury: Shire), and B. Spears (1995) *100 Years on the Road* (New York: Yale University Press).
93 J. L. Hammond and B. Hammond (1911) *The Village Labourer and the Town Guild* (London: Guild Books), pp. 37–204; Mayall, *Gypsy-Travellers in the Nineteenth-Century*; and D. Mayall (1995) *English Gypsies and State Politics* (Hatfield: University of Hertfordshire Press).
94 Billy 'Two Hats' – Kent, 1990.
95 Earle *et al.*, *A Time to Travel*, pp. 50, 129.
96 Ibid., p. 51.
97 See Ibid.; G. McKay (1996) *Senseless Acts of Beauty* (London and New York: Verso); and K. Hetherington (2000) *New Age Travellers: Vanloads of Uproarious Humanity* (London and New York: Cassell).
98 See A. Sampson (1997) *The Scholar Gypsy* (London: John Murray (Publishers) Ltd) for example.
99 See Mayall, *Gypsy-Travellers in the Nineteenth-Century.*
100 Orwell, *The Road to Wigan Pier.*
101 Clebert, *The Gypsies*; D. Kenrick and G. Puxon (1972) *The Destiny of Europe's Gypsies* (Hatfield: Sussex University Press); and K. Fings, H. Heuss and F. Sparing (1997) *From 'Race Science' to the Camps* (Hatfield: University of Hertfordshire Press).
102 Minster, 1997.
103 M. Weber (1922) *Economy and Society (vol. I)* (Berkeley, CA: University of California Press).

104 L. Kalaydjieva and colleagues (1998) in 'Univation, Gypsies and Genetics: New Paths to Understanding' (July 1998). Internet: http://www.avcc.edu.au/avcc/pubs/univation/ jul98/page9.htm p1.

105 Ibid.

106 Ibid.

107 Ibid.

108 Ibid., p. 2.

109 Ibid.

110 L. Kalaydjieva, G. Gresham and F. Calafell (2001) *Genetic Studies of the Roma (Gypsies): A Review* (BMC Medical Genetics 2:5.1471-2350/2/5).

111 J. Okely (1994) 'An Anthropological Perspective on Irish Travellers', in M. McCann, S. O'Siochain and J. Ruane (eds), *Irish Travellers: Culture and Ethnicity* (Belfast: Institute of Irish Studies, The Queen's University Belfast), p. 9.

112 Ibid.

113 A. Heymowski (1969) *Swedish 'Travellers' and Their Ancestry: A Social Isolate or Ethnic Minority?* (Stockholm: Almqvist and Wiksell).

114 A. Cottaar (1998) 'Dutch Travellers: Dwellings, Origins and Occupations', in L. Lucassen, W. Willems and A. Cottaar, *Gypsies and Other Itinerant Groups* (Basingstoke: Macmillan), p. 174.

115 Ibid., p. 175.

116 Ibid., p. 183.

117 Ibid., pp. 182–5.

118 Ibid., pp. 187–8.

119 Ibid.

120 The National Gypsy Council and so on.

121 Cottaar, 'Dutch Travellers'.

122 Ibid., p. 114.

123 Ibid., p. 115.

124 Ibid., p. 118.

125 Ibid.

126 Ibid., p. 120.

127 Ibid., p. 122.

128 Ibid., p. 123.

129 Ibid., p. 124.

130 Ibid., p. 125.

131 Ibid., p. 126.

132 See Chapter Four.

133 Cottaar, 'Dutch Travellers', p. 129.

134 Ibid., p. 120.

135 See Chapter Four.

136 Cottaar, 'Dutch Travellers', p. 127.

137 Ibid., p. 129.

138 This interprets as 'our interest'.

139 Cottaar, 'Dutch Travellers', p. 128.

140 Ibid., p. 131.

141 Ibid., p. 132.

142 See Chapter Four.

143 Chartered Institute of Public Finance and Accountancy (1978–96) *Homeless Statistics Actuals* (London: Chartered Institute of Public Finance and Accountancy).

144 R. Skellington in R. Dallos and E. McLaughlim (eds) (1995) *Social Problems and the Family* (London: Sage Publications), p. 240.

145 Greve, *Homelessness in Britain*, p. 12.

146 Shelter (1996) *Homelessness in England, the Facts* (London: Shelter), p. 7.

147 Skellington *et al.*, *Social Problems*.
148 See S. Hutson and D. Clapham (eds) (1999) *Homelessness: Public Policies and Private Troubles* (London: Cassell); S. Hutson and M. Liddiard (1994) *Youth Homelessness* (London: Macmillan); and M. Liddiard, 'Youth Homelessness: The Press and Public Attitudes', *Youth and Policy*, 1(59) (1998), pp. 57–69).
149 S. J. Blackman (1998) 'Young Homeless People and Social Exclusion', *Youth and Policy*, 59, 1(7).
150 See Chapter One.
151 This group may include retired, traditionally non-itinerant people who find it expedient to travel in the summer and people employed on a temporary basis by Travellers or who are working with Travellers on casual contract work for example. It may also encompass traditional Travellers who, although having access to conventional housing, maintain a penchant for travelling through a part-time option or who undertake seasonal itinerancy because of sentimental attachments, facilitating contact with friends, current or former business relationships and relatives etc.
152 See Chapter Four.
153 D. T. Goldberg (1993) *Racist Culture* (Malden, MA and Oxford: Blackwell Publishers), p. 206.
154 M. Hyman (1989) *Sites for Travellers* (London: London Race and Housing Research Unit).

4 Legislative regulation of the Traveller population

1 D. Hawes and B. Perez (1995) *The Gypsy and the State* (Bristol: SAUS Publications), pp. 17–23.
2 Ibid., p. 121.
3 J. Okely (1983) *The Traveller Gypsies* (Cambridge: Cambridge University Press), pp. 105–6.
4 Hawes and Perez, *The Gypsy and the State*, pp. 17–52.
5 N. N. Dodds (1966) *Didikois and Other Travellers* (London: Johnson Publications), p. 142.
6 The Thatcherite paranoiac nightmare of the 'enemy within'.
7 D. Kenrick and C. Clark (1995) *The Gypsies and Travellers of Britain* (Hatfield: University of Hertfordshire Press), p. 93.
8 Ibid., pp. 103–12.
9 See Appendix Four.
10 G. McKay (1996) *Senseless Acts of Beauty* (London and New York: Verso), pp. 159–82.
11 R. Morris and L. Clements (eds) (1999) *Gaining Ground: Law Reform for Gypsies and Travellers* (Hatfield: University of Hertfordshire Press).
12 Ministry of Housing and Local Government.
13 Okely, *The Traveller Gypsies*, pp. 20–1; and A. Fraser (1992) *The Gypsies* (Oxford and Malden, MA: Blackwell Publishers).
14 See Appendix Four.
15 Okely (1983) *The Traveller Gypsies*, p. 22. The need to control caravan sites demonstrates the growth of such provision in the light of housing shortages. This amounts to a confirmation that a drift from conventional housing to caravan-dwelling was taking place.
16 A number of whom were themselves caravan-dwellers.
17 See B. Adams, J. M. Okely, D. Morgan and D. Smith (1975) *Gypsies and Government Policy in England* (London: Heinemann), pp. 9–10.
18 M. Smith (1975) *Gypsies: Where Now?* (London: Fabian Society), p. 7.
19 Ibid.
20 Adams *et al.*, *Gypsies and Government Policy*, p. 11.

21 See T. Acton (1974) *Gypsy Politics and Social Change* (London: Routledge and Kegan Paul), pp. 134–6, 148, 166, 174–9; and M. Hyman (1989) *Sites for Travellers* (London: London Race and Housing Research Unit), pp. 160–1.
22 Adams *et al.*, *Gypsies and Government Policy*.
23 Adams *et al.*, *Gypsies and Government Policy*; and Smith, *Gypsies: Where Now?*, p. 9.
24 The main source of site provision before the 1968 Act.
25 Adams *et al.*, *Gypsies and Government Policy*; Acton, *Gypsy Politics*; J. Okely (1975) 'Gypsies Travelling in Southern England', in F. Rehfisch (ed.), *Gypsies, Tinkers and Other Travellers* (London: Academic Press).
26 Often Travellers camped on county boarders, crossing over alternatively as they were moved on by each local authority in turn.
27 Okely, *The Traveller Gypsies*, p. 106.
28 Hawes and Perez, *The Gypsy and the State*, Chapter 7.
29 See Okely, *The Traveller Gypsies*, p. 110.
30 Adams *et al.*, *Gypsies and Government Policy*, pp. 13–14.
31 With whom the Gypsy Council had affiliated.
32 Ministry of Housing and Local Government/Welsh Office (1967) *Gypsies and Other Travellers* (London: HMSO).
33 It assumed many families did not want to live full-time in a caravan.
34 Acton, *Gypsy Politics*, p. 175.
35 Its powers were applicable only to England and Wales.
36 Notably the Police Criminal Evidence Act 1984 and the Public Order Act 1986.
37 Okely, *The Traveller Gypsies*, p. 105.
38 Control powers could be applied to 'any person being a Gypsy'.
39 Section 12, 1968 Caravan Sites Act.
40 G. Orwell (1937) *The Road to Wigan Pier* (London: Victor Gollancz) and pp. 80–5 above.
41 Adams *et al.*, *Gypsies and Government Policy*, p. 17.
42 As he was then.
43 This definition was later applied to the boundary of highways.
44 Prepared by Alan Williams MP and Alistair MacDonald MP for a Labour Back-Bench committee on local government – July 1967.
45 Acton, *Gypsy Politics*, p. 180.
46 Smith, *Gypsies: Where Now?*, p. 9.
47 Section 10, Caravan Sites Act 1968.
48 Ibid., Section 11.
49 Smith, *Gypsies*.
50 The legislation made it an offence for any person 'being a Gypsy' to station a caravan on land without the consent of the owner of that land.
51 Hawes and Perez, *The Gypsy and the State*, Chapter 2.
52 See Adams *et al.*, *Gypsies and Government Policy*.
53 Ibid., p. 246.
54 Department of the Environment and Welsh Office 1977, pp. 6, 8.
55 London boroughs were, in any case, not obliged to provide more than fifteen pitches, no matter how many Gypsies had been residing in or resorting to their area of jurisdiction.
56 Okely, *The Traveller Gypsies*, p. 110.
57 Ministry of Housing and Local Government/Welsh Office, *Gypsies and Other Travellers*.
58 Fraser, *The Gypsies*, p. 283.
59 R. Morris and L. Clements (2001) *The Cost of Unauthorized Encampments* (Cardiff: TLRU, Cardiff Law School).
60 Okely, *The Traveller Gypsies*, p. 124.
61 See Chapter Three.

62 Typical was *West Glamorgan County Council* v. *Rafferty* in 1987. Here the court prevented a local authority from carrying out an eviction of Gypsies from its land because it had not provided adequate site provision.

63 *Buckley* v. *UK* No. 20348/93 decision 3 March 1994.

64 Hyman, *Sites for Travellers*, pp. 85–6.

65 See Appendix Four.

66 Ibid.

67 For example the Highways Act 1980, the Law of Property Act 1925 (camping on common land) and the Environmental Protection Act 1990.

68 Which provides restricted provision for security of tenure on public Gypsy sites (Mobile Homes Act 1983, 5(1), excludes public sites from the security of tenure provisions of the Mobile Homes Acts).

69 See Appendix Four for a detailed analysis of this legislation.

70 Formally embodied in caravan-dwelling terms in the local authority site.

71 Adverse occupation of residential premises and *ex parte* interim possession orders.

72 F. Earle, A. Dearling, H. Whittle, R. Glasse and Gubby (1994) *A Time to Travel* (Dorset: Enabler Publications), p. 154.

73 Gary in Earle *et al.*, *A Time to Travel*.

74 Ibid.

75 Orwell, *The Road to Wigan Pier* and pp. 80–5 above.

76 The early 1990s seem to qualify.

77 Part of a group that lived (were accommodated) literally on the periphery of society.

78 See for example M. Wilson (1998) *A Directory of Planning Policies for Gypsy Site Provision* (Bristol: The Policy Press), p. 104.

79 According to the Department of the Environments' biannual caravan counts between 1986 and 1996 there was a fall of about 1,100 caravans on unauthorized sites.

80 See Chapter Three.

81 See Department of the Environment 1991, p. 32.

82 As argued by Smith, *Gypsies: Where Now?*, p. 4.

83 This would likely need to be the case for this population to have sustained such a growth rate.

84 See Hawes and Perez, *The Gypsy and the State*, p. 107.

85 A detailed analysis of the Bill may be found in Appendix Four.

86 From hence forward, in this section, to be known as 'the Bill'.

87 See Gypsy Organizations in Chapter One and Appendix Two.

88 Niall Crowley (then Projects Manager, Pavee Point Travellers Centre, Dublin; now Chief Executive Officer of The Equality Authority in Ireland) in L. Clements and P. Smith (1997) *Traveller Law Reform: TLAST and TLRU Conference and Consolation Report* (Cardiff: Traveller Law Research Unit, Cardiff Law School), p. 1.

89 Morris and Clements, *The Cost of Unauthorized Encampments*.

90 Ministerial advice issued by Nic Raynsford MP (May 1998) and Chris Mullin MP (Sept. 1999) Department of the Environment, Transport and the Regions, London.

91 October 1998.

92 HSC 2000/10 and LAC (2000) 9.

93 1998 SI 2998.

94 Speech, DETR Minister Nic Raynsford MP, 29 October 1998.

95 See L. Clements in *Travellers' Times*, 9, August 2000.

96 The report included a catalogue of the substantial legal prejudice experienced by Gypsies and Travellers in the United Kingdom and concludes:

> In the face of these difficulties, the itinerant life style which has typified the Gypsies is under threat. As Justice Henry observed when he cited the need for the policy embodied in Britain's Caravan Sites Act 1968 (now abandoned) of making adequate provision for caravan sites: 'If there are not sufficient sites

where Gypsies may lawfully stop, then they will be without the law whenever and wherever they stop. This will result either in them being harried from place to place, or in them being allowed to remain where they should not lawfully be.'

(*R* v. *Hereford and Worcester CC ex parte Smith* (1988) transcript, pp. 24–5)

97 Morris and Clements, *The Cost of Unauthorized Encampments*, suggest that from the perspective of 'Best Value' a national site provision strategy may be significantly more cost efficient than the previous practice. The consultation paper preceding the 1994 legislation emphasized the cost to the public purse of providing sites for Gypsies, indicating that (since 1970) this had amounted to £56 million. No research existed to assess whether the cost to the public purse of not providing sites would be any more or less costly. However, local authorities, the police and government departments as well as private individuals and businesses have expended considerable resources evicting Gypsies and Travellers who have had no lawful place to site their caravans.

98 See for example *West Glamorgan County Council* v. *Rafferty* [1987] 1 All ER 1015.

99 See the analysis of the Bill in Appendix Four.

100 For instance, the measures in clauses 14–15 (which extend the Housing Corporation's funding remit to include caravan site construction) could be incorporated into a general Housing Bill; or the necessary amendments to the criminal trespass provisions (in clause 13) could be incorporated into a general Criminal Justice Bill.

101 In 1999 the Joseph Rowntree Charitable Trust supported a research project which sought to develop consultation of and discussion with Gypsies and Travellers, their representative organizations and service providers, with the aim of transforming a selection of the reform proposals into a draft parliamentary Bill. Following 18 months of consultation and discussion by way of regional meetings, private correspondence and oral submissions, the annual Traveller Law Reform Conference took place on 19 September 2000 in London.

102 See p. 111 above. After becoming a Knight of the Realm Joseph would become one of the architects of the Thatcher Conservative dynasty that would preside over the effective dismantling of social housing provision in Britain, the strangulation of the Trade Union movement and the rise of the State intervention into and control of public life by way of the Criminal Justice Acts of the 1980s and 1990s.

103 Orwell, *The Road to Wigan Pier* and pp. 80–5 above.

104 Although as J.-P. Liegeois (1986) *Gypsies: An Illustrated History* (London: Al Saqi Books) and Hawes and Perez, *The Gypsy and the State*, have pointed out, this is not a necessary adjunct in terms of Gypsy culture.

5 Power, knowledge, truth and the prison

1 D. Hawes and B. Perez (1995) *The Gypsy and the State* (Bristol: SAUS Publications).

2 M. Foucault (1977) *Discipline and Punish* (Harmondsworth: Penguin), pp. 293–308.

3 K. Marx quoted in T. Carver (1982) *Marx's Social Theory* (Oxford: Oxford University Press), p. 22.

4 See H. Marcuse (1968) *Reason and Revolution* (Boston, MA: Beacon Press), pp. 389–98; Carver, *Marx's Social Theory*, pp. 45–8; A. Brewer (1984) *A Guide to Marx's Capital* (Cambridge: Cambridge University Press), pp. 2 and 185.

5 B. Brect (1985) *Mother Courage and Her Children* (London: Methuen).

6 Including the 1994 Criminal Justice Act and the Traveller Law Reform Bill 2002.

7 B. Mussolini (1935) *Fascism: Political and Social Doctrine* (Rome: Ardita), pp. 27–9.

8 Hawes and Perez, *The Gypsy and the State*.

9 K. Marx (1849) in A. Meyer (1954) *Marxism: The Unity of Theory and Practice* (Cambridge, MA: Harvard University Press), p. 8.

10 K. Marx (1935) *The Eighteenth Brumarie of Louis Nonaparte* (New York: International Publishers), p. 13.
11 L. McNay (1994) *Foucault: A Critical Introduction* (Cambridge, MA: Polity Press), p. 88.
12 M. Foucault (1972) *The Archaeology of Knowledge* (London: Tavistock Publications), p. 55.
13 M. Foucault, 'Nietzche, Genealogy, History', in P. Rabinow (ed.) (1986) *The Foucault Reader* (London: Peregrine), p. 89.
14 A. Fraser (1992) *The Gypsies* (Oxford and Malden, MA: Blackwell Publishers).
15 McNay, *Foucault: A Critical Introduction*, p. 89.
16 Ibid., see also Fraser, *The Gypsies*, pp. 84–5.
17 Hawes and Perez, *The Gypsy and the State*.
18 McNay, *Foucault*.
19 This is an echo of the thought of Pico Della Mirandola (1463–94), who undertook the great oration, *On the Dignity of Man, On Being and the One Heptaplus* (Indianapolis, New York, Kansas City: The Bobbs-Merrill Company, 1965) one of the seminal humanist texts of the Renaissance concept of man, which argues that God did not make human-beings fixed, but fluid and changing.
20 Foucault, 'Nietzche, Genealogy, History', p. 85.
21 McNay, *Foucault: A Critical Introduction*, p. 91.
22 Of which the State has a monopoly.
23 McNay, *Foucault*.
24 For example see T. Acton (1974) *Gypsy Politics and Social Change* (London: Routledge and Kegan Paul); and Fraser, *The Gypsies*.
25 Foucault, 'Nietzche, Genealogy, History', p. 83.
26 See Chapters One and Two.
27 As exemplified in Acton, *Gypsy Politics and Social Change*; Hawes and Perez, *The Gypsy and the State*; and J. Okely (1983) *The Traveller Gypsies* (Cambridge: Cambridge University Press).
28 Hawes and Perez, *The Gypsy and the State*.
29 Quoted in C. Gordon (ed.) (1980) *Power/Knowledge: Selected Interviews and Other Writings 1972–1977 by Michel Foucault* (New York: Pantheon), p. 102.
30 In 1972 the National Council for Civil Liberties, 'Gypsies and Civil Liberties 1967–72' (memorandum), concluded that the site-building programme was more than a problem, it was a national disgrace.
31 That the Caravan Sites Act only required 15 pitches per local authority as minimum provision can be seen as part of the problem.
32 See Chapter Four and Appendix Four.
33 D. Kenrick and C. Clark (1995) *The Gypsies and Travellers of Britain* (Hatfield: University of Hertfordshire Press).
34 Foucault, *Discipline and Punish*.
35 As the site is taken to be the 'natural' place for Gypsies, as exemplified in the Traveller Law Reform Bill 2002.
36 The 'truth' as framed by Hawes and Perez, *The Gypsy and the State* for instance.
37 Housing that feeds or is set within the capitalist nexus.
38 Chiefly by theorists but also professionals involved in Traveller issues.
39 Foucault, *Discipline and Punish*.
40 This exemplifies power saturated knowledge.
41 Perhaps this is why those involved with Traveller affairs are so keen to campaign for sites instead of, for example, widespread social housing. The successful accomplishment of provision of sites may confirm their credentials as Champions of the downtrodden Gypsies and subdue the unconscious guilt (cradled in white European history) of fostering the notion of human differentiation.
42 Foucault, *Discipline and Punish*, pp. 170–1.
43 Ibid.

44 Ibid., p. 194.
45 Established in the school, prison, the site etc.
46 J. Okely (1983) *The Traveller Gypsies* (Cambridge: Cambridge University Press), p. 77.
47 Foucault, *Discipline and Punish*, p. 208.
48 Hawes and Perez, *The Gypsy and the State*.

Conclusion

1 J. O'Connell (1994) 'Ethnicity and Irish Travellers', in M. McCann, S. O'Siochain and J. Ruane (eds), *Irish Travellers: Culture and Ethnicity* (Belfast: Institute of Irish Studies, The Queen's University Belfast), pp. 111–12.
2 D. Hawes and B. Perez (1995) *The Gypsy and the State* (Bristol: SAUS Publications), p. 12.
3 W. Willems (1997) *In Search of the True Gypsy: From Enlightenment to Final Solution* (London: Frank Cass Publishers); and J. Lucassen, W. Willems, A. Cottaar (1998) *Gypsies and Other Itinerant Groups: A Socio-Historical Approach* (Basingstoke: Macmillan).
4 H. O'Nions (1995) 'The Marginalization of Gypsies', *Web Journal of Current Legal Issues* (London: Blackstone Press), p. 13.
5 Hawes and Perez, *The Gypsy and the State*, p. 4.
6 T. Acton (1974) *Gypsy Politics and Social Change* (London: Routledge and Kegan Paul), pp. 55–7; A. Fraser (1992) *The Gypsies* (Oxford and Malden, MA: Blackwell Publishers), pp. 2–27.
7 J. Okely (1994) 'An Anthropological Perspective on Irish Travellers', in M. McCann, S. O'Siochain and J. Ruane (eds), *Irish Travellers: Culture and Ethnicity* (Belfast: Institute of Irish Studies, The Queen's University Belfast), pp. 68–9, 72–4.
8 Ibid., pp. 78–86.
9 Ibid., pp. 76–86.
10 S. Hall (1981a) 'Cultural Studies: Two Paradigms', in T. Bennett, G. Martin, C. Mercer, C. Woollacott (eds), *Culture, Ideology and Social Process* (Milton Keynes: Open University/ Batsford).
11 K. Malik (1996) *The Meaning of Race* (Basingstoke: Macmillan), p. 13.
12 A. D. Smith (1992) *Ethnic and Racial Studies* (London: Routledge), p. 13.
13 A. Rehfisch and F. Rehfisch (1975) 'Scottish Travellers or Tinkers', in F. Rehfisch (ed.), *Gypsies, Tinkers and Other Travellers* (London: Academic Press).
14 See also F. Barth (1975) 'The Social Organization of a Pariah Group in Norway', in F. Rehfisch (ed.), *Gypsies, Tinkers and Other Travellers* (London: Academic Press), p. 28.
15 The 'oppressors' – see O'Nions, 'The Marginalization of Gypsies'.
16 D. Kasler (1988) *Max Weber* (Cambridge: Polity Press), p. 150.
17 F. Parkin (1979) *Marxism and Class Theory* (London: Tavistock).
18 M. Foucault (1977) *Discipline and Punish* (Harmondsworth: Penguin).
19 Parkin, *Marxism and Class Theory*, Chapter 4.
20 F. Fanon (1952) *The Wretched of the Earth* (Harmondsworth: Macgibbon and Kee/ Penguin); and F. Fanon (1961) *Black Skins, White Masks* (London: Pluto Press).
21 L.-P. Liegeois (1994) *Roma, Gypsies, Travellers* (Strasbourg: Council of Europe Press), p. 45.
22 A. Montagu (1997) *Man's Most Dangerous Myth: The Fallacy of Race* (Walnut Creek, CA: AltaMira Press).
23 G. Orwell (1937) *The Road to Wigan Pier* (London: Victor Gollancz).
24 A. Cottaar (1998a) 'The Making of a Minority: the Case of Dutch Travellers', in L. Lucassen, W. Willems and A. Cottaar, *Gypsies and Other Itinerant Groups* (Basingstoke: Macmillan).
25 Foucault, *Discipline and Punish*.
26 Ibid.
27 Hawes and Perez, *The Gypsy and the State*, p. 17 for example.

28 P. Gilroy (2000) *Between Camps: Race, Identity and Nationalism at the End of the Colour Line* (London: Allen Lane), pp. 327–58.
29 Gilroy, *Between Camps*.
30 It seems likely that Travellers do not constitute a population as such but are a number of sometimes overlapping, sometimes separate groups. However, for brevity's sake, I refer to these very disparate groups as a population.
31 See Chapter Four.
32 Willems, *In Search of the True Gypsy*.
33 K. Hetherington (2000) *New Age Travellers: Vanloads of Uproarious Humanity* (London and New York: Cassell), pp. 92–3.
34 M. Weber (1922) *Economy and Society (vol. I)* (Berkeley, CA: University of California Press), p. 389.
35 Montagu, *Man's Most Dangerous Myth*.
36 Ibid.

Appendix 1

1 J. Okely (1994) 'An Anthropological Perspective on Irish Travellers', in M. McCann, S. O'Siochain and J. Ruane (eds), *Irish Travellers: Culture and Ethnicity* (Belfast: Institute of Irish Studies, The Queen's University Belfast), p. 15.
2 Ibid., p. 11.
3 The validity of this method again dates back to the Chicago School with Nels Anderson's 1921 study on hobos and the work of Howard Becker and more recent work on feminist biography. See R. Rauty (ed.) (1998) *Nels Anderson: On Hobos and Homelessness* (Chicago, IL and London: University of Chicago Press); J. Ribbens and R. Edwards (eds) (1998) *Feminist Dilemmas in Qualitative Research: Public Knowledge and Private Lives* (Thousand Oaks, CA: Sage Publications); H. S. Becker (1963) *Outsiders* (New York: Free Press) and H. S. Becker (1964) *The Other Side* (New York: Free Press).
4 Okely, 'An Anthropological Perspective'.

Appendix 2

1 Of Chapter One, pp. 43–6.
2 D. Hawes and B. Perez (1995) *The Gypsy and the State* (Bristol: SAUS Publications), p. 60.
3 C. Kiddle (1999) *Traveller Children: A Voice for Themselves* (London and Philadelphia, PA: Jessica Kingsley Publishers), p. 50.
4 T. Acton (1974) *Gypsy Politics and Social Change* (London: Routledge and Kegan Paul), p. 225.
5 J. Okely (1983) *The Traveller Gypsies* (Cambridge: Cambridge University Press), pp. 22–3.
6 Acton (1974) *Gypsy Politics and Social Change*, p. 183.
7 The cost of affiliation ranged from five shillings (25p) to one pound.
8 Acton, *Gypsy Politics*.
9 Whose interest had in large measure been aroused by the writings of George Borrow, see W. Willems (1997) *In Search of the True Gypsy: From Enlightenment to Final Solution* (London: Frank Cass Publishers). 'George Burrows (1803–81): the walking lord of Gypsy lore', pp. 93–170.
10 A. Fraser (1992) *The Gypsies* (Oxford and Malden, MA: Blackwell Publishers), p. 256.
11 Hawes and Perez, *The Gypsy and the State*, pp. 63–4.
12 Ibid.
13 Ibid.
14 Ibid.

Appendix 3

1 'The Social Generation of the Traveller Population', pp. 59–107.
2 pp. 100–2.
3 p. 106.

Appendix 4

1 See Chapter Four.
2 L. J. Clements and S. Campbell (1995) 'Traveller Law and the Criminal Justice and Public Order Act 1994', Paper for 'Save the Children' seminar (Cardiff: Cardiff Law School, University of Wales: Unpublished).
3 For exceptions see First Schedule Caravan Sites and Control of Development Act and Schedule 2 Part V Town and Country Planning General Development Order 1968.
4 Section 172 Town and Country Planning Act 1990.
5 Even if appealed.
6 *Mole Valley* v. *Smith*, 1992.
7 Clements and Campbell, *Traveller Law*.
8 D. Hawes and B. Perez (1995) *The Gypsy and the State* (Bristol: SAUS Publications), Chapter 2.
9 Ibid., Chapter 6.
10 Clements and Campbell, *Traveller Law*.
11 See R. Lowe and W. Shaw (1993) *Travellers: Voices of the New Age Nomads* (London: Forth Estate).
12 Hansard (7.9.94) House of Lords: cols. 1121–2.
13 Clements and Campbell, *Traveller Law*.
14 Hansard – Lord Avebury, House of Lords, 7.6.94, col. 1118. In the year before April 1967, Wolverhampton, for example moved 1,456 caravans from its area, in 251 separate operations, 5 evictions per week on average. This of course meant that Walsall, next door to Wolverhampton, was involved in similar type and level of activity – B. Adams, J. M. Okely, D. Morgan and D. Smith, *Gypsies and Government Policy in England* (London: Heinemann), p. 200.
15 Section 6.
16 Section 9.
17 Sections 10–12.
18 Clements and Campbell, *Traveller Law*.
19 Hansard (26.7.93), House of Commons: volume 229, adjournment debate: cols. 972.
20 Letter from the Association of Chief Police Officers to Labour Campaign for Travellers Rights, 15.1.93.
21 Police Gazette Editorial, September 1992.
22 Hansard (7.6.94), House of Lords: Lord Avebury, cols. 1117.
23 It did not matter if their presence on the land was legal.
24 Hansard (2/94), House of Commons: Standing Committee B: col. 533.
25 Twelve had been the former limit.
26 Chief Constable Guidance, Home Office Circular 37/1991: 22/5/91. Clements and Campbell, *Traveller Law*.
27 See Hansard (11.7.94), House of Lords: cols. 1526–7 and 1560.
28 *Krumpa* v. *Anderson* (1989) Criminal Law Record 295.
29 Clements and Campbell, *Traveller Law*.
30 Hansard (31.3.93), House of Commons: Written answer: col. 292.
31 Being loud and taking place over a prolonged period of time.
32 This might be understood as a direct attack on what G. McKay (1996) *Senseless Acts of Beauty* (London and New York: Verso), p. 2, refers to as 'Counter Culture' and 'cultures of resistance', as described by T. Roszak, *The Making of Counter Culture: Reflections of the*

Technocratic Society and Its Youthful Opposition (London: Faber and Faber), which is embodied in, for example, New Age Travellers.

33 Ibid., p. 9.

34 *Observer*, 19.6.94, p. 3.

35 See Chapter Four, pp. 123–8.

36 With the benefit of Housing Corporation financial support if needs be.

37 Which include temporary stopping places.

38 Clause 6(1)(d).

39 Reinstating but adjusting local authority funding that existed within the 1968 Caravan Sites Act.

40 The current pattern of provision.

41 Under clause 3: This provision is modelled on the Housing (Traveller Accommodation) Act 1998 in the Republic of Ireland, although the present Bill creates a less elaborate scheme.

42 Clause 2(1)(b)(i).

43 It remedies the anomalous situation created by *R* v. *Brighton Council ex p Marmont* (1998) and *R* v. *Hillingdon LBC ex p McDonagh* (1998) which suggested that the duty to follow governmental good practice guidance did not apply to certain forms of enforcement action.

44 Article 8(2).

45 As part of their educational development plans.

46 Of whatever age and including vocational training.

47 Twelve or more persons and 12 or more vehicles.

48 Their local site, or the site where they 'came from'.

49 Now known as registered social landlords.

50 To facilitate the provision of accommodation for Travellers.

51 See L. Clements and P. Elkin (2001) *Human Rights Act – Gypsies and Other Travellers* (Cardiff: TLRU, Cardiff Law School), p. 2.

Bibliography

Acton, T., *Gypsy Politics and Social Change* (London: Routledge and Kegan Paul, 1974).
—— *The Social Construction of the Ethnic Identity of Commercial Nomadic Groups* in J. Grumet (ed.), *Papers from the 4th and 5th Annual Meetings of the GLSNAC* (1985).
—— 'Categorising Irish Travellers', in M. McCann, S. O'Siochain and J. Ruane (eds), *Irish Travellers: Culture and Ethnicity* (Belfast: Institute of Irish Studies, The Queen's University Belfast, 1994).
Adams, B., Okely, J. M., Morgan, D. and Smith, D., *Gypsies and Government Policy in England* (London: Heinemann, 1975).
Anderson, N., *The Hobo: The Sociology of the Homeless Man* (Chicago, IL: University of Chicago Press, 1923).
Azoulay, K. G., *Black, Jewish and Interracial: It's Not the Color of Your Skin, but the Race of Your Kin, and Other Myths of Identity* (Durham, NC and London: Duke University Press, 1997).
Banton, M., 'The Idiom of Race', in S. Back and J. Solomos (eds), *Theories of Race and Racism: A Reader* (London and New York: Routledge, 2000).
Barnes, B., 'Irish Travelling People', in F. Rehfisch (ed.), *Gypsies, Tinkers and Other Travellers* (London: Academic Press, 1975).
Barth, F., *Introduction to Ethnic Groups and Boundaries* (St Albans: Allen and Unwin, 1969).
—— *Ethnic Groups and Boundaries* (London: George Allen and Unwin, 1970).
—— 'The Social Organization of a Pariah Group in Norway', in F. Rehfisch (ed.), *Gypsies, Tinkers and Other Travellers* (London: Academic Press, 1975).
Becker, H. S., *Outsiders* (New York: Free Press, 1963).
—— *The Other Side* (New York: Free Press, 1964).
Biko, S., *I Write What I Like* (London: Heinemann, 1987).
Blackman, S. J., 'Young Homeless People and Social Exclusion', *Youth and Policy*, 59, 1(7) (1998).
Boas, F., *The Mind of Primitive Man* (New York: Free Press, 1911).
Brah, A., *Cartographies of Diaspora: Contesting Identities* (London: Routledge, 1996).
Brecht, B., *Mother Courage and Her Children* (London: Methuen, 1985).
Brewer, A., *A Guide to Marx's Capital* (Cambridge: Cambridge University Press, 1984).
Burns, T., *Erving Goffman* (London: Routledge, 1992).
Burrows, R., Pleace, N. and Quilgers, D., *Homelessness and Social Policy* (London: Routledge, 1997).
Carver, T., *Marx's Social Theory* (Oxford: Oxford University Press, 1982).
Castells, M., *The Power of Identity* (Malden, MA and Oxford: Blackwell Publishers, 1997).
Chapman, M. (ed.), *Social and Biological Aspects of Ethnicity* (Oxford: Oxford University Press, 1993).

Chartered Institute of Public Finance and Accountancy, *Homeless Statistics Actuals* (London: Chartered Institute of Public Finance and Accountancy, 1978–96).

Clebert, J.-P., *The Gypsies* (London: Readers Union Ltd, 1963).

Clements, L., 'The Traveller Law Reform Bill' in *Travellers' Times* magazine (TLRU, Cardiff Law School, Issue 9, August 2000).

Clements, L. J. and Campbell, S., 'Traveller Law and the Criminal Justice and Public Order Act 1994', Paper for 'Save the Children' seminar (Cardiff: Cardiff Law School, University of Wales: Unpublished, 1995).

Clements, L. and Elkin, P., *Human Rights Act – Gypsies and Other Travellers* (Cardiff: TLRU, Cardiff Law School, 2001).

Clements, L. and Smith, P., *Traveller Law Reform: TLAST and TLRU Conference and Consolation Report* (Cardiff: Traveller Law Research Unit, Cardiff Law School, 1997).

Clifford, J., *Routes Travel and Translation in the Late Twentieth Century* (Cambridge, MA: Harvard University Press, 1997).

Cornell, S. and Hartmann, D., *Ethnicity and Race: Making Identities in a Changing World* (London and New Delhi: Pine Forge Press, Sage Publications, 1998).

Cottaar, A., 'The Making of a Minority: the Case of Dutch Travellers', in L. Lucassen, W. Willems and A. Cottaar, *Gypsies and Other Itinerant Groups* (Basingstoke: Macmillan, 1998a).

—— 'Dutch Travellers: Dwellings, Origins and Occupations', in L. Lucassen, W. Willems and A. Cottaar, *Gypsies and Other Itinerant Groups* (Basingstoke: Macmillan, 1998b).

Cottle, T. J., *Private Lives and Public Accounts* (Amherst, MA: University of Massachusetts Press, 1977).

Department of the Environment, *Counting Gypsies* (London: HMSO, 1991).

—— *The Biannual Caravan Counts* (London: HMSO, 1978 to 1996).

Dodds, N. N., *Didikois and Other Travellers* (London: Johnson Publications, 1966).

Dublin Travellers Education and Development Group, *Traveller Ways Traveller Words* (Dublin: Pavee Point Publications, 1992).

Durkheim, E., *Elementary Forms of Religious Life* (St Albans: Allen and Unwin, 1915).

Earle, F., Dearling, A., Whittle, H., Glasse, R. and Gubby, *A Time to Travel* (Dorset: Enabler Publications, 1994).

Encarta Online, *Social Science: Anthropology Roma*, in *Encarta Concise Encyclopaedia* (Encarta Online, 1998).

Fanon, F., *The Wretched of the Earth* (Harmondsworth: Macgibbon and Kee/Penguin, 1952).

—— *Black Skins, White Masks* (London: Pluto Press, 1961).

Fenton, S., *Ethnicity: Racism, Class and Culture* (Basingstoke: Macmillan, 1999).

Fings, K., Heuss, H. and Sparing, F., *From 'Race Science' to the Camps* (Hatfield: University of Hertfordshire Press, 1997).

Fonseca, I., *Bury Me Standing* (London: Chatto and Windus, 1995).

Foucault, M., *The Archaeology of Knowledge* (London: Tavistock Publications, 1972).

—— *Discipline and Punish* (Harmondsworth: Penguin, 1977).

—— in C. Gordon (ed.), *Power/Knowledge: Selected Interviews and Other Writings 1972–77 by M. Foucault* (New York: Pantheon, 1980).

—— 'Nietzche, Genealogy, History', in P. Rabinow (ed.), *The Foucault Reader* (London: Peregrine, 1986).

Fraser, A., *The Gypsies* (Oxford and Malden, MA: Blackwell Publishers, 1992).

Geertz, C., *The Interpretation of Cultures* (New York: Basic Books, 1973).

Gilroy, P., *The Black Atlantic* (London and New York: Verso, 1993).

—— *Between Camps: Race, Identity and Nationalism at the End of the Colour Line* (London: Allen Lane, 2000).

Goldberg, D. T., *Racist Culture* (Malden, MA and Oxford: Blackwell Publishers, 1993).

Goldschmidt, W., *The Human Career: The Self in the Symbolic World* (Malden, MA and Oxford: Blackwell Publishers, 1990).

Gordon, C. (ed.), *Power/Knowledge: Selected Interviews and Other Writings 1972–77 by Michael Foucault* (New York: Pantheon, 1980).

Greve, J., *Homelessness in Britain* (York: Rowntree, 1991).

Greve, J., Page, D. and Greve, S., *Homelessness in London* (Edinburgh: Scottish Academic Press, 1971).

Guy, W., 'Ways of Looking at Roms: The Case of Czechoslovakia', in F. Rehfisch (ed.), *Gypsies, Tinkers and Other Travellers* (London: Academic Press, 1975).

Hall, S., 'Racism and Reaction', in Commission for Racial Equality (eds), *Five Views of Multi-cultural Britain* (London: Commission for Racial Equality, 1978).

—— 'Cultural Studies: Two Paradigms', in T. Bennett, G. Martin, C. Mercer, C. Woollacott (eds), *Culture, Ideology and Social Process* (Milton Keynes: Open University/ Batsford, 1981a).

—— 'Teaching Race', in A. James and R. Jeffcoate (eds), *The School in the Multicultural Society – A Reader* (London: Harper and Row, 1981b).

—— 'Cultural Identity and Diaspora', in J. Rutherford (ed.), *Identity, Community, Culture and Difference* (London: Lawrence and Wishart, 1990). First published in *Framework*, 1(36).

—— 'The Local and the Global', in A. D. King (ed.), *Culture, Globalization and the World System* (London: Macmillan, 1991).

—— (1992) 'Our Mongrel Selves', *New Statesman and Society*, supplement, 19 (June 1996), pp. 6–8.

Hall, S. and du Gay, P. (eds), *Questions of Cultural Identity* (London: Sage, 1996).

Hammond, J. L. and Hammond, B., *The Village Labourer and the Town Guild* (London: Guild Books, 1911).

Hancock, I., Dowd, S. and Djuric, R. (eds), *The Roads of the Roma* (Hatfield: University of Hertfordshire Press, 1998).

Hansard (31.3.93) House of Commons: Written answer: col. 292.

Hansard (26.7.93) House of Commons: volume 229, adjournment debate: cols. 970–6.

Hansard (2/94) House of Commons: Standing Committee B: col. 533.

Hansard (7.9.94) House of Lords: cols. 1121–2.

Hansard (7.6.94) House of Lords: Lord Avebury, cols. 1117 and 1118.

Hansard (11.7.94) House of Lords: cols. 1526–7 and 1560.

Hansard (7.6.94) House of Lords: cols. 1121–2.

Hansard – Lord Avebury, House of Lords, 7.6.94, col. 1118 – in the year before April 1967.

Harvey, D. C., Jones, R., McInroy, N. and Milligan, C. (eds), *Celtic Geographies: Old Cultures, New Times* (London: Routledge, 2002).

Hawes, D. and Perez, B., *The Gypsy and the State* (Bristol: SAUS Publications, 1995).

Henderson, H., *Alias MacAlias* (Edinburgh: Polygon, 1992).

Hetherington, K., *New Age Travellers: Vanloads of Uproarious Humanity* (London and New York: Cassell, 2000).

Heymowski, A., *Swedish 'Travellers' and Their Ancestry: A Social Isolate or Ethnic Minority?* (Stockholm: Almqvist and Wiksell, 1969).

Hobsbawn, E. and Ranger, T. (eds), *The Invention of Tradition* (Cambridge: Cambridge University Press, 1983).

Hoggart, R., *The Uses of Literacy* (London: Chatto and Windus, 1957).

Huges, E. C., 'On Work', in L. A. Coser (ed.), *Race and the Sociological Imagination* (Chicago, IL: University of Chicago Press, 1994).

Huseby-Darvas, E. V., 'The Search for Hungarian National Identity', in L. Romanucci-Ross and G. DeVos (eds), *Ethnic Identity* (Walnut Creek, CA: AltaMira Press, Sage Publications, 1995).

Hutchinson, J. and Smith, A. D. (eds), *Ethnicity* (Oxford and New York: Oxford University Press, 1996).

Hutson, S. and Clapham, D. (eds), *Homelessness: Public Policies and Private Troubles* (London: Cassell, 1999).

Hutson, S. and Liddiard, M., *Youth Homelessness* (London: Macmillan, 1994).

Hyman, M., *Sites for Travellers* (London: London Race and Housing Research Unit, 1989).

Jenkins, R., 'Rethinking Ethnicity: Identity, Categorization and Power', *Ethnic and Racial Studies*, 17(2) (1994), pp. 197–223.

—— *Social Identity* (London: Routledge, 1996).

Jinadu, A. L., *Fanon: In Search of the African Revolution* (London: KPI, 1986).

Jones, S., *The Language of the Genes* (London: HarperCollins, 1993).

Jusserand, J., *English Wayfaring Life in the Middle Ages* (Corner House Williamstown MA and London: Methuen, 1988, repr. of 1974).

Kalaydjieva, L. and colleagues in Univation, '*Gypsies and Genetics: New Paths to Understanding*' (July 1998). Internet: http://www.avcc.edu.au/avcc/pubs/univation/jul98/page9.htm.

Kalaydjieva, L., Gresham, G. and Calafell, F., *Genetic Studies of the Roma (Gypsies): A Review* (BMC Medical Genetics 2:5.1471-2350/2/5, 2001).

Kasler, D., *Max Weber* (Cambridge: Polity Press, 1988).

Kenrick, D., *Gypsies: From India to the Mediterranean* (Paris: Gypsy Research Centre CRDP Midi Pyrenees, 1993).

Kenrick, D. and Bakewell, S., *On the Verge: The Gypsies of England* (London: Runnymede Trust, 1990).

Kenrick, D. and Clark, C., *The Gypsies and Travellers of Britain* (Hatfield: University of Hertfordshire Press, 1995).

Kenrick, D. and Puxon, G., *The Destiny of Europe's Gypsies* (Hatfield: University of Hertfordshire Press, 1972).

Kiddle, C., *Traveller Children: A Voice for Themselves* (London and Philadelphia, PA: Jessica Kingsley Publishers, 1999).

Kornblum, W., 'Boyash Gypsies: Shantytown Ethnicity', in F. Rehfisch (ed.), *Gypsies, Tinkers and Other Travellers* (London: Academic Press, 1975).

Kuper, A., *Anthropology and Anthropologists: The Modern British School* (London: Routledge, 1983).

Laparge, G., 'The English Folklore Corpus and Gypsy Oral Tradition', in T. Acton and G. Mundy (eds), *Romani Culture and Gypsy Identity* (Hatfield: University of Hertfordshire Press, 1997).

Lansley, S., *Housing and Public Policy* (Beckenham: Croom Helm, 1979).

Lee, K., 'Australia – Sanctuary or Cemetery for Romanies?', in T. Acton and G. Mundy (eds), *Romani Culture and Gypsy Identity* (Hatfield: University of Hertfordshire Press, 1997).

Lee, P. J., *We Borrow the Earth: An Intimate Portrait of the Gypsy Shamanic Tradition and Culture* (London: Thorsons, 2000).

Lee, W., *Dark Blood; A Romany Story* (London: Minerva, 1999).

Leeson, R. A., *Travelling Brothers* (St Albans: George Allen and Unwin, 1979).

Liddiard, M., 'Youth Homelessness: The Press and Public Attitudes', *Youth and Policy*, 1(59) (1998), pp. 57–69.

Lieberman, L., Littlefield, A. and Reynolds, L. T., 'The Debate over Race: Thirty Years and Two Centuries Later', in A. Montagu (ed.), *Race and I.Q.* (New York: Oxford University Press 1975).

Liegeois, J.-P., *Gypsies and Travellers* (Strasbourg: Council of Europe Press, 1985).

—— *Gypsies: An Illustrated History* (London: Al Saqi Books, 1986).

—— *Roma, Gypsies, Travellers* (Strasbourg: Council of Europe Press, 1994).

Lowe, R. and Shaw, W., *Travellers: Voices of the New Age Nomads* (London: Fourth Estate, 1993).

Lucassen, J., Willems, W. and Cottaar, A., *Gypsies and Other Itinerant Groups: A Socio-Historical Approach* (Basingstoke: Macmillan, 1998).

McCann, M., O'Siochain, S. and Ruane, J., 'Introduction', in M. McCann, S. O'Siochain and J. Ruane (eds), *Irish Travellers: Culture and Ethnicity* (Belfast: Institute of Irish Studies, The Queens University Belfast, 1994).

McKay, G., *Senseless Acts of Beauty* (London and New York: Verso, 1996).

McLoughlin, D., 'Nomadism in Irish Travellers' Identity', in M. McCann, S. O'Siochain and J. Ruane (eds), *Irish Travellers: Culture and Ethnicity* (Belfast: Institute of Irish Studies, The Queen's University Belfast, 1994).

McNay, L., *Foucault: A Critical Introduction* (Cambridge: Polity Press, 1994).

Malik, K., *The Meaning of Race* (Basingstoke: Macmillan, 1996).

Mallory, J. P., *In Search of the Indo-Europeans: Language, Archaeology and Myth* (London: Thames and Hudson, 1989).

Manby, J., *Pamphlet 188*, Fabian Research Series (London: Fabian Society, 1956).

Mandel, E., *Introduction to Marxist Economic Theory* (London: Pathfinder, 1979).

Mann, M., *The Macmillian Student Encyclopaedia of Sociology* (Basingstoke: Macmillian, 1983).

Marcuse, H., *Reason and Revolution* (Boston, MA: Beacon Press, 1968).

Marx, K., *Capital, Vol. 1* (Moscow: Foreign Language Publishing House, Lawrence and Wishart, 1818).

—— *The Eighteenth Brumarie of Louis Nonaparte* (New York: International Publishers, 1935).

Mayall, D., *Gypsy-Travellers in the Nineteenth-Century Society* (Cambridge: Cambridge University Press, 1988).

—— *English Gypsies and State Politics* (Hatfield: University of Hertfordshire Press, 1995).

Merrett, S., *State Housing in Britain* (London: Routledge and Kegan Paul, 1979).

Meyer, A., *Marxism: The Unity of Theory and Practice* (Cambridge, MA: Harvard University Press, 1954).

Miller, C., 'American Rom and the Ideology of Defilement', in F. Rehfisch (ed.), *Gypsies, Tinkers and Other Travellers* (London: Academic Press, 1975).

Ministry of Housing and Local Government/Welsh Office, *Gypsies and Other Travellers* (London: HMSO, 1967).

Montagu, A. (ed.), *Culture: Man's Adaptive Dimension* (Oxford and New York: Oxford University Press, 1968).

—— (ed.), *The Concept of Race* (London: Collier Books, Collier-Macmillan, 1969).

—— (ed.), *Race and I.Q.* (New York: Oxford University Press, 1975).

—— *Man's Most Dangerous Myth: The Fallacy of Race* (Walnut Creek, CA: AltaMira Press, 1997).

Morris, R. and Clements, L. (eds), *Gaining Ground: Law Reform for Gypsies and Travellers* (Hatfield: University of Hertfordshire Press, 1999).

—— *The Cost of Unauthorised Encampments* (Cardiff: TLRU, Cardiff Law School, 2001).

Mussolini, B., *Fascism: Political and Social Doctrine* (Rome: Ardita, 1935).

Nando.net, 'Mrs. Clinton tells Gypsies not to give up' (Associated Press, 1996).

Neat, T., *The Summer Walkers* (Edinburgh: Canongate Books, 1996).

Noonan, P., 'Policy-making and Travellers in Northern Ireland', in M. McCann, S. O'Siochain and J. Ruane (eds), *Irish Travellers: Culture and Ethnicity* (Belfast: Institute of Irish Studies, The Queen's University Belfast, 1994).

O'Baoill, D. P., 'Travellers' Cant – Language or Register', in M. McCann, S. O'Siochain and J. Ruane (eds), *Irish Travellers: Culture and Ethnicity* (Belfast: Institute of Irish Studies, The Queen's University Belfast, 1994).

O'Connell, J., 'Ethnicity and Irish Travellers', in M. McCann, S. O'Siochain and J. Ruane (eds), *Irish Travellers: Culture and Ethnicity* (Belfast: Institute of Irish Studies, The Queen's University Belfast, 1994).

Office of Population Censuses and Surveys, *Biannual Caravan Counts* (London: Department of the Environment, 1975–95).

Office of Population and Surveys, *Census Information* (London: HMSO, 1961, 1971, 1991).

Okely, J., 'Gypsies Travelling in Southern England', in F. Rehfisch (ed.), *Gypsies, Tinkers and Other Travellers* (London: Academic Press, 1975).

—— *The Traveller Gypsies* (Cambridge: Cambridge University Press, 1983).

—— 'An Anthropological Perspective on Irish Travellers', in M. McCann, S. O'Siochain and J. Ruane (eds), *Irish Travellers: Culture and Ethnicity* (Belfast: Institute of Irish Studies, The Queen's University Belfast, 1994).

O'Nions, H. 'The Marginalization of Gypsies', *Web Journal of Current Legal Issues* (London: Blackstone Press, 1995).

Orwell, G., *The Road to Wigan Pier* (London: Victor Gollancz, 1937).

Oxford English Dictionary (New York: Oxford University Press, 1999)

Parker, J. and Mirrlees, C., 'Housing' in A. H. Halsey (ed.), *Trends in British Society Since 1900* (Basingstoke: Macmillan, 1972 and 1988).

Parkin, F., *Marxism and Class Theory* (London: Tavistock, 1979).

Pico Della Mirandola, G., *On the Dignity of Man, On Being and the One Heptaplus* (Indianapolis, IN: The Bobbs-Merrill Company, 1965).

Rabinow, P. (ed.), *The Foucault Reader* (London: Peregrine, 1986).

Rao, A., 'Some Manus Conceptions and Attitudes', in F. Rehfisch (ed.), *Gypsies, Tinkers and Other Travellers* (London: Academic Press, 1975).

Rauty, R. (ed.), *Nels Anderson: On Hobos and Homelessness* (Chicago, IL and London: University of Chicago Press, 1998).

Rehfisch, A. and Rehfisch, F., 'Scottish Travellers or Tinkers', in F. Rehfisch (ed.), *Gypsies, Tinkers and Other Travellers* (London: Academic Press, 1975).

Reid, W., 'Scottish Gypsies/Travellers and Folklorists', in T. Acton and G. Mundy (eds), *Romani Culture and Gypsy Identity* (Hatfield: University of Hertfordshire Press, 1997).

Renfrew, C., *Archaeology and Language: The Puzzle of Indo-European Origins* (London: Cape, 1987).

Rex, J., *Race and Ethnicity* (Milton Keynes: Open University Press, 1986).

Ribbens, J. and Edwards, R. (eds), *Feminist Dilemmas in Qualitative Research: Public Knowledge and Private Lives* (Thousand Oaks, CA: Sage Publications, 1998).

Roszak, T., *The Making of Counter Culture: Reflections of the Technocratic Society and Its Youthful Opposition* (London: Faber, 1970).

Sampson, A., *The Scholar Gypsy* (London: John Murray, 1997).

Samuels, A., 'Gypsy Law', *Journal of Planning and Environment Law*, 719 (1992).

Sandford, J., *Gypsies* (London: Martin Secker and Warburg, 1973).

Scruton, R., 'In Defence of the Nation', in J. C. D. Clark (ed.), *Ideas in Politics in Modern Britain* (Basingstoke: Macmillian, 1990).

Sennett, R., *Authority* (New York: Knopf, 1980).

Shelter, *Homelessness in England, the Facts* (London: Shelter, 1996).

Skellington, R. in R. Dallos and E. McLaughlin (eds), *Social Problems and the Family* (London: Sage Publications, 1995).

Smith, A. D., *Ethnic and Racial Studies* (London: Routledge, 1992).

Smith, M., *Gypsies: Where Now?* (London: Fabian Society, 1975).

Sollors, W. (ed.), *The Invention of Ethnicity* (New York and Oxford: Oxford University Press, 1989).

—— (ed.), *Theories of Ethnicity: A Classical Reader* (Basingstoke: Macmillan, 1996).

Southwark Traveller Women's Group *Moving Stories* (London: Traveller Education Team, 1992).

Spears, B., *100 Years on the Road* (New York: Yale University Press, 1995).

Spicer, E. H., 'Persistent Cultural Systems', *Science*, 174 (4011, 1971), pp. 795–800.

Stepan, N., *The Idea of Race in Science: Great Britain 1800–1960* (London and Basingstoke: Macmillan, 1982).

Sutherland, A., 'The American Rom', in F. Rehfisch (ed.), *Gypsies, Tinkers and Other Travellers* (London: Academic Press, 1975).

Toulson, S., *The Drovers* (Aylesbury: Shire, 1980).

—— *Lost Trade Routes* (Aylesbury: Shire, 1983).

Weber, M., *Economy and Society (vol. I)* (Berkeley, CA: University of California Press, 1922).

Willems, W., *In Search of the True Gypsy: From Enlightenment to Final Solution* (London: Frank Cass Publishers, 1997).

—— 'Ethnicity as a Death-Trap: the History of Gypsy Studies', in L. Lucassen, W. Willems and A. Cottaar, *Gypsies and Other Itinerant Groups,* (Basingstoke: Macmillan, 1998).

Wilson, M., *A Directory of Planning Policies for Gypsy Site Provision* (Bristol: The Policy Press, 1998).

Legislation

Halsbury's Statues (4th edn) (London: Butterworths, 1997).

Town and Country Planning Act 1947, 1951, 1954 (2 & 3 Eliz 2 c 72).

Caravan Sites Act 1960 (1960 Eliz 2 c 62).

Scrap Metal Dealers Act 1964 (1964 c 69).

Caravan Sites and Control of Development Act 1968 (1968 c 52).

Highways Act 1980 (1980 c 66) – Consolidates the Highways Acts 1959 to 1971.

Public Order Act 1986 (1986 c 4).

Children Act 1989 (1989 c 41).

Criminal Justice and Public Order Act 1994 (1994 c 33).

Index

For Product Safety Concerns and Information please contact our EU
representative GPSR@taylorandfrancis.com
Taylor & Francis Verlag GmbH, Kaufingerstraße 24, 80331 München, Germany

www.ingramcontent.com/pod-product-compliance
Lightning Source LLC
Chambersburg PA
CBHW070415270326
41926CB00014B/2814